# Writings from Another Saint Paul

*This book is dedicated to Margaret Bredberg Harrington who has enriched and supported my life, my family, and my ministry in more ways than one can imagine. She has truly been an amazing gift to me and to all who know her. I thank God every day for her kind, calm, and loving presence in my life.*

A word from the author: While many books are read from cover to cover, please feel free to pick and choose those of your liking as you review the many titles in the table of contents. Also, you will note some pieces are more current than others as the book spans several decades of my writing. You may also notice a small amount of repetition in this book. Having written over a 50-year period, it is quite understandable that I would on occasion return to some of my favorite themes and theologies. And finally, feedback (positive or negative) is always welcome. Enjoy the read.

About the book's title: Over the centuries the Church has used the word "saint" to describe someone who has lived an especially holy or exemplary life. However, it should be noted that the Bible most often uses the word "saint" to describe ALL of God's people, any and all who have experienced the unconditional grace and mercy of God through our Lord, Jesus Christ. In short, a forgiven sinner. It is this definition of the word that I wish to ascribe to the title of this book.

# Writings from Another Saint Paul

## A Pastor Shares his Insights
## From Five Decades of Parish Ministry

### PAUL L. HARRINGTON

First Printing: Feb. 2024
First Edition

Paperback: 978-1-955541-14-5
eBook: 978-1-955541-15-2
Hardcover: 978-1-955541-16-9
LCCN: 2023918729

Cover and interior design by Ann Aubitz

Published by FuzionPress
1250 E 115th Street
Burnsville, MN 55337
FuzionPress.com
612-781-2815

# TABLE OF CONTENTS

# INTRODUCTION

W hen I was in high school and college, I had the good fortune of having outstanding English teachers who introduced me to the joy of creative writing and thoughtful composition. I also recall taking a Latin language course focusing on word derivation, illustrating how words came into being. I found it all to be fascinating. (I didn't particularly appreciate conjugating Latin verbs.)

The love of writing began slowly at first, but, like many things in life, the more we do something, the more we improve. And, as it happens, the vocation I felt most called to (Christian ministry) gave me ample opportunities to compose and write. This included monthly and even weekly articles for the church newsletter, daily correspondence with church officials, friends, family members, neighbors, contractors, parishioners, annual reports, constant emails, and more than a few letters to the editor. Over the next five decades, I wrote hundreds of articles on diverse topics, including a co-authored book, "Behind the Pulpit," published by Kirk House Publishers.

As the subtitle of this book indicates, I have selected a number of articles from this trove, some of which are personal, some theological, some political, and some that seek to address the many questions and challenges of daily life—all filtered through a prism of Christian thought and experience. One of the significant challenges of any clergyperson these days is to demonstrate how the Christian gospel of the first century can apply itself meaningfully to all the struggles, fears, doubts, confusion, and disappointments of the twenty-first century. In an age of skepticism and cynicism, people today are looking for helpful and instructive words that give them hope, courage, faith, and the strength to meet the arrival of each new day. I trust that the reader of this volume will find hope and courage in their daily lives.

I remind people we are created as a mind, body, and spirit trilogy. And all three parts of our being must be regularly nourished, or some part of us will soon die. We are fortunate to live in a place and time where mind and body are generally well-fed. However, the human spirit, psyche, soul, and inner person are often malnourished. I hope that this book may in some way feed your soul as well as your mind. If so, I will be most pleased as its author.

*—plh—*

# Section One

## FAITH AND LIFE

# CALLING ALL DISCIPLES

W ith the fall season now upon us and summer something of a
memory, we turn again to the many tasks of parish life
which support and undergird the various ministries of our
church. A host of people are needed in any church to plan and imple-
ment its programs and projects, and sometimes, if we are honest with
ourselves, we may wonder about those whom God has enlisted to do the
work of his Kingdom. We may wonder about our own qualifications or
the qualifications of those around us. We may think the church is a
strange enterprise that sometimes recruits the most unlikely people to
perform specific tasks. It is good to be reminded that through the ages,
God has made some surprising selections in choosing his servants.
Some improbable candidates have proven themselves faithful, and that,
of course, is all that matters.

The following letter has a powerful message for all the church.
God's primary concern is not our ability but our availability and willingness to look to him for the necessary resources to accomplish the
task.

TO: Jesus, Son of Joseph, Woodcrafters Shop, Nazareth

FROM: Jordan Management Consultants, The Solomon Building,
Jerusalem

Thank you for submitting the resume's of the Twelve men you have
picked for management positions in your new organization. All of them
have now taken our battery of tests, and we have not only run the results
through our computer but also have arranged personal interviews for
each of them with our psychologist and vocational aptitude consultant.

The profiles of all the tests are included, and you will want to study each of them carefully. We made some general comments as part of our service and for your guidance. It is the staff's opinion that most of your nominees lack background, education, and vocational aptitude for the type of enterprise you are undertaking. They do not have a team concept. We recommend you continue searching for people with managerial experience and proven capability. Simon Peter is emotionally unstable and given to fits of temper. Andrew has absolutely no qualities of leadership. The two brothers, James and John, the sons of Zebedee, place personal interest above company loyalty. Thomas demonstrates a questioning attitude that tends to undermine morale. We feel that we must tell you that Matthew has been blacklisted by the Jerusalem Better Business Bureau. James, the son of Alpheus, and Thaddaeus, have radical leanings, and they both registered a high score on the depressive scale. One of the candidates, however, shows enormous potential. He is a man of ability and resourcefulness, meets people well, has a keen business mind, and has a contact in high places. He is highly motivated, ambitious, and responsible. We recommend Judas Iscariot as your controller and trusted assistant. All the other profiles are self-explanatory.

We wish you every success in your new venture.

# Four Pictures of the Crucifixion

As we begin another season of Lent, I am reminded of a conversation I had with a woman not long ago. She asked me, "Why did Jesus have to die for us?" I began with the answer we all learned in church school: he died to take upon himself the sins of the world. But she pressed me for more. "Yes, but was there more to it than that?" What else can we say about this act of redemption? Two books came to my mind. *His Only Son, Our Lord* by Kent Knutson, and *Christus Victor* by Gustav Aulen. Each author lays out several different "pictures" of why the crucifixion had to be as it was. Let me briefly share them with you today.

The first picture is that of **Christ, The Victor**. In this motif, the world is a great battlefield wherein God and Satan fight for control. In Christ, God enters into the battle to defeat evil. But unfortunately, he chooses to fight on the devil's own turf, the world of broken and sinful humanity. We are slaves to sin. Our minds are darkened, and our wills are perverted. We are helpless to rescue ourselves from this terrible prison. Enter Christ, the Victor who defeats the enemy, frees humanity from Satan's tyranny and transfers us into the glorious Kingdom of God. He moves us from slavery to freedom, from darkness to light, from certain death to certain life. St. Paul says, "Thanks be to God who gives us the victory through our Lord Jesus Christ."

The second picture of the crucifixion is that of the **Ransom Paid**. Here, Christ comes to literally pay the debt to set us free. It's as if we were trapped in some cosmic pawn shop waiting for someone to come and pay the price to get us out. We are redeemed when Christ pays the price (and he alone can do this). Jesus said he came to give his life as a ransom for many (Matthew 20:28). Paul tells us in I Corinthians 6:20 that we were "bought with a price." God was in Christ, reconciling the world to himself. Luther tells us in his Catechism that Christ bought and freed us, not with silver and gold, but with his own precious blood, that we might be his forever and live under him in his kingdom.

A third picture of the crucifixion is the **Perfect Sacrifice.** This motif comes originally from St. Anselm, one of the early church fathers. Christ is seen as the one worthy sacrifice offered by God for our sins. Christ is the substitution for us, who rightfully deserved punishment. He has fully satisfied the demands of the law. This theory of the death of Christ brings to mind such verses as Isaiah 53:6, "and the Lord has laid on him the iniquity of us all," or Romans 4:25, "It was he (Jesus) who was put to death for our trespasses." Or the old hymn: "There was no other good enough to pay the price of sin; he alone could unlock the gate of heaven and let us in."

Finally, there is the **Magnet Motif** in which Jesus is understood to be the fullest revelation of God's love, which draws humanity back to himself. This motif is prevalent in our time when people want to know God in simple and uncluttered terms. This understanding of Christ's work also speaks to our deep need to be in communion with our Creator. We sense that there must be more to life than an endless round of events best defined by our years, fears, and tears. Something deep within us calls out for communion with God. We think of such verses as: "We love because he first loved us" (I John 4: 19) or when Jesus said, "When I am lifted from the earth, I will draw all men to myself" (John 12:32). Or maybe it's as simple as a little child declaring that "Jesus loves me, this I know, for the Bible tells me so." Who can honestly say they are not moved by this grand promise, regardless of age?

The crucifixion's full meaning will always be a mystery, but the Bible offers several interpretations of this powerful event. Whichever you choose, they all tell of "What wondrous love is this, O my soul, O my soul, what wondrous love is this."

# LET THE BEATITUDES BE YOUR ATTITUDES

A new year lies before us. How will you use this gift of twelve months, fifty-two weeks? There are so many choices to make, some selfish and some selfless. The following is a modern interpretation of the Beatitudes of Jesus from Matthew, chapter five. Ponder these words as you think about the year before you.

Blessed are you if you're struggling to pay the bills but insist on making time to be with your children whenever they need you. You may never own a vacation home or a Lexus, but heaven will be yours.

If you are overwhelmed by the care of a dying spouse, a sick child, or an elderly parent, and you are determined to make a loving home for them, blessed are you. One day, your sorrow will be transformed into joy.

If you willingly give your time to cook at a soup kitchen, vacuum at the church, help in a classroom, if you befriend the uncool, the unpopular, the perpetually lost, blessed are you. Count God among your friends and biggest boosters.

If you refuse to take shortcuts when it comes to doing what is right, if you refuse to compromise your integrity and ethics, if you refuse to take refuge in the rationalization that "everybody does it," blessed are you. You will triumph.

If you try to understand things from the perspective of the other person and manage to find a way to make things work for the good, if you're feeling discouraged and frustrated because you are constantly worrying, always waiting, always bending over backward, always paying the price for loving the unlovable and forgiving the undeserving, blessed are you. God will welcome, affirm, and love you.

If you struggle to discover what God asks of you in all things, if you seek God's presence in every facet of your life and every decision you make, if your constant prayer is not 'give me' but 'help me,' blessed are you. God will always be there for you.

If you readily spend time listening and consoling anyone who looks to you for support, guidance, and compassion; if you manage to heal wounds and build bridges; if others see in you graciousness, joy, and serenity; if you can see the good in everyone and seek the good for everyone, blessed are you. You are nothing less than one of God's own.

If you are rejected or demeaned because of the color of your skin or the sound of your name, if your faith automatically puts you at odds with some people, if you refuse to compromise to 'get along' or 'not make waves,' blessed are you. One day, you will live with God.

"Rejoice and be glad," Jesus tells those who have gathered around him, for "you are the blessed of God. In the end, heaven will surely be yours."

(Author Unknown)

# LEARNING TO NURTURE OUR FAITH

L utheran pastors sometimes find themselves in a funny position. As those who preach the saving gospel of Jesus Christ and seek to set forth the truths of the Protestant Reformation, we firmly proclaim God's unconditional and unmerited grace as a gift with no strings attached. Anyone who has come close to the writings of St. Paul knows to what great lengths he goes to show us that our righteousness *is* a gift from God, pure and simple. Over and over again, Paul declares that righteousness before God is unattainable through human effort. One of Paul's clearest statements comes from his letter to the Ephesians (2: 8), where he says, for by grace have you been saved through faith; and this is not your own doing, lest any man should boast, it is a gift from God.

But now the dilemma. The moment we grasp this life-altering insight, we are in danger of an error in the opposite direction. We may be tempted to say there is nothing more I can or need to do. But, if our human strivings to find favor with God are in moral bankruptcy (and we know this is true), and if righteousness is a gracious gift from God (as the Bible tells us), then is it not logical to conclude that we ought to do nothing but wait for God to come and transform us? Strangely enough, the answer is no. Our analysis is correct: human striving is insufficient, and righteousness is a gift from God. But our conclusion is faulty, for happily, there is something we can do and should do. God has given us wisdom to nurture our faith and help us receive his grace. These disciplines allow us to place ourselves before God so that he can do his transforming work within us.

A brief analogy from Richard Foster's book, *Celebration of Discipline,* may help us with this truth. Any good farmer knows that he cannot grow grain on his own. It is God who performs that miracle, and God is alone. God gives and sustains all plant and animal life. But the farmer most certainly can help provide the conditions for grain growth. He plows, cultivates, fertilizes, and observes the proper growing seasons. God causes the grain to grow, but he partners with the farmer. So, too, with the Christian life. God desires to grant us His righteousness and cause his grace to grow within us. But let us also remember that we have a response here. The cultivation of the soil of our hearts should include regular worship, celebration of the sacraments, prayer, service to others, confession, fellowship with other believers, the study of the Word, times for personal devotions, and perhaps even fasting. And always a deep desire to love and serve our neighbor.

# SUBJECT OF PRAYER

In a sermon on the subject of prayer, I received a great deal of positive feedback. As someone noted, prayer is so obvious that we sometimes overlook it. What follows are some further comments on this topic. May I encourage you all to continue to be faithful and diligent in your own personal life of prayer. Your heavenly Father waits to hear from you and me.

1. We pray because God is our Friend. The death and resurrection of Jesus broke down the dividing walls between God and humankind. God invites us to view him as a personal friend willing to help with any need. Prayer is a form of conversation that helps maintain this relationship. Without prayer, the relationship slowly dies. How sad this can be.

2. We pray because we have been invited to. God, as our Father, is honored when we ask. Would an earthly father not be disappointed if his children never asked him for anything? It is no accident that the prayer Jesus taught us is full of petitions asking for God's good gifts.

3. We pray in order to be put in touch with the very source of life itself. God created us and gave us life; we genuinely draw strength from him. But, without prayer, we "pull the plug" on this vital source of our being.

4. We pray because our prayers influence God. This is a huge subject, but I am convinced that God's will is a good will, and when I ask for things that please him, he will grant them. However, a word of caution is needed lest we view God as a sugar daddy in

the heavens. God answers all prayers in one of three ways: yes, no, and wait.

5. I pray because it changes me. If I have an enemy and I am able to pray for him, I will be changed inwardly. Prayer is a powerful healer of relationships.

6. Prayer is a very accurate gauge of how I am doing spiritually. When there is little prayer, I grow little. The chances are good that when there are many prayers I am growing in my faith. As someone noted, seven days without prayer makes one weak. Even seven hours without prayer is too long. In this Lenten season, let's all make better use of this beautiful gift our Father gave.

*I got up early one morning.*
*And rushed right into the day,*
*I had so much to accomplish.*
*I didn't have time to pray.*
*Problems just tumbled about me.*
*And heavier became each task.*
*"Why doesn't God help me?" I wondered.*
*He answered, "You didn't ask. "*
*I woke up early this morning.*
*And paused before entering the day.*
*I had so much to accomplish.*
*That I had to take time to pray.*

# LIVING WITHIN OUR MEANS

W e Americans find it very difficult to live within our means. We are constantly being encouraged to move far beyond our means. A thousand ads are aired daily on television and online, and all are trying to do one thing: separate us from our money, and they are very effective.

The per capita credit indebtedness of the average American has never been more outstanding than it is today. We are asked to live way beyond our means, and the stresses that result can often be harmful, if not downright destructive. Some years ago, a good friend gave me a tip on how to live life, and I have never forgotten his words. He said, "When God gives you a dollar, give a dime back to him, save or invest a dime, and go have a good time with the other eighty cents." His advice is not easily kept, but it is a wise and healthy way of life. A dime out of a dollar doesn't sound like much, but when you truly get serious about tithing to church and charity, you face some interesting challenges. You will likely have to reorder some of the priorities of your life. So what? It's all for the good.

When Jesus challenged the Rich Young Ruler to give his wealth to people experiencing poverty, he didn't compromise his request because he knew it was in the best interest of this young man. Discipleship can be costly, but it also has some significant rewards. I have learned some things over the years about how God works in our lives. I know that I can never outgive him. No matter how generous I may become, he will find new and exciting ways to bless me. I know I can never hurt myself by giving too much, but I can hurt myself by giving too little. Perhaps most of all, I have discovered freedom regarding money matters. It all belongs to God, and I am only a manager or trustee of that wealth for a short time. I need not become greedy, selfish, or uptight. I can relax, celebrate, and discover that giving is more of a blessing than receiving. Take a walk on the wild side. Discover the joy of giving without resentment or regret. Give freely and joyously as God has first given to you. You will be blessed in return—I guarantee it.

Secondly, learn how to save or invest with that second dime. Saving 10% of your income will require further prioritizing. That's okay. We all need this kind of discipline. The average American family saves less than 3% of its annual income. An NPR report recently stated that the average family in the US saves no more than $2,400 a year. Compare this with Germany, where the average family saves about 9% of annual income, and Japan, which is close to 19%. (No wonder Japan is buying out the world. They have so much capital in their financial institutions.) Only about three in every one hundred Americans retires with any great degree of financial independence.

To digress, let me say that taxes and inflation often eat up savings (sadly). Wise investing, on the other hand, can often stay ahead of these two "monsters." Then enjoy the other eighty cents from every dollar of your income. Is it possible to live within our means these days? I think so. It will surely mean foregoing certain purchases that may be frivolous or selfish in the first place. It will cause us to think long and hard about what we value. Jesus once said that where your treasure is, there will your heart be also. Just where is your treasure today? While adopting the 10/10/80 lifestyle may sound risky, I am sure that once we show our Lord how serious we are about Him and His work, He will continue to respond to us in ways we never dreamed possible. And always remember, the greatest gifts in life are nonmaterial. Tithing our income to the church and our savings program is not usually done in one fell swoop. I suggest boosting your current level of giving each year by one, two, or three percentage points. You will be surprised how quickly you will attain your goals. Consider these words as you consider giving to the church for the coming year. Remember that the accurate measure of a person's life is not duration but donation. May God grant us all much joy in our giving.

# Happy Homes, Happy Marriages

All of us involved in family life (however you may wish to define the term) know that maintaining a healthy family unit is hard work. Perhaps it was never easy, but the stresses and strains of the last half of the twentieth century have taken their toll on the best of families. I recently read an article outlining six secrets of a strong family. (After I share them with you, they won't be secrets anymore, but they are too important not to share.) Here they are:

1. **Communication**—This one does not have to be a big mystery. Family members can sit down and learn to talk openly as well as to listen. Good communication demands both. A professionally trained "third party" is well worth the time and expense if walls and defenses constantly increase.

2. **Commitment**—Crucial to any family's success is investing time, energy, and heart, better known as commitment. People can will themselves to remain in a committed relationship. In an age of rampant infidelity and broken promises, commitment is absolutely fundamental.

3. **Time Together**—When one thousand five hundred children were asked what they wanted most from Mom and Dad, it was "time together." Healthy families spend lots of time together. What you are doing isn't too important; it's just that you do it together.

4. **Appreciation**—I also like the word "affirmation." We need it more than food, especially in the growing-up years. Hug your kids daily (even in high school) and tell them you love them and

are proud of them. The more you affirm, the less you will have to discipline, but your affirmation has to be genuine.

5. **Spiritual Wellness**—A foolish parent will assume that the church has nothing to offer their child. We were created as spiritual beings, and only God can fill that God-shaped void within us. Likewise, family members who grow in faith and love for God will also grow in love for one another. It's a time-honored truth.

6. **Coping with crisis**—Life is never a bed of roses. Trauma and crisis hit the best of families. Coping skills are essential. Don't overreact. A sense of humor can be helpful. Try to define the problem and then work together on creative solutions. Again, get professional help if necessary. Ask God for help. Draw on the support of friends and loved ones. And remember, no crisis goes on forever.

# THE CURSE OF DOMESTIC VIOLENCE

A few years ago, about twenty women inmates of the California prison system asked Governor Pete Wilson to review their cases and grant them all amnesty. Their crimes? All had murdered their husbands or boyfriends. At first hearing, one might wonder why such women should be set free. But I must tell you that while I certainly believe our courts must administer justice, there are unusual circumstances when they must also administer mercy. This may be just such a time.

Margaret and I both work in professions where we deal with instances of domestic violence. Over the years, I have learned some things that cause me to be very sympathetic to women who live out their lives in abusive situations. Here is a typical scenario and why it is difficult for women to break out of their "prisons of fear."

1. Many women go into marriage wanting security, companionship, and family. They are reluctant to give up that dream and tend to tolerate abuse, hoping that "things will one day get better."

2. Strange as it may seem, many women blame themselves when beaten or otherwise violated. They wrongly believe "they caused it all" and decide to tell no one. As a result, a conspiracy of silence sets in that can be deadly.

3. Women with children often feel economically trapped. If they lose their husband, abusive as he may be, they have great fears about how they will ever survive with children, little income, no roof over their heads, and perhaps a family that will offer little or no help to them. One woman once told me that her parents told her she was now an adult and had to work out all her problems independently—a small comfort for a trapped woman.

4. Abused women often tell how they fear the physical strength of their mates. Men are often physically stronger and can literally subdue a woman of weaker physical ability.

5. Abused women often tell how their husbands threaten them to such a degree that they literally fear being killed (and many women are killed each year in America by husbands or boyfriends). For example, one woman I knew some years ago told me how she tried to run away late one night, and when her husband caught up to her, he bluntly told her that if she ever tried anything like that again, he would "slit her throat."

6. Until recently, abused women found little support from the police or the court systems. Our culture has been male-dominated for centuries, and women's rights have been greatly diminished.

Some men honestly believe it is right to strike their wives and children. When the prevailing culture allows for this kind of thinking, it is no wonder women have struggled so hard to break out of this destructive system of victimization. Even if some think women are the "weaker sex," this gives no one the right to exploit them in any way.

Much more is to be said on this subject, but I trust I have made my point. Frankly, I hope they do a case-by-case review of all those women in California. I believe that at least some of those women should be exonerated. While I certainly do not condone murder, for not a few women, it has become the one act of desperation that allows them to break free of that terrible prison in which they have been held captive. Let me close with this one statement: There has never been nor will there ever be an acceptable reason for striking a spouse. Those who hit their spouses for any reason whatsoever are people who need help immediately. I can't say it more clearly than that.

**National Domestic Violence Hotline**
Hours: 24/7. Languages: English, Spanish, and 200+
through interpretation service
800-799-7233

# PRISONS OF FEAR

One issue of the Community Action Council newsletter carried a gut-wrenching story of a woman telling of over fifty years of physical, verbal, and psychological abuse from her own father and then later from her husband. As I read her story, I wondered what a private hell this woman had lived in for half a century. I envisioned her in a prison of fear, just as real as any prison with walls.

A few years ago, a bar owner in Carver, MN, shot his wife, daughter, and then himself. Further investigation revealed years of abuse and domestic violence on the home front. And, of course, the case of Ricky and Kate Hebert reminds us again of how pervasive and destructive this societal problem can be. A jury recently found Ricky Hebert guilty of first-degree manslaughter for the death of his wife. Physical abuse was carried to its ultimate conclusion.

After nearly twenty years of parish ministry, I have realized that far too many women (and some men) live with the paralysis of fear and intimidation. They live in prisons of fear and perceived powerlessness. It is time for society to rise up and say, "Enough of this and no more." No human being ever has the right to exploit, manipulate, oppress, or otherwise abuse another person.

The Bible teaches that genuine love frees; it does not seek to control or dominate. "There is no fear in love, but perfect love casts out fear." (1 John 4:18). Real love allows another person to be all they can be.

Anything that tries to control, demean, manipulate, or intimidate another person can hardly be called love. It is sick and should have no place in our lives whatsoever. Women (and children, too) must know their options. Physically hitting another person is never acceptable. Society is slowly waking up to an idiotic double standard it held to for centuries: if I were to hit my neighbor's wife, I would likely end up in court or jail, but if I hit my own wife, somehow, that was okay. Nothing could be further from the truth, and we are just now figuring out how wrong our thinking on this matter has been over the years. Wives and children are to be loved and affirmed, not beaten and oppressed, and any man who thinks otherwise needs serious help.

Again, let me say that it is never okay to strike a spouse. **Call 911,** the **National Domestic Violence Hotline,** a trusted friend or relative, or your church when such events happen. But don't just accept such abuse. Help today is more available than ever, and good counseling can often improve a marriage. Let's all do whatever it takes to eliminate these terrible prisons of fear and abuse. Let me also state that verbal abuse can often be just as destructive as physical abuse. The wounds of the body may heal in time, but the wounds of the spirit or the psyche may never heal completely.

Centuries ago, St. Paul wrote some words that, tragically, society seems slow to understand. He said, "There is now neither Jew nor Gentile, slave nor free man, and neither is there male nor female; for we are all one in Christ." (Galatians 3:28). When Christ rules in our lives and our homes, there is a love that enables us to regard others as equals, It is also a love that seeks to build up others and not tear them down. Gone is the desire to exploit, dominate, and belittle. In truth, Christ's love compels us to serve and love others and to encourage and develop healthy human relationships. And when that happens, the home and society, in general, will greatly benefit. Tell me that Christianity doesn't teach a very practical and beneficial lifestyle.

# SOME WHYS AND WHEREFORES OF WORSHIP

I have experimented with worship at churches from time to time. I want to assure you that we don't make changes for the sake of change. A lot of thought and planning goes into the worship life of our church. Whenever we do something new at the church (an institution that is known for its "traditional" qualities), there is always the tendency to say those seven famous words: "We never did it that way before." Sometimes, as I get older," I am inclined to speak those words myself.

The world does seem to change too rapidly at times. But please remember that worship over the centuries has gone through numerous transformations. What form of worship was used in the catacombs of ancient Rome? Can you imagine what it was like for the German people in Luther's day to suddenly switch from the Latin Mass, where the choir did all the singing, to a German Mass, where the congregation did most of it? That must have raised a few eyebrows (though many also saw this change as needed and progressive.) Many Catholics underwent a similar change in this country in the 1960s when Rome approved the English Mass for use here in America. In the past few decades, many different liturgies and other forms of worship have been introduced to churches in the US and worldwide. Indeed, there is today a flood of different styles, instruments, and liturgies to choose from. Our Lutheran Book of Worship, first introduced in 1978, has served us well for nearly a quarter of a century. I also recall the red hymnal before the green and the black hymnal before the red one. *So,* we do change, and often for the better. Varying worship styles can be found in nearly every part of the Christian Church today. Our experimenting will continue at SOTVLC. Liturgy is not an end in itself but a means to an end. And there is no one set liturgy for all time and eternity. Instead, the liturgy must be user-friendly, melodic (easy to sing), possess theological depth, and lets me worship God in *"spirit and truth."* If these criteria are met, I can be happy with just about any liturgical setting.

Of course, we hope you, too, find joy and meaning in your weekly worship experience. As I said, your comments are always welcome. And your openness to new things is also appreciated. May our Lord continue to bless us all as we gather each week to be nourished by the Word and the Sacraments. "I was glad when they said unto me, Let us go up to the House of the Lord." (Psalm 122:1)

I close with ten reasons why you and I need to worship at least once a week. I invite you to add your own to this listing:

1. In worship, we shift the focus of our lives off of self and onto God, where it rightly belongs.
2. In worship, we hear God's word read, proclaimed, and applied to our lives.
3. In worship, we celebrate and receive the Sacraments.
4. In worship, we spend an essential hour together with family and friends.
5. In worship, we tell the world which side we are on; Jesus once declared that we are either for or against him.
6. In worship, we fulfill the commandment to remember and keep the Sabbath day holy.
7. In worship, we have a marvelous opportunity to give thanks to God for the blessings of life.
8. In worship (before, during, and after), we can comfort, support, and otherwise encourage one another in our journey through life.
9. In worship, we make an offering to God, a serious attempt to return to him a generous portion of what he has first given to us.
10. In worship, we make visible the body of Christ on earth today. When you are missing, the Body is not complete.

# SEX AND CHASITY

Some weeks before Christmas, a parishioner asked me why the Lutheran Church doesn't say more about sex. It took me a minute to figure out what this person was getting at, but it became more apparent as we discussed it. Her concern was that the church not be so silent on such an essential issue in our lives. I agree, so let me respond.

Our society is swimming in a sea of mixed messages about sex and sexuality; most are either sick or unproductive. Some soap operas and prime-time TV routinely air programs that are nearly X-rated. Movies portray sexual activity as one big game with no serious consequences. Talk shows become ever more sensational as they try to boost their ratings. Advertising literally drips with sexual imagery or the premise of instant love on reality dating shows. A headline read, "Desperate CBS lowers standards." Great. That is all America needs. Yet, according to a Minnesota Department of Education survey, more than one in four ninth graders and three out of five high school seniors have experienced sexual intercourse. Can such statistics be accurate? And, of course, we hardly need to mention the rock bands that have now taken us to a new low or the explosion of pornography and sex-related crimes.

Well, what does the church say about all this? Just what the church has been saying for the past two thousand years: Chastity (purity) before marriage and fidelity (faithfulness) during marriage. The teachings of the Scriptures are immutable and given by a God who knows what is best for His world. Yet, sometimes, the church doesn't say much on this subject because the facts speak loudly for themselves. Just look at our society today. We have an epidemic of abortions, venereal diseases, shotgun weddings, extra-marital affairs, sexual additions, sexual abuse, the killer AIDS, and unwanted teenage pregnancies. The human pain and sorrow caused by illicit sex seems to know no boundaries. How God must weep for us. How slow we are to learn.

So let me say it again: Purity before marriage and faithfulness during marriage. Practice this scriptural, time-honored plan, and you will avoid so much of the hurt society is today inflicting upon itself. Remember, God gave his laws, not because he is a killjoy, but for our benefit. As some wise person once said, it's not that we break the commandments; the commandments have a way of breaking us. Live by the commands of God and discover the real joys of life. Twenty centuries ago, St. Paul wrote: "Whatever is pure…think on these things." (Phil. 4:8).

Words to live by in any century.

# THE SEASON OF PENTECOST

We now celebrate Pentecost Sunday and the beginning of the most extended season of the church year. From May until November, we will observe this festival, emphasizing our response to the Gospel and our growth in discipleship. Pentecost is the third great festival of the church year. We sometimes complain that the two other great festivals, Christmas and Easter, have been commercialized and secularized to the point that their significance is almost lost. But such is not the case with Pentecost. This is one holy day (and season) that has not been commercialized. If anything, it has been neglected or even forgotten.

To help us better understand the significance of Pentecost, we need to think again about what happened on that first Pentecost Sunday so vividly described in the second chapter of the book of Acts. Pentecost reminds us of the indispensable role of the Spirit of God, not only in the conversion of the sinner but also in the lifelong development of the believer's spiritual life. Luther called this whole process sanctification. It is our daily walk of faith, nurtured by the Holy Spirit, who seeks to help us pattern our lives ever more closely after that of our Lord. God's Spirit must assist us in this task. The Bible makes it clear that no one can step from spiritual death to spiritual life unless they are brought into this new life by the work of the Holy Spirit. St. Paul talks about this distinction in his first letter to the Corinthians (2:14) when he writes, "The unspiritual man does not receive the gifts of the Spirit of God, for they are folly to him, and he is not able to understand them because they are spiritually discerned." The scriptures teach that spiritual life comes only through repentance for sin and trust in Jesus Christ as Lord and Savior. The Bible also teaches that "no one can say 'Jesus is Lord,' but by the Holy Spirit." Without the Spirit's work, there can be no faith.

How about your life? Has the Spirit been allowed to perform his work within you? Has your heart been receptive to his promptings? Have you heard again that still small voice that speaks to all who truly take time to listen? Have you experienced the many "fruits of the Spirit" that can make life worth living?

Luther tells us the Spirit is the one who calls, gathers, and enlightens all who give him even the slightest opportunity. If you have not felt the Spirit's presence in your life, Pentecost is most certainly for you. Come to worship. Hear the Gospel. Work at your prayer life. Ponder the scriptures. And place your heart, soul, and mind under the persuasion of the Holy Spirit. And He will give you new life. Call upon the Spirit, and He will surely come to you.

# DA VINCI CODE BALONEY

The Da Vinci Code movie has an award-winning director, a star-studded cast, and a large budget. It was a blockbuster success. But, ironically, the tagline for the movie is: "Seek the Truth." What a farce!

Much has already been written about this movie, especially regarding its claims concerning the divinity of Jesus Christ and the history of the early Christian Church. Unfortunately, the claims made by the book (and the film) are often highly misleading. For example, "a relatively close vote" decided the Council of Nicaea. It was not. Or the patently false claim that no Christians believed Jesus was divine before Constantine around 313 AD. Absurd. Worse yet, Jesus renounced his calling from God, married Mary Magdalene, and even fathered a child. Utterly ridiculous.

While many mature Christians will be able to understand this book and film as purely fictional, others, not so rooted in the faith or having no roots at all, may find it difficult to separate fact from fiction, truth from falsehood. Much like some of the Oliver Stone films (noted for playing fast and loose with the truth), this film will also confuse, confound, and distort the truth to the benefit of no one except those reaping the profits from this production.

Worse yet, it may well sow the seeds of doubt for an entire generation that already espouses enormous skepticism and cynicism. It is pure fabrication and has no factual basis whatsoever. I assure you that if the claims of Jesus Christ were bogus, they would have been revealed centuries ago. The validity of the New Testament has stood the test of time in every century. We can all take comfort in knowing that when the hammer strikes the anvil of God's truth, it is always the hammer that shatters.

# The Quiet Sermon

A member of a certain church, who previously had been attending services regularly, stopped going. After a few weeks, the pastor decided to visit him. It was a chilly evening. The pastor found the man at home alone, sitting before a blazing fire. Guessing the reason for his pastor's visit, the man welcomed him, led him to a comfortable chair near the fireplace, and waited. The pastor made himself at home but said nothing. Instead, in the silence, he contemplated the dance of the flames around the burning logs.

After some minutes, the pastor took the fire tongs, carefully picked up a brightly burning ember, and placed it alone on one side of the hearth. Then he sat back in his chair, still silent. The host watched all this in quiet contemplation. As the one lone ember's flame flickered and diminished, there was a momentary glow, and then its fire was no more. Soon, it was cold and dead. Not a word had been spoken since the initial greeting.

The Pastor glanced at his watch and realized it was time to leave. He slowly stood up, picked up the cold, dead ember, and placed it back in the middle of the fire. Immediately, it began to glow again with the light and warmth of the burning coals around it.

This simple little parable has profound significance for our lives. The Christian life is designed to be lived out in a Christian community.

# LENT: SACRED SEASON FOR CHRISTIANS WORLDWIDE

Pick up a Bible dictionary, and you will not find the word Lent. The word never appeared in the Bible. And yet, for Christians worldwide, it is one of the most sacred of all seasons of the church here. What was the origin of Lent, and what significance does it have for our lives today?

The church developed the forty-day season of Lent, which begins on Ash Wednesday and ends with Easter, over several centuries. Early on, the followers of Christ realized that the events surrounding his life, suffering, and death were of prime importance to their faith. So, it should not surprise us that, even in the earliest centuries, special attention was given to the passion of Jesus. The word lent comes from an old Anglo-Saxon word, meaning to lengthen, referring to days getting longer in the spring. I am unsure where the number came from, but it may have been the forty hours between the crucifixion and resurrection. Forty is also a relatively common biblical number as in the forty days of the flood, the forty days of Jesus' temptation in the wilderness, and the forty days between the resurrection and the ascension.

This season, as one might expect, was a somber time in which the faithful reflected on the agony and death of Jesus on the cross. Ashes were often placed on the foreheads of the faithful. Hence, Ash Wednesday reminds them of the sober and penitential nature of the season. Ashes in the Jewish and Christian context suggest God's judgment of our sin, our human frailty, the need for repentance, and dependence upon God.

As Christians are signed with ashes on their foreheads, even today, we hear the words, "dust thou art, and to dust thou shalt return."

For many Christians, Lent became a time of strict discipline and self-sacrifice. This emphasis is much less prevalent today.

Fasting and other forms of self-denial during Lent are an old custom that grew from the catechetical instruction while preparing candidates for baptism at Easter.

It seems that the discipline of those preparing for membership in the body of Christ became so attractive to the entire congregation of believers that it was decided to make this special time of commitment for all the faithful, not just those ready for baptism. Denial of self is also a natural outgrowth of the apparent sacrifice made by Jesus on behalf of the whole world. To this day, the Mardi Gras festivities in New Orleans symbolize one last time of celebration before the more contemplative days of Lent.

Years ago, one heard the question: what are you giving up for Lent? Today, that question is seldom posed in conversation.

But this is not to suggest that the season has no meaning. In her book, *The Downward Assent*, Edna Hong says of Lent. "The purpose of Lent is to arouse awareness of our sin, to arouse humble contrition for the guilt of the sin that makes forgiveness possible, to arouse the sense of gratitude for the forgiveness of sin, and to arouse or motivate the works of love and justice that one does out of gratitude for the forgiveness we received." Interestingly, the three traditional disciplines of Lent, prayer, fasting, and alms, still play an essential role in addressing the needs of a sick and broken world.

Prayer is a conversation with God, seeking his will for our lives, and fasting allows us to identify more closely with the needy. And almsgiving implies a generous gift to people experiencing poverty as an act of justice and mercy. All three can significantly add to the meaning of Lent as we've come to see the suffering of Christ in the face of those about us.

This is a healthy focus for any Lenten season, but perhaps the Old Testament prophet Micah states the issue most clearly when he asks (6:8), "What does the Lord require of you?" And then the profoundly simple answer, "Do justice, love kindness, and walk humbly with your God."

# MAN TO MAN

O kay, guys, listen up. I have some info for you that I hope will be helpful to both you and your spouses. Over thirty years of parish ministry, I have worked with several hundred couples as they try to develop and enhance the daily skills needed for a healthy marriage. I have concluded that men generally have much to learn about "nurturing a relationship." Forgive me if this sounds a bit sexist, but I still believe that women generally have stronger "nesting" instincts, understand the dynamics of healthy relationships, and are better able, as a rule, to appreciate what it takes to keep relationships healthy, growing, and satisfying. This is not always *so* true for men. Men often have to learn these skills; it comes slowly and painfully for some.

Let's start with some universal truths. One, it is never okay to hit your wife. If this is happening in your home, you need some serious help. At last, we now have some laws to prevent or punish such behavior. No matter how your father treated your mother, hitting is never an option. Never, never, never. Secondly, talking to your wife in a degrading, demeaning, or dehumanizing manner is never acceptable. Maybe your father did it to your mother or your grandfather to your grandmother. They were wrong, and so are you if you do this to your wife. Listen carefully to your words. Better yet, listen to your wife. How does she feel about the conversations you have? Are your words critical, hurtful, judgmental, degrading, angry, disrespectful, crude, or pain-inducing? If so, you must take note.

Over time, such treatment of your spouse could destroy your marriage. (Yes, I know women can have a biting tongue too.) Sometimes, I have told couples to forget about being husbands, wives, and lovers. Just think of yourselves as best friends. Sort of like those carefree days when you were dating. How did you treat each other then? Think of yourselves as good friends for life. How do you nurture a friendship? How do you treat your best friend?

To put it another way, who is your best friend outside your marriage? How do you treat that person? Treat your spouse at least as well as you treat your best friend, and it should do wonders for your marriage.

Remember, too, that nurturing a relationship will demand time and sacrifices. The biggest challenge in a marriage is to stop thinking as a ME and start thinking as a WE. Marriage is going to change your life and your commitments. If you are not ready for this change, don't consider getting married. For the guys, it will mean you need to give MORE time to your wife and LESS time to the softball league, golf, hunting, football games, hanging out with your buddies, or canoeing in the Boundary Waters. It's not that you give these up entirely. But there will be less time for such activities because you must continue to nurture that one all-important relationship in your life. Think of all the time you spent together during dating and courtship. Why do you think that should all stop now that you have spoken your vows? You have to work at your marriage. If you don't, you will likely lose it. One other word of warning. If and when children come, you must spend even more time nurturing your wife and child (ren). This is often a critical time in many marriages. Your wife is not the only caregiver. This task must be shared as equally as possible. If not, forget about having a family. You cannot be a self-centered person and be a good parent. It just won't work. The bottom line is that maintaining good relationships within the family will likely be one of the most demanding tasks you have ever undertaken. It doesn't "just happen." It takes time and a deep desire to help make the family circle a place of warmth, affirmation, and support.

Some years ago, I found a poem entitled *The Wall*. It is a reminder that each day, we are either building a nurturing and responsive relationship with our spouse or building a wall that may become impenetrable, one brick at a time.

### The Wall

*Their wedding picture mocked them from the table,*
*these two, whose minds no longer touched each other.*
*They lived with such a heavy barricade between them,*
*that neither a battering ram of words nor*
*artilleries of touch could break it down.*
*Somewhere between the oldest child's first tooth*
*and the youngest daughter's graduation,*
*they had lost each other.*
*Sometimes, she cried at night and begged the*
*whispering darkness to tell her who she was.*
*He lay beside her, snoring like a hibernating bear,*
*unaware of her lonely winter.*
*She took a course in modern art, trying to find herself*
*in colors splashed upon a canvas and complained*
*to other women about men who were insensitive.*
*He climbed into a tomb called "the office," wrapped*
*his mind in a shroud of paper figures and*
*buried himself in customers.*
*Slowly, the wall between them rose, cemented*
*by the mortar of indifference.*
*One day, reaching out to touch each other,*
*they found a barrier they could not*
*penetrate, and recoiling from the coldness of the stone,*
*each retreated from the stranger on the other side.*
*For when love dies, it is not in a moment of angry battle,*
*nor when fiery bodies lose their heat.*
*Instead, it lies panting, exhausted at the bottom*
*of a wall it could no longer climb over.*
~Author Unknown

Marriage today is hard work. No one in their right mind would deny this. The pressures and stresses on home and family can be enormous. But marriages can succeed when two people are genuinely committed to each other. A good marriage asks us to be faithful, generous, caring, patient, and kind. These qualities may not always flow freely from within us, but they are worth all the time and energy required.

May our Lord bless your marriage with all the resources needed to keep it strong, healthy, and responsive.

# GLOSSOLALIA

## (Speaking in Tongues)

*"Now, concerning spiritual gifts, my friends, I do not want you to be uninformed..,* "Corinthians 12: I*

O ccasionally, I get asked about a spiritual gift called glossolalia, commonly known as "speaking in tongues." For many people, this spiritual gift, spoken of extensively in I Corinthians, chapters 12-14, sounds foreign and even incomprehensible. But I assure you, it is a spiritual phenomenon that should be taken seriously. It is not a joke, and many people across the ages have benefited from this gift. There are, however, some essential boundaries that should be noted regarding this gift.

First, the Bible talks about both the "fruits" of the Spirit and the "gifts" of the Spirit. In all such references, it is clear that the fruits of the Holy Spirit (love, joy, peace, patience, kindness, gentleness, faithfulness, and self-control) are to be the most desired. These fruits are for all people, and God desires that we all have them. However, the gifts of the Spirit are something entirely different.

These include wisdom, healing, miracles, prophecy, tongues, and the interpretation of tongues (I Cor. 12: 8-11). Notice that tongues are always last or next to the last in all such lists of these gifts. What does it mean to speak in tongues? This gift often indicates a particular manifestation of the work of the Holy Spirit and cannot be generated by a person on their own. Speaking in tongues is deemed as someone who is involuntarily speaking in a tongue or language that appears to most to be unintelligible. This experience often makes no sense unless there is someone present who can interpret what has been said.

It should be noted that there seem to be periods of history (as in the church's earliest days) when such gifts were very pervasive. There are also times when such gifts appear to be almost nonexistent. Again, this is a gift, pure and simple. It appears only as the Holy Spirit desires. And while tongues can be a spiritually uplifting experience for some believers, they also come with some dangers.

One is the likelihood that this gift can cause division within the church when used publicly. You and I both know something about human nature. If you have a gift and I don't, there is always the potential for arrogance, jealousy, or misunderstanding. This is why St. Paul clarifies that this gift is best accepted in a private setting, not public worship. St. Paul clearly states his position in chapter 14, verse 19, when he says, "I would rather speak *five* intelligible words with my intellect, to instruct others, than ten thousand words in a tongue."

Paul sees the pitfalls and dangers in this gift. And in 14:28, Paul says that when no one is available to interpret, the use of tongues should not be employed even if given the gift to avoid confusion within the church. The main concern of Paul is for unity and goodwill within the church. He sees the downside of this gift and wants to be sure that it will be used in a context that will not harm anyone.

Even more to the point is how Paul desires to emphasize the first fruit of the Spirit. After talking about tongues and other related matters in chapter 12, he concludes with these noteworthy words: "I now want to show you a still more excellent way (in which to live.)" (12:31). Paul then launches into his very famous love chapter 13. "If I should speak in the tongues of men or angels but have not love, I am a noisy gong or clanging symbol." 13:1

For Paul, the gifts of the Spirit are far less important than the fruits. And the fruit of love is the one actual litmus test for all Christians. If you can't love freely, joyfully, and unconditionally, Paul says, you have not fully grasped the Christian faith. All else is secondary to the practice of love in our daily lives. Paul concludes the thirteenth chapter in this way: "So faith, hope, love abide, these three, but the greatest of these is love." Gifts of the spirit may or may not come to us. But the fruit of love must belong to all who call themselves Christians.

# Body or Soul: Which is Being Cheated?

Have you ever considered how much time, energy, and cold, hard cash our society gives to preserving and beautifying the human body? Accurately calculating the totals would be staggering, if it were possible. Consider, for a moment, the tens of millions spent each year on cosmetics, perfumes, and hair treatments for both males and females. A recent trip to the drugstore tells you they come in every imaginable kind and variety.

To remain in vogue, millions are spent yearly on clothing, accessories, and other general apparel. We put a high priority on appropriately adorning the body. Then, millions more are spent on health spas, diet plans, athletic clubs, and so-called "bodybuilding" salons to maintain that youthful and always-illusive physique we desire.

I am confronted with two very discomforting questions when pondering our society's massive investment in such activities. First, is it wise (or even moral) to spend so much on something that will one day be laid into a grave to decay? And secondly, do we spend anywhere near this amount of time, energy, and money in preserving, enhancing, and beautifying our inner life—the soul?

A strong case could be made for the fact that Americans today have never been more "body conscious." Within reasonable limits, this is good. St. Paul refers to our bodies as temples for the Spirit of God. Indeed, proper care of the body can be a wise and even worshipful thing to do. After all, we are to care for the gifts God has given us. But there is also an inner being, soul, and spirit destined to live forever. Are we doing much of anything to preserve its future? Would that Americans today seek to preserve and enrich their souls as much as they do their bodies!

In the parables, Jesus frequently reminds us that while we are to take this life and this world seriously, our tenure on this planet is temporary at best. Unfortunately, the rich man (Rich Man & Lazarus parable) learned this lesson too late. Another wealthy man who had built bigger barns for his many holdings also found life to be abruptly concluded. Of him, Jesus said, "You fool! This night shall your soul be required of you." What is the condition of your soul today? Even more to the point, what are you doing to beautify, strengthen, and preserve it? In this season of Pentecost, let us use every opportunity to allow God's Spirit to have His way in our lives. Let us be diligent in worship, prayer, Bible study, celebrating the Sacraments, finding fellowship with other believers, and being sensitive to our neighbor's needs. Listen to our Lord's voice and heed the Spirit's prompting. And resolve now to give at least as much care to your soul as you do your body.

# BEING A TEEN—THEN AND NOW

*The article was written years ago,*
*but it is still relevant today.*

I will be fifty-five in a few months, and remembering my teen years is no longer easy. But of this, I am sure: being a teen today is quite different from being a teenager forty years ago. I suspect that nearly every generation would make this same comment, but the changes we are witnessing today are among the most dramatic ever. So, let me share some of them with you in hopes that we might all better understand today's youth.

1. Drugs and Alcohol: Alcohol has always been with us, doing its share of damage, but the drug scene is new. Indeed, it was not a part of my teen years. I personally fail to see the attraction to drugs, but I also know that peer pressure can be enormous, and otherwise good kids can get hooked after only one or two experimentations. A life wasted on drugs is a genuine tragedy.

2. The President demeans himself and his office while mocking marriage's sacred vows. On the eve of the Super Bowl, one of its star players is arrested for trying to hustle a prostitute who happened to be an undercover police officer. Jerry Springer and company offer the most disgusting "guests" you can imagine. Is it any wonder that our youth are often confused about what is right and wrong with sex? If our youth look to our culture for their values, they will be greatly disappointed or confused.

3. Materialism/Narcissism (an excessive love of self) ads today tell us to "buy it because you are worth it." At every turn, youth are told that happiness is to be found in "things" and that you should have it because you need it and deserve it. Hopefully, teens will also hear the words of Jesus when he reminds us that

the true joy of life "is not found in the abundance of possessions" but in a right relationship with God,

4. Violence: I grew up with John Wayne, Roy Rogers, and the Lone Ranger. There was violence, but it was not nearly so graphic, gory, or gratuitous. Unfortunately, today's youth are exposed to violence (via the media, gaming, or the entertainment industry) that almost numbs the senses. How else can we explain bizarre events that often make the evening news? When we witness enough violence, we not only accept it, we may even begin to practice it as though it were a "normal" part of life.

5. Pornography: Strip joints and "girly" magazines have long been around, but today, we are witnessing something entirely different. Pornographic books, magazines, films, and the internet are booming businesses. We seem to have an insatiable appetite for all things sexual. Is sex a bad thing? Of course not. It is a gift from God. But like all of God's gifts, sex can be perverted and distorted. The desires of the flesh need boundaries, as does every area of our lives.

6. Gambling: The so-called "gaming industry" is undoubtedly new for this generation. In my youth, it was Vegas, Atlantic City, or, for the very rich, Monte Carlo. Today, it's online, at the gas station or at the casino just down the street. Again, we need to guard against the addictive power of gambling. For the most part, it is an immoral act because for me to win, someone else has to lose. I do not believe this practice is in keeping with the Christian life.

7. Body Image: Most people try to look their best most of the time, but today, we seem to have entered a new realm altogether. Cosmetic surgery has become a high-growth industry. The legacy of Ken and Barbie is still very much with us. Clothing ads now display the "waif look", models so thin they look emaciated or anorexic with glassy-eyed stares suggestive of someone on drugs. They look lifeless. All of us, especially our youth, are pushed by a continuous barrage of advertisements to buy the right clothes (designer, of course), use the right cosmetics, wear

the latest hairstyle, join the right fitness club, maintain the proper diet, and be seen with the right people. This could become unbearable, unhealthy, and downright destructive after a point. How many of our youth feel like failures before they even get started in life? How refreshing the words of Jesus who asked, "Is not life *more* than food and the body more than clothing?" (Matthew 6:25)

What is the point of this discussion? Simply to remind our youth that while many voices will try to influence them in those formative teen years, there is one voice they should always listen to: the voice of God. His will and his word will never disappoint you. So, remember to pray each day, asking *for* his guidance. Read your Bibles to discover his will for your fife. Worship each week and find hope, strength, encouragement, fellowship, and peace. Every Sunday may not be a "barn burner," but worship will make a profound difference in your life.

If I had one word for today's youth, it would come from St. Paul: "Do not be conformed to this world but be transformed by the renewal of your mind," Commit your life to Jesus Christ, and you will never regret it. Let me tell you about one more change that I find very encouraging. So many of our youth are willing to share their faith with their peers. High school youth often bring their Bibles to school and pray together. FCA (Fellowship of Christian Athletes) and other campus organizations joyfully celebrate the Christian faith. In Juarez, Mexico I was privileged to spend a week with some of the finest Christian youth I have ever known. There is much to be thankful for. But there are also dangers aplenty. So, pray for the youth of our nation each day.

# Section Two

# FAITH AND LIFE

# WHY IS THERE SUFFERING?

I consider this to be the most challenging question in all of the world. You already know the question too well, and so do I. It is the question that thousands ask daily around the world. It is usually asked in the wake of some terrible event. The question goes like this. *Why is my mother suffering from cancer? Why did my brother have to die in that hunting accident? Why did that plane have to crash? Why are innocent children sometimes afflicted with terribly debilitating diseases? Why has my life been so full of pain? Why God? Why?*

It is the most pervasive question of life and is most often asked of the clergy. So, let me attempt an answer that I believe is accurate and faithful to the teachings of the Bible. The question is this: *Why does God allow terrible things to happen?* The answer is relatively simple. Bad things happen in our world because God is not entirely in control. When I was in Confirmation as a youth, I learned, as you did, that God is omnipotent and all-powerful. He is limited by nothing. I do not deny this fundamental biblical truth. But I am also declaring that God, for whatever reason, has chosen to limit his power in the world temporarily. (Note: It was not taken from him; he willingly gave it up.)

If God were entirely in control, it would be a different world. But he is not entirely in control. God has chosen to grant each of us a free will. It is this gift that makes us human. We are not puppets, droids, or robots. We are free moral agents and can use this freedom to destroy or enhance life, obey God, or disobey. Then add this one whom we call the Devil or Satan to the mix. He, too, has a free will and desires to confound, disrupt, deceive, and destroy. And he does it well.

So why did God structure the world in this manner? We can only speculate about that. But God had to give us the freedom to be authentically human. By giving us a free will, God can know that our response to him (positive or negative) is genuine. God took a risk in giving us the freedom to make choices, distinguishing us from the animal kingdom. Will we use our freedom wisely and productively or not? God waits to see how every generation responds. If you doubt my assertion that God is not entirely in control, please consider the following texts from the Bible.

One day, Jesus taught his disciples to pray like this: "Thy kingdom come, thy will be done, on earth as it is in heaven." In other words, Jesus acknowledges that God's rule is not now fully established. So, we pray for the day when God's will will be done on earth as it now is in heaven.

A second text involves the temptation of Jesus in the wilderness. Satan tells Jesus to bow down and worship him, and he will give him all the world's kingdoms. Jesus does not fall victim to the temptation, but neither does Jesus question Satan's assertion that he (Satan) is in some sense in control of the world.

A third text is the parable of the wheat and the weeds in the same field. You recall the story (Matthew 13:24 to 30). The wheat seed is sown in the story, but an enemy comes at night, and sows weed seeds in the same field. The field is the world in the parable. When the seeds sprout, the servants tell the landowner (God) what happened. They suggest pulling up the weeds immediately. But the landowner says no. Rather, he says, let the wheat and the weeds grow together, and they will be separated on the day of the harvest. What a powerful insight into life. God is saying that good and evil will co-exist for a time but that a day of justice will undoubtedly come. In the meantime, you and I live in a bitter-and-sweet world. We live daily with the realities of life and death, sickness and health, pleasure and pain, truth and falsehood, hope and despair, good and evil, joy and sorrow, sin and grace.

Does this mean that God has forsaken us? Not at all. God promises to be with us always, even to the end of time. But this parable also gives us an essential insight into the true nature of life on this planet. It is an imperfect world where God has temporarily chosen to limit his power. We may wish for it to be different and one day, it will be. But, for now, we recall the words of the poet Robert Frost: "Life is like an onion. You peel it one layer at a time, and sometimes you cry."

Is it God's will if my sister dies in a car crash? Of course not. God never wills evil for his people. The crash likely happened because of ice, speed, mechanical failure, alcohol, inattention, drowsiness, or other reasons. But amidst all the pain of life, two great certainties have sustained God's people for centuries:

1. God is with us through the best and worst of times.
2. The day will come when all this life's hurts, sorrows, and injustices will be permanently banished. We will all stand in the glorious light of God's eternal presence and know life as we have never known it before. In John's Gospel (10:18), Jesus says, "I willingly lay down my authority, and I willingly take it up again."

When that happens, we will surely experience a new world order.

# THE TRUTH OF THE RESURRECTION

During Easter week, one or more national news magazines or online news sources run stories focusing on the life of Christ and particularly the myth or truth of the resurrection. As a preacher, I seldom try to defend the faith by using empirical and verifiable data because I know that in the last analysis, we accept the stories of the Bible not by "proof" but by faith. Never once, for example, does the Bible ever try to prove the existence of God. Ultimately, you either believe or you don't. But this is not to say that the Bible has left itself without witnesses. Indeed, many skeptical scholars have set out to prove that Jesus never arose from the dead, only to become a believer after examining the evidence. For the record, let me share some historical facts that give much credence to our faith. This is not an exhaustive list, but I trust you will find it helpful in fully appreciating the credibility of our faith.

Let's start with the Lord's Day. For over a thousand years, the Jewish people held the Sabbath as the seventh day of the week (now called Saturday). Suddenly, we find a group of early Christians (who were Jews) changed the day of worship from the seventh day to the first. What could account for their changing a custom they had so tenaciously held, if not an event as monumental as the resurrection, which took place, as the Bible tells us, on the first day of the week? Pentecost also occurred on "the first day of the week," as did Jesus' first appearance in the Upper Room.

Secondly, there was the dramatic switch from celebrating Passover (another one-thousand-year-old tradition) to celebrating Easter. What caused those early Jews to abandon this sacred holy day and replace it with Easter, which dates back to the first century AD? Only the conviction that Christ has truly risen could cause such a change.

Third, I offer the Christian sacraments, which point to Jesus' suffering, death, and resurrection. The practice of these sacraments can be traced back in an unbroken line to the very earliest days of the Church. Would such practices ever have been maintained based on the notion of a dead Christ?

Fourth, I offer the fact of Christian art. The catacombs of Rome, for example, date to the church's earliest days and were filled with depictions of the resurrection of Jesus. Some of these can still be seen to this very day.

Fifth, I offer the facts about the martyrs. The persecution of early Christians, often by the emperors of Rome, is an undeniable fact of history. Some persecutions claimed thousands of lives. Who would be willing to die for a myth? Or a falsehood? Or a fairy tale? I submit that no one would do such a thing. But many in history have died for the truth. And these people have often changed history dramatically. The truth of the resurrection so convicted the early Christians that they gladly laid down their lives to further the cause of the Gospel.

Sixth, there is the fact of the Christian Church itself. By any measurement, the Church is the largest and oldest organization in all human history. Today, about one and a half billion people claim allegiance to Jesus. Is it possible that such an incredible organization could be built upon a lie? Jesus stated that the gates of Hell could not prevail against his Church. History has proven him correct because history is, after all, his story.

Seventh, I offer the fulfilled prophecies of the Old Testament. Hundreds of prophecies in the Old Testament concerning the coming messiah point to the motif of death and resurrection. All were fulfilled in this one we call Jesus.

Eighth, I invite you to consider Pentecost, the birth of the Church. Peter spoke, and his sermon focused mainly on the resurrection of Christ. Undoubtedly, many in his audience had been eyewitnesses of the living Christ. Had Peter been telling a lie, he would indeed have been challenged. The Bible tells us that Jesus appeared to as many as five hundred persons after the resurrection. Had this been a falsehood, had Peter and the others been telling a lie, they would indeed have been found out. On the contrary, the truth was so compelling that ordinary men and women went out around the Roman world and did extraordinary things in His name.

Ninth, there is the testimony of hostile witnesses. The centurion at the cross declared, "surely this was the Son of God." The Romans, who cared nothing for Jesus or his cause, admitted that the tomb was empty. Even the Sanhedrin concedes to the truth by asking the Roman soldiers to tell a lie and state that Jesus' disciples had come and stolen his body. If there is falsehood here, it comes not from the early believers but from the enemies of Christ who wanted to keep him entombed but could not.

Perhaps the most convincing truth comes through the Christian experience itself. The risen Christ, whom we praise and honor each Easter, has touched and transformed the lives of countless millions across the centuries. The living Christ has brought millions of people love, hope, healing, truth, and forgiveness. Once again, this kind of reality could never be based on a hoax.

Ultimately, we still believe by faith and not necessarily because of verifiable facts. Still, the resurrection did not take place in a vacuum. The preponderance of evidence supporting the reality of the resurrection is nothing short of overwhelming. Moreover, it happened in a valid historical context, which has left us with many credible clues if we are willing to look for them. Christ is risen! He is risen indeed!

# SOME THOUGHTS ON THE NEW YEAR

Over the years, I have kept a file for the coming of the New Year. So, naturally, our thoughts turn to the value of time. Here are a few gleanings that I think are worth your consideration.

*The great use of life is to spend it on something that outlasts it.*
~William James

*Teach us to number our days and recognize how few they are; help us to spend them as we should.* Psalm 90:12

*I trust in Thee, O Lord; Thou art my God. My times are in your hands.* Psalm 31: 14, 15

*He does not lead me year by year,*
*Nor even day by day.*
*But step by step, my path unfolds,*
*My Lord directs my way.*
*Tomorrow's plans, I do not know.*
*I only know this minute.*
*But he will say, "This is the way,*
*By faith now, walk ye in it."*
*What needs to worry then or fret?*
*The God who gave his Son*
*He holds all my moments in his hand.*
*And gives them one by one.*
~Author unknown.

*For a thousand years in thy sight are but as yesterday when it is past...* Psalm 90:4


*For the New Year,*
*I would wish to have strength enough to battle with difficulties and overcome them, love enough to move me to be valuable and helpful to others, faith enough to make the things of God real, and hope enough to remove all anxious fears concerning the future.*
~Johann Wolfgang Von Goethe

**The Future**
*There's an unknown path before me*
*And yet I fear it not;*
*I know through all the years gone by,*
*Whate'er has been my lot;*
*That a kind and Heavenly Father,*
*Planned out the way for me;*
*And I know that in the future,*
*watched over, I will be.*
*To everything, there is a season,*
*a time for every matter under heaven;*

*It is good to know that in the midst of all the changes of life, "Jesus Christ is the same yesterday and today and forever."* Hebrews 13:8

*I said to the man who stood at the gate of the new year: Give me a light that I may tread safely into the unknown. And he replied: "Go out into the darkness and put your hand into the hand of God. That shall be to you better than any light and safer than any known way."*
~M. Louise Haskins

## A Prayer for the New Year

*Lord, this year, teach me the art of taking minute vacations—of slowing down to look at a flower, to chat with a friend, to pet a dog, to read from the Bible. Remind me daily that the race is not always swift and that there is more to life than increasing its speed. Let me look upward into the branches of the towering oak and know that it grew slowly and well. Slow me down, Lord, and inspire me to send my roots deep into the soil of eternal values so that I may grow toward my eternal home.*
*Through Jesus Christ our Lord, Amen*

# EVIL IN OUR WORLD

As I sat at breakfast the other morning, I read in the newspaper about a thirty-one-year-old man who was convicted and sentenced for the killing of two older women. It is a heinous crime that leaves everyone asking the age-old question: why? One sentence in the article stood out among all the others. It simply read: the defendant did not explain the killings. And do you know why? Because there isn't an explanation. Who in their right mind would do such a horrible thing? The murderer is now going to jail for at least thirty-nine years, and he should. But what we also see here is a terrible manifestation of evil that is sadly so much a part of our world. This man is guilty without question. But there is something bigger going on here, something demonic.

Satan has reared his ugly head once more and ruined at least three lives, likely many more. As Lutherans, we don't dwell a lot on Satan because we prefer to emphasize the power of the Gospel of Jesus Christ to bring about change in our lives. But there are critical times to discuss Satan and his power in our world. I have to believe that, somehow, this man fell under his spell. Commandments are broken, blood is spilled, lives terminated, and Satan is delighted.

My point is simply this. Let us not be naïve about the world we live in. St. Paul tells us in Ephesians 6 that we daily battle with the "powers and principalities" of this thwarted old world. The Devil prowls about like a hungry lion seeking someone to devour. We need to be on guard constantly. Sometimes, people tell me about something they did that is so out of character. Stealing, lying, cheating, a brief affair, a terrible lapse of judgment. Momentary but often with painful consequences. We cannot be casual or uninformed about the real world. God calls on us daily to renounce Satan and all his evil ways. Give him just an inch, and he will take more than a mile. He will take your very life. It amazes me how casually people treat the weapons of defense God gave us including weekly worship and the Lord's Supper. The study of scripture. Prayer. Fellowship with other Christians. Seeking out others who can help us through the tough times of temptation.

A good offense is still the best defense. Practice your faith daily, and God will give you the weapons you need to avoid the destructive power of Satan. Put on the armor of God—the sword of the Spirit, the breastplate of Righteousness, the belt of Truth, the helmet of Salvation, and the shield of Faith. Don't think for one second that your enemy will go away and leave you alone. He will stalk you like a tiger, awaiting an opportune moment to pounce and destroy.

Keep the faith and practice the faith. The Word and the Sacraments are two of your best tools. Don't neglect them. See you at church this week, where we can practice our faith and learn how to resist the temptations of the Evil One.

# THE PRICE OF FAITH

You and I live in a land of incredible freedom. We have our founding fathers to thank for such wisdom and insight. Democracy for the "common man" was a radical experiment over two hundred years ago, but it worked well. One of those great freedoms we enjoy is the freedom of religion.

It isn't easy to imagine what it would be like to be persecuted for our faith. Or worse, to be put to death for practicing our faith. But unfortunately, in some places in the world, even today, religious persecution is still very real.

I came across several quotes from ancient Roman historians who detail how many of the early Christians were treated. We ought to be thankful for their witness and their tenacity. Yet, in many cases, their faithfulness to Jesus Christ cost them dearly. I often wonder how I would fare in similar circumstances.

The Roman historian Tacitus, who was not a Christian, records in his Annals (XV,44) the persecution of the Christians under Nero in A.D. 64; (the translation is a bit stilted) "Nero put in his own place as culprits and punished with most ingenious cruelty, men whom the common people hated for their shameful crimes and being called Christians. Christians, from whom the name was derived, had been put to death in the reign of Tiberius by the procurator Pontius Pilate. Having been checked for a time, the deadly superstition began to break out again, not only in Judea, where this mischief first arose but also in Rome, where all things scandalous and shameful met and become fashionable from all sides.

Therefore, in the beginning, some were seized who made confessions; then, on this information, a vast multitude was convicted. And they were not only subjected to insults, that they were either dressed up in the skins of wild beasts and perished by the cruel mangling of hungry dogs or else put on crosses to be set on fire, to be burned, being used as torches at night. Nero had thrown open his gardens for that spectacle and gave a circus play, mingling with people dressed as charioteers..."

And this *quote* from Pliny the Younger: "These Christians in Thynia (a Roman province) were tested by the authorities under Emperor Trajan, as shown in this letter of Pliny the Younger to the Emperor about A.D. 112: The method I have observed towards those who have been turned over to me as Christians is this: I interrogated *them* as to whether they were Christians or not; if they confessed, I repeated the question two more times, adding the threat *of* capital punishment; if they still persevered, I ordered them to be executed."

As I read these two accounts, taken from actual Roman histories, I am reminded again that faith has come to us with a price tag. How casually we treat this gift, which some were willing to die for so that it might be preserved and shared with succeeding generations. I used to say it was the blood of the martyrs that nourished the seeds of the early church.

As I wrote these lines, the words of Luther's great hymn kept running through my mind:

*God's Word forever shall abide.*
*No thanks to foes who fear it.*
*For God himself fights by our side*
*With weapons of the Spirit*
*Were they to take our house*
*Goods, honor, child, or spouse*
*Though life be wrenched away*
*They cannot win the day.*
*The Kingdom's ours forever!*

Let this bracing promise sustain your life today, and let us all be mindful of the great sacrifices formerly made on our behalf.

How much we have to be thankful for.

# CREMATION: GOOD OR BAD?

I want to address two questions that have been asked of me. I trust you will find the answers to be of help to you.

1. What does the Lutheran Church teach regarding the practice of cremation? Officially, the church neither endorses nor opposes this practice. Because we believe that this mortal body does indeed return to the dust from whence it came, there is no solid opposition to cremating the earthly remains of a loved one.

When we confess our belief in the "resurrection of the body," we speak of a new and glorified body free of all physical encumbrances, such as pain, aging, sickness, disease, wounds, and even death. Therefore, it may be that cremation would be preferable where the high cost of a funeral could be a deciding factor. In short, a Christian should not think of cremation as unfavorable. I would, however, add this one word of caution.

In some instances, it may be essential for family members to be able to gaze upon and even touch the deceased's body. This is not a morbid practice. Instead, it helps us come to grips with the finality of death and that we ought to have no illusions about the person being dead. I know of a case where two children were never allowed to view the body of a deceased parent (their father), and years later, they began to have real doubts about whether or not he had died. In most cases, I recommend that family and close friends be allowed to view the physical remains of the deceased person. Then, having purchased a relatively inexpensive casket, cremation can occur or the family may forego a public reviewal altogether.

I also think it wise to bury the "cremains" and not spread them over some lake or field, for example. I think it is helpful for survivors to visit the remains, usually at a cemetery or burial plot. This may not always be important, but we grieve over many months or years, and returning to the burial site can often be helpful to the healing process.

2. Another question, often asked by teens and confirmands, has to do with the origin of God. Where did God come from? (I sometimes chuckle at this question, though I respect those who ask it.) God, by definition, has no point of origin and no point of termination.

If God had a beginning or an ending, he would not be God. He would be finite as we mortals are finite. But the God of the scriptures is infinite. Psalm 90:2 states it well: Lord, thou has been the dwelling place of all generations. From everlasting to everlasting, Thou art God. If that boggles your mind a bit, it should. Lord Balfour once declared that "any God that I can fully comprehend is surely too small a God for me."

Humans have sometimes become too impressed with our accomplishments and have taken God's work for granted. I remember looking at the night skies in 1958 when the Russians launched the first Sputnik. How impressed we were while at the same time forgetting the One who created the vastness and the majesty of the heavens beyond. The Hubble Telescope discovered two million new galaxies in our universe. That should humble us all. However, it is also helpful to remember that we mortals are always confined to two constant realities: time and space.

These two pervasive boundaries in life limit everything we do. Now, if you are able, imagine a realm in which there is neither time nor space. Let your mind run to the outer limits of your imagination. Even then, you will have only begun to understand how God functions. Time, space, and distance mean nothing to him. *In* the end, we accept the sovereignty and authority of God by faith. But to think of God as being limited in any way as we humans are, is to view a God very unlike that whom we find in the Bible.

# What do you Know
# About Our Creeds?

Every weekend, when we gather for worship, we rise to affirm and confess our faith in the words of one of the three great creeds of the church. All three of these can be found in the front part of our hymnal. Though we use them often, people do not know much about their origin. Perhaps a few thoughts on this subject will be helpful in better understanding these excellent summations of our faith. The creeds, you may know, do not appear in the Bible. All three have been drafted during the early centuries of the church's history, and two seemed to have been written in response to some heresy that had arisen in the early church. As you study the character of each creed, you begin to understand better what issues they seem to address or redress. A summary of each:

1. The Apostle's Creed is the oldest, best-known, and most widely accepted of all the creeds of Christendom. It was also the slowest to develop into its present form. Its first appearance was likely sometime in the second century, but its final or "received" form was no earlier than the fifth or sixth century. Tradition has it that the Apostles' Creed was composed shortly after the Ascension of Jesus and that all twelve apostles had a hand in authoring it. While there may be a bit of truth to this theory, the earliest known copy of the Creed is traced no earlier than 700 AD. This creed seems to have originated in some baptismal formula. It may be rightly regarded as the summary of what the early church believed to be fundamental to the Christian faith.

2. The Nicene Creed was first drafted at a general ecumenical council of the church at Nicea in Asia Minor in the year 325 AD. Its final form was approved at the Council of Constantinople in 381 AD. This creed was a pointed response to Arius, who was teaching that Jesus was not originally a part of the Trinity but was only a later creation of the Father. This teaching, in essence, undermined the divinity of Christ. Later, the Council of Chalcedon in 451 AD sought to finally settle the controversy by affirming both the divinity and the humanity of Christ, one person with two natures (true God and true man.)

3. The Athanasian Creed was initially attributed to the hand of Athanasius, who died about 373 AD. However, this connection is generally held to be incorrect. Like the Apostles' Creed, it originated in the West, rather than Palestine, sometime after the late fourth century. This creed seeks to set forth the doctrine of the Trinity. The reason is that Arius continued, even after the Council of Nicea, to undermine the divinity of Jesus. In defense of the faith and scripture, Bishop Athanasius of Alexandria spoke out against Arius. Because he later became known as the Father of Orthodoxy, Athanasius' name was given to this remarkable creedal statement.

Though centuries old, these creeds have strengthened believers' faith immeasurably. Indeed, there is a certain joy and comfort in knowing that these words have given the church guidance and continuity across the centuries. As our ancestors confessed these words, we pray that generations to come will confess and celebrate the Christian faith in these ancient, yet ever timely creeds.

# BIBLE INTERPRETATION

When we last talked, we touched on several topics but did not dwell on any of them long enough to do them justice. With this in mind, I would like to elaborate on this whole subject of Bible interpretation so that we might better understand where each of us is coming from.

Some years ago, I saw a bumper sticker that said, "The Bible says it, I believe it, and that settles it." Now, if only it were that simple. The Bible is a book (actually a book of books) that demands serious study and thoughtful interpretation. Let's start with some guiding principles for understanding how best to grasp the full message of the Bible.

1. The Bible is most certainly the Word of God, but the Word of God is not limited to the Bible. Jesus Christ is the living Word of God and the final arbiter for all matters of faith and life. He is the standard by which all else is judged. "The Word became flesh and dwelt among us full of grace and truth…" (John 1:14)

2. All verses in the Bible are essential, but not all verses are of equal value.

3. There are verses in the Bible that are pre-Christian, sub-Christian, and even non-Christian. Again, this is why interpretation is so critical.

4. A friend of mine likes to say that he takes the Bible so seriously that he cannot take all of it literally.

5. Remember that the Bible is both divinely inspired and humanly written. God did not dictate every single word to the writers of the Bible. (Muslims claim that Allah dictated every word of the Koran to Mohammed; we Christians make no such claim.) Remember, too, that not one of the authors of any of the books of

the Bible woke up one morning and said, "I think I am going to write the Bible today." It just did not happen that way. It is helpful to think of the Bible more like a painting and not so much as a photograph. The two are not the same.

6.  Further, if you think the Bible is forever immutable, consider how Jesus himself reinterprets the Bible six different times in the Sermon on the Mount. For example, "You have heard that it was said, an eye for an eye and a tooth for a tooth, but now I say unto you love your enemies and pray for those who would do you harm." (Matt 5:44) Jesus himself is reinterpreting some of the basic teachings of the Old Testament. Again, how important it is to interpret the Bible rightly. Jesus himself even found it necessary to do so.

7.  Rather than think of the Bible as a chain of almost twenty-nine thousand verses (and if one link in the chain is broken, the whole chain is broken), it is much better to think of the Bible as a target. The Bible's outer rings (verses) are essential, but there are much more significant, life-changing, and revealing verses closer to the center of the target.

8.  Today, Christians (and indeed clergy) are called upon to state just what the Bible says about abortion, capital punishment, stem cell research, taking another human life in times of war, prolonging life artificially, gay and lesbian issues, physician-assisted suicide (legal in Oregon), use of contraception and birth control methods, gender equality, gun violence, (we must stop this madness), critical race theory, drug abuse, climate change, immigration, and a host of other timely issues. Yet, again, anyone who takes the Good Book seriously knows that it demands thoughtful interpretation.

9.  Finally, let me remind you just how many times in history the Bible was used to justify a certain belief, only to discover later that we were wrong. The Bible was used to justify the nine very bloody Crusades, the Spanish Inquisition, the Salem Witch trials, and human slavery here in America and around the world.

Some have used the Bible to ban women from the ordained ministry (and still do, as you well know), a ban on racially mixed marriages, that a divorced clergy person could never again serve in the pulpit, a ban on gay/lesbian relationships, a ban on most forms of contraception. For a time, the Roman Catholic Church discouraged using anesthesia for women in childbirth, citing the text in Genesis stating that women should suffer such pain. When immunizations became common in the 1950s, the RCC discouraged their usage, stating that if God wanted someone to die, who were we to interfere?

10. The RCC taught that unbaptized babies went to Limbo (a bogus doctrine) and that the earth was the center of our solar system, (Galileo was placed under house arrest for his "heresy" in declaring correctly that the sun was the center of our solar system.) We used the Bible to support the false notion of the "divine right of kings" all across Europe, that suicide victims all went to hell, that no baby could be baptized if born out of wedlock, and that divorced persons should never again be allowed to partake of Holy Communion. That women should be silent in the church (as St. Paul states in Corinthians), and smoking, dancing, playing cards, going to movies, wearing makeup or jewelry, working on Sundays, and wearing shorts…at one time or another, we used the Bible to forbid any of these activities. And did you know there are no less than thirty-nine Bible verses that call for someone to be put to death for any number of infractions, many of which we now consider rather petty? Do you now see how many times we were SURE the Bible said one thing, and now we know we were WRONG on almost all of these issues?

11. So, let me close with one more. I officiated at a wedding at the Landmark Center in downtown St. Paul, MN. Eric and James had been in a life-giving, totally committed, monogamous relationship for over nine years when the Supreme Court ruled in favor of gay marriage. So now it was legal for them to marry.

Eric and James are two of the finest young Christian men you would ever want to meet. Well educated, gifted, good jobs, faithful in worship, generous in every aspect of their lives, and just a pleasure to know. The last time I talked with James just before Christmas (they now live on the north side of the Twin Cities), they were adopting a little five-year-old boy born with multiple congenital disabilities. That little boy will be the luckiest kid in Minnesota to have Eric and James as his parents. They are taking on a huge responsibility, and I have nothing but admiration for both of them.

12. I forgot to mention this: six months ago, our congregation called a gay pastor who is also in a committed, monogamous, life-giving marriage. As a result, Pastor Julie was overwhelmingly approved as one of our five pastors.

# GIFTS AND FRUITS

In the last couple of weeks, several people have asked me about "speaking in tongues" and what it means. Books have been written on this subject, but let me explain briefly. In a couple of the New Testament letters, there are references to a phenomenon called "glossolalia," or speaking in tongues. St. Paul thoroughly describes it in his first letter to the Corinthians, specifically chapters twelve, thirteen, and fourteen. "Now concerning spiritual gifts, I do not want you to be uninformed." (12:1). Paul talks about the gifts: speaking in tongues, interpreting tongues, prophecy, works of healing, and the like. Now, what should the Church do with such gifts? First, remember that they are gifts given by the Holy Spirit and not something we should seek to appropriate on our own.

If given by the Spirit, fine, but let us not seek ways to manipulate the Spirit to our own advantage. Paul himself offers a similar warning. He stresses that these gifts, if genuinely given, are not usually practiced in a public forum like worship. These gifts can be divisive and have often been used by people in a self-righteous manner. (i.e., I speak in tongues, and you don't; therefore, my spirituality exceeds yours). This kind of thinking is dangerous and hurtful to the church's unity. Even Paul says he would rather speak five words using his mind than ten thousand words in tongues because, in the long run, it is better for the whole church. (14: 19)

Perhaps the most essential point of all centers on chapter thirteen. Amid his commentary, Paul stops to remind us that the fruits of the Spirit are more to be desired than the gifts. And what are the fruits of the Spirit? Love, joy, peace, patience, kindness, goodness, gentleness, faithfulness, and self-control. What would the world be like if these fruits were more prevalent? Paul writes, "I will show you a more excellent way." And he goes on to tell us about love, utilizing the entire thirteenth chapter. (Don't just take my word for it; read it yourself in I Corinthians 13.)

So, what is the bottom line? The gifts of the Spirit are given to certain people for specific purposes, but they have never really been normative in the Church. If the Spirit gives them, we receive them with thanksgiving and use them appropriately. But the fruits of the Spirit are always desired and ought to be the goal of every Christian at every stage in their life. There have been times when the gifts have divided the church (that's why Paul was writing as he did to the Corinthians), but the fruits of the Spirit never divide. On the contrary, they unite, encourage, build up, and bless. The fruits of the Spirit will always be needed and never go out of style.

# LORD, TEACH US HOW TO PRAY

O ne day, the disciples came to Jesus and asked, "Lord, teach us (how) to pray." And he did. He taught them what we now call the Lord's Prayer. It is recorded twice in the New Testament. First, it is the prayer with seven petitions or seven requests.

Interestingly, only one of the seven petitions asks for a material gift: give us this day our daily bread. The other six petitions ask for spiritual or non-material blessings. What follows is a short explanation of this prayer. Most of these thoughts are mine, and a few are from a book by Nicky Gumbel (the founder of the Alpha program) entitled *Questions for Life*.

1. **Hallowed (holy) be your name.** God is very concerned that his name be used properly. This first petition and the Second Commandment both speak to this important issue. In the Old Testament, the Hebrews were so fearful of profaning God's name that they made up another word that signified God's name. Even it was used with the utmost respect. A person's name is really an extension of who that person *is*. We all value a good name. If we want our name used respectfully, how much more should God's name be used with reverence and awe? And yet, think about it. God's name is often used in the most degrading and profane ways. How long will God endure a people who abuse his name so shamelessly? We must pray that God's name be honored above all other names in our lives, homes, and nations.

2. **Your kingdom come.** God's kingdom exists in our hearts and wherever his rule is recognized. God's kingdom came into the fullest view when Jesus entered the world. Jesus spoke constantly of his Father's kingdom. Many of his parables begin with, "The kingdom of God shall be like..." His kingdom

includes praying for people to be reconciled, healed, set free from evil, filled with the Holy Spirit, and given the fruits and gifts of the Spirit to the end that one day, everyone will see this powerful spiritual reality that can transform our lives like nothing else in the entire world.

3. **Your will be done on earth as it is in heaven.** What is most important here is the acknowledgment that God wishes to bring his kingdom of love, hope, mercy, and *justice* to bear upon this broken and sinful world. By implication, not only do we pray for this, but we are also invited to work as hard as we can to make it happen. The kingdom and the Church are not necessarily the same, but they do overlap in great measure when the Church is being true to *its* "servant" calling.

4. **Give us this day our daily bread.** Martin Luther declared that this petition was not just about "spiritual" bread. It also includes food and clothing, shelter and family, peace and good government, and everything needed for our safety and well-being. The word 'daily' is not included by accident. God wants us to trust him daily for all the necessities of life. He will surely meet our needs, though not our greeds. Ask yourself when God last failed to provide for your daily needs. And when did you last thank him with all the sincerity of your heart?

5. **Forgive us our sins as we forgive those who sin against us.** Surely Jesus taught us to ask God to forgive us for our sinful thoughts, words, and deeds. "If you forgive people when they sin against you, your heavenly Father will also forgive you. But if you do not forgive others their sins (against you), your Father will not forgive your sins." (Matthew 6:14,15). The text does not imply that forgiving others can earn forgiveness. We can never earn forgiveness. Jesus achieved that for us on the cross. But the sign that we are forgiven is that we are willing to forgive others. If we are unwilling to forgive other people, that is evidence that we do not know forgiveness ourselves. If we really know God's forgiveness, we cannot refuse forgiveness to someone else.

6. **And lead us not into temptation.** Scholars have long debated just what this phrase means. God does not tempt us (James 1:13), but he is in control of how much exposure we have to the devil (see Job one and two, for example). Every person on this earth has at least one or more points of vulnerability in their lives. These may include selfish ambition, greed, pride, fear, lust for the flesh, gossiping, cynicism, anger, or idolatry. If we know our weaknesses, we can pray for protection against them and take action to avoid unnecessary temptation. The grocer told the little boy, "If you find the candy counter too tempting, go stand by the fruits and vegetables." Simple but profound advice. How much pain and sorrow could be averted if people were more aware of Satan's deep desire to entrap, ensnare, and destroy them?

7. **But deliver us from evil.** St. Paul tells us that Satan is like a roaring lion that prowls around us daily, seeking to devour us. It is a rather graphic but pointedly accurate illustration. How do we defend ourselves? Remember that the best defense is still a good offense. Play your trump cards. Worship weekly. Pray daily. Read your Bible. Seek the counsel and wisdom of other Christians. Stay away from people whose lifestyles may tempt you in the wrong direction. Stand for something, or you will fall for anything. "And put on the whole armor of God," St. Paul tells us. Satan does not have to have the last word. God has given you a free will, and you can make choices that align with God's will and your best interests.

It's a fairly short prayer. Just seventy words in all. But it has spoken powerfully to millions of people across the centuries. But that shouldn't surprise us. After all, it is the Lord's Prayer.

# DRUGS! DRUGS! DRUGS!

America has a serious drug problem now made even worse because of opioids and fentanyl. In 2021, there were over one million overdoses in America, many of which ended as a fatality. This is a national tragedy by any measure. So, how did we get into this mess? Look no further than Big Pharma. Only two nations on the planet foolishly allow for the mass advertising of prescription and over-the-counter drugs. As a result, children and adults alike are constantly exposed to very persuasive messaging that there is literally a pill for any malady under the sun. We now have enough of a problem dealing with illegally imported drugs, so why should drugs of any kind be mass-advertised?

But Big Pharma discovered long ago (with the blessing of Congress) that billions of dollars will be made every year if they can get more Americans to buy their drugs whether they need them or not. So, companies like Perdue, McKesson, and Mallinckrodt deliberately inundated our nation with over seventy-six billion highly addictive oxycodone pills from 2006 to 2012. McKesson was happy to ship over five million pain pills in two years to Kermit, West Virginia, a village of less than four hundred people. Were any of these companies self-monitoring such outrageously large orders of drugs? Of course not.

They were just making too much money ever to question such lucrative orders. So, is there a solution? At least one step would be to ban the mass advertising of drugs in America. And a second would be to hold these companies more accountable for the drugs they dispense to an often unsuspecting nation. Economist Milton Friedman once stated, "American corporations' sole purpose is to make money for its shareholders." We can all hope that our corporations have more of a conscience than that.

To be sure, many American companies are "good citizens" of this nation. But not all of them are…

# Why We Seem to Be Losing a Generation of Church Goers

1. It has become very "cool" and fashionable to be skeptical and cynical about "all things institutional," including the Church.
2. Some prominent authors have written bestselling books denouncing anything that smacks faith and religion. These include Sam Harris, Christopher Hitchens, Richard Dawkins, and Stephen Hawking (now deceased).
3. Significant scandals in some of our mainline churches, including the Roman Catholic Church and the Southern Baptist Convention, disillusioned our youth. i.e., clergy abuse of children, sexual assault of women, Indian Schools, etc.
4. So-called TV preachers always begging for money while living in multi-million-dollar mansions, owning private jets, and being caught up in repulsive sex scandals.
5. Phony TV "faith healers" like Benny Hinn, Mike Murdoch, Jimmy Swaggart, and Oral Roberts (deceased).
6. Devout young Christians who now see the Christian faith being hijacked by an ultra-conservative, far rightwing, politically motivated group of "believers." Some of this was witnessed when the Capitol was attacked on January 6, 2021.
7. Some college and university professors who no longer regard religious faith as having any real value and who, knowingly or not, degrade and demean all things religious.
8. Cultural "props" of years gone by are no longer in place. i.e., whole families, from grandparents to grandchildren, attended worship because it was "the right thing to do." Also, organized sports have almost totally pre-empted Sunday mornings.

9. The Church itself has failed at times. Strong and life-changing preaching seems to be on the wane. Little passion for worldwide evangelism today. And the Church not knowing how to evangelize in the twenty-first century.

10. Diversity and inclusivity are huge words in today's world. Some of my grandchildren attend schools that are very diverse ethnically, culturally, and religiously. This is a very different world than those of us who grew up in mostly White Anglo-Saxon Protestant (and Catholic) communities. So do my grandchildren, whose friends embrace a very different religion than theirs, ask themselves, "What is so unique about my Christianity?"

11. It could also be argued that some churches today take such far right-wing or far left-wing political positions that they tend to alienate young people whose politics are primarily centrist. Another challenge for the church today.

12. Almost all media forms today (TV, movies, plays, books, music, etc.) seem to delight in lampooning all things religious. Try to think of any movie or TV show that recently portrayed the clergy as anything but incompetent and insincere. PBS' Father Brown comes to mind, but he would be a rare exception.

# BACK TO BASICS

## (The Five Great Disciplines of True Christian Living)

As we begin another fall season, I need to remind some of our members just what it means to be a member of the Christian Church. It sometimes astonishes me how casual people can be in this regard—the words disciple and discipline are derived from the same root word. There are certain disciplines to our life of faith. I will list some of them as we consider the year before us.

The first is weekly worship. For Christians, this is not an optional exercise we participate in whenever it is convenient. You might be surprised if I told you some of the flimsy excuses I have heard for why people avoid weekly worship over the years. Worship is the lifeblood of the Christian. Without it, our faith soon falters and often even dies. Like a burning coal removed from a fire, it quickly cools and dies. And we, too, jeopardize our faith when we neglect worship. This notion that we can maintain faith in God in isolation is nonsense. You need the church, and the church needs you. The cross is a powerful symbol for all ages: the vertical portion reminds us of our relationship with God, while the horizontal reminds us of our relationship with one another. And we need both whether we know it or not. Jesus, the Bible tells us, went to the synagogue "as was his custom." (Luke 4:16). Now, if he needed the experience of worship, how much greater is our need? I find it interesting that in the wake of events like the Columbine shootings and 9/11, people suddenly flocked to the church. While I am glad they have come, I also ask, where have you been for the last weeks, months, or even years? Do we rush to God in times of crisis but ignore him when things are going smoothly? Is God some sugar daddy we call on only in times of great need? To me, we greatly dishonor God by treating him so casually. Worship is a weekly event as we all "remember the Sabbath day and keep it holy."

Secondly, we need to pray daily. Prayer is a very accurate barometer of a person's spiritual life and growth. Little prayer equals little growth. Much prayer equals much growth. Prayer is that wonderfully simple medium that allows us to be in touch with the God who created us, redeemed us, and now desires more than anything to live in daily communion with us. Like a father who is honored when his children ask him for his love and blessings, so is God honored when we ask. God will not meet our greeds but will surely meet our needs. And remember, prayer is more than a shopping list of wants and desires. Thank God for his blessings, praise him, confess your sins, and pray for others, not just ourselves.

Thirdly, read the Bible daily. God's written word has been a source of hope, comfort, wisdom, truth, and encouragement for almost three thousand years. As the Psalmist says, "Thy word is a lamp unto my feet and a light unto my path." So read just one chapter a day, and don't rush it. Instead, savor its meaning; I promise your faith will grow and deepen. And don't forget all the weekly Bible study opportunities your church offers.

Fourthly, do at least one act of loving service a day. As Christ gave himself for others without reservation, so should his followers. And by doing so, we will discover the real meaning of life. In giving, we do receive. In losing ourselves on behalf of others, we truly find the joy and meaning of life. Jesus once declared, "As you have done it unto the least of one of these persons, you have also done it unto me." One of the primary reasons for our existence is to console and care for one another. And remember that a joy shared is a joy doubled, and a burden shared is a burden halved.

Finally, give 10% of your income to the church's work. Margaret and I started this discipline the first year we were married and have never regretted it. While both students in 1968 and living on a very meager income, we joined the Lutheran Church of Hope near Dinky Town and pledged $ 9.50 a week. We believe this is the wisest and most satisfying thing we could do with our money. (I acknowledge that people with very meager incomes may find it harder to tithe simply because they have a tiny "pie" to begin with. But ironically, these same people are often the most generous in their giving.) Such giving also reminds me that I am only returning to God what I never owned in the first place. It all belongs to him. As the Psalmist says, "The earth is the Lord's and the fullness thereof." This notion that I own anything in any ultimate sense is a lie. I am only a manager of these gifts, and even that isn't for very long. How selfish and faithless the human race can often be. How we love to hoard what isn't ours to begin with. Remember that humans work from an economy of scarcity while God always works from abundance. We need to trust him much more than we do. As Jesus said, "Seek first my kingdom and my righteousness, and all else will be added unto you." Do you really believe this promise that he makes to us?

There is only one way to find out how all this works: just try it. I promise it will be the journey of a lifetime. So, there is worship, scripture, prayer, service, and stewardship. The big five. It's a model for godly living that has served God's people for centuries. And there is absolutely no reason to start doubting its value now.

# THE BRIDGE OPERATOR STORY

The season of Lent is upon us once again. Among other things, it is a time for reflection and meditation. With this in mind, I invite you to contemplate the following story. For me, it captures the essence of Lent, especially Good Friday.

A certain man was the operator of a railroad drawbridge that spanned a great river. The bridge was normally kept in a raised position to allow for ships and boats to freely move up and down this important waterway, but when the train whistle blew in the distance and the signal was given, the operator would lower the bridge to allow the train to swiftly and safely cross the river.

One day, the bridge operator brought his son with him to work, and, as little boys often do, he quickly went about exploring the bridge. In the course of time, an approaching train sounded its whistle, alerting the operator that the bridge must be lowered into position. But as he prepared to do so, the operator looked down in horror to see his son playing in amongst the huge gears that would lower the bridge into position. A terrible, gut-wrenching choice suddenly faced the operator—either lower the bridge and crush his son in the process or leave it upright and witness the death of hundreds of passengers in what would certainly be a horrible train wreck. In the agonizing moments that followed, the operator did what he knew he had to do. He lowered the bridge and covered his ears to block out the dying screams of his son below.

I want to tell you that I'm not fond of this story. It is one of pain, sorrow, and a terrible choice. And God forbid that any parent should ever have to make such an excruciatingly painful decision. (Incidentally, that very word excruciating comes to us from the ancient Romans; the Latin ex-crusis literally refers to the intense pain and suffering experienced by those being crucified). I am not sure I could have acted as nobly as did the bridge operator. But that is just the point. God did for us what we could not do for ourselves. God paid a terrible price for you and for me on the cross of Calvary. It will always be a mystery, but God gave up his Son's life so that you and I might have life. It is likely the first Bible verse you learned was "For God so loved the world that he gave his only Son..." (John 3:16); or as St. Paul wrote, "And being found in human form, Jesus humbled himself and became obedient unto death, even death upon a cross." (Phil. 2:8) We may never know how this was all accomplished. Still, for centuries, millions of people have discovered profound hope and comfort in this incredible rescue mission performed on your behalf and mine.

There is one other aspect of this story to be noted. As the train sped on, few passengers likely realized what an enormous sacrifice had just been made so that they might live. Many have heard the story, but many have not. And for some who have heard, it seems to have little meaning for them. Let us double our efforts to keep telling the whole world this old, old story that is ever new. This is our calling and our commission for life. Go forth and tell the good news and a blessed Lenten season to you and yours.

# Israel, Biblical Prophecy, and the Second Coming of Christ

I want to clear up a matter today that some of you have asked about and many of you have no doubt thought about.

Within the "right-wing" of the Christian Church, there are several fundamentalist preachers and teachers who, in recent years, have set forth the premise that the re-establishment of the state of Israel in 1948 is somehow a sure sign that the end of the world is near and, therefore, the fulfillment of some great Biblical prophecy. Worse yet, they have embarked upon a campaign that is so pro-Israel and anti-Arab that they have turned a blind eye to the terrible suffering of the Palestinian people, some of whom are Christians. (Many Palestinians embrace the Muslim faith, but some Palestinians are Christians.) In either case, these people, who have inhabited the Holy Lands for over thirteen centuries, are now treated as aliens in their own country. You may be interested to know that before 1948, about 80% of Israel's land belonged to the Palestinians. Today, that number is down to about 30% and still shrinking—no wonder they are frustrated and outraged.

Let me say this as clearly as I can. The re-establishment of the state of Israel has nothing to do with the Second Coming of Christ and the fulfillment of Biblical prophecy. Anyone who tells you otherwise is simply misinformed.

Yes, this small piece of real estate on the eastern shore of the Mediterranean Sea is holy to Jews, Muslims, and Christians alike. The Temple Mount and the Wailing Wall are especially sacred sites. But that is precisely the problem. These places are no more important to our Lord than any other part of our globe. These places, for some, have become idolatrous creations that make all this bloodshed in Israel doubly tragic. God is not interested in real estate (he owns it all anyway). But he is interested in human hearts. Does the city of Jerusalem have historical value? Of course. And so does the log cabin that Abe Lincoln was born in. But no one should have to die fighting over it.

Do you recall the words of Jesus as he spoke to the woman at the well of Samaria? "Woman," he said, "the hour is coming when neither on this mountain nor in Jerusalem will you worship the Father." John 4:21). Jesus was trying to tell this woman that God was now to be worshipped "in spirit and truth" (vs. 24) and that a particular "holy site" would no longer be of any great importance.

How pathetic and provincial we humans can be. Jesus could not have said it more plainly. His kingdom is not territorial, geographical, political, or even ecclesiastical. His kingdom is a spiritual kingdom in which Christ calls upon all people to practice the fruits of the Spirit: love, joy, peace, patience, kindness, gentleness, faithfulness, and self-control.

Christ is saying to us in no uncertain terms: your "holy city" means little to me, especially if you use it as an excuse to kill each other. Remember what I said, "I will destroy this temple, and in three days, I will raise it up again." (Matt. 26:61) But we didn't get the message. "I am God's true Temple," Jesus is telling us. And, wonder of wonders, so are we. Paul reminds us. "Do you not know that your bodies are the temple of the Holy Spirit?" (I Cor. 3:16). It is as if Jesus is saying, "So forget about all your sacred shrines and make yourselves holy by inviting me into your life without reservation and without condition. Then you will begin to understand what my kingdom is all about."

Jesus calls upon us to renounce all sin and selfishness, to forget about all the cheap treasures of this world, to renounce all hatred, bigotry, and prejudice, and to learn to love others as he first loved us: fully, joyfully, unconditionally, sacrificially, and even recklessly. Jesus says, in my kingdom, the lion and the lamb will lie down together. In my kingdom, the child will play with the serpent and not be bitten. So go now and be "little Christs" in the world. Be salt and leaven and light. Be peace, hope, and joy. Be truth and mercy and goodness. Be wise and understanding and merciful. And know for a certainty that I will be with you always, even to the end of time.

God must weep over our silly and idolatrous ways. He wants a changed heart. Everything else is incidental. St. Paul says: "If anyone is in Christ, they are a new creation. The old has passed away, and the new has come." (II Cor. 5:17). Praise God for his challenge to us to change. So may we heed his call today.

# THE ORIGIN OF THANKSGIVING DAY

This Thanksgiving, millions of Americans will once again gather with family and friends to enjoy their traditional holiday meal. But many know little about the events that brought this day into being. So, as a means of enhancing our understanding of this observance and for the refreshment of our memories, let us again examine some of its origins.

Any serious consideration of our nation's day of Thanksgiving must focus on two different events separated in time by almost two and a half centuries. First, our national holiday, which falls on the last Thursday of each November, was not signed into law until 1863. This portion of the story began in 1850 when a determined young woman named Sarah Hale felt that the United States should pause once a year for a National Day of Thanksgiving and prayer. She earnestly petitioned Presidents Fillmore, Pierce, Buchanan, and Lincoln for over a dozen years, urging them to declare a National Day of Thanksgiving. During the Civil War's dark days, Sarah Hale continued to ask for just one day of peace amidst the bloodshed and strife. Finally, her efforts were rewarded when Abraham Lincoln, a man much respected for his faith in God, signed the Thanksgiving Day Proclamation into law.

But perhaps even more fascinating is the story of that first gathering of Pilgrims who had come to the new land seeking religious and political freedom. Having fled from England to Holland, the Separatists, as they were called, waited over a decade for the opportunity to sail to the new world. Finally, after an aborted start in which a smaller companion ship, the Speedwell, nearly sank, the Mayflower sailed out of Plymouth Harbor on September 6, 1620, with a manifest of one hundred and two passengers. Sixty-six days later, on November 11th, the Mayflower

Pilgrims first sighted what is now Cape Cod, laying to rest serious fears that they had become lost at sea.

Arriving late in the fall, the Pilgrims barely had time to build shelters for the coming winter. While many stayed aboard ships, stricken with such probable illnesses as pneumonia and tuberculosis (aggravated by scurvy), others scouted the coastland, looking for the most suitable place to build the new colony. A decision was finally made, and the first construction began in late December 1620.

During the terrible months that followed, the colonists faced famine, bitter cold, disease, and deep despair. At one point, only a handful of people were well enough to tend to the sick, much less work on the Common House, the first structure erected. So decimated were their numbers that over half of the company lay in their graves by late winter. Burials occurred at night to prevent the Indians from noting their continued losses.

The advent of spring, however, brought much needed relief and an excellent growing season, accompanied by some sound agricultural advice from friendly Indians, culminating in the first Thanksgiving celebration in mid-October 1621. It was out of these remarkable events that the first Thanksgiving was born.

I am moved in some way by these two stories. Undoubtedly, the faith of our forebears ought to cause us all to ponder again what it means to give thanks to God. Instead, for far too many Americans, Thanksgiving Day has been reduced to a time for stuffing turkeys and families and quarterbacking televised football games. How carelessly we regard this day and how casual we are about those opportunities to worship God in the true spirit of thankfulness. Houses of worship throughout our land should be filled. Instead, many will see only modest numbers of worshippers. How is it that the Pilgrims called for a day of thanksgiving following a devastating first winter in the new world, and we who live with daily abundance find less and less time for genuine thanksgiving?

Another historical note given to us by the Pilgrims merits retelling. Letters and diaries relate that the colonists first entered Massachusetts Bay on a Saturday. A party of sixteen men went ashore to do an initial exploration. The next day being Sunday, the Pilgrims remained on the Mayflower for worship and prayer. Remembering that the Pilgrims had been at sea for over two months living in cramped and unhealthy quarters, one might expect they would have scrambled ashore the first moment they were able. Instead, they observed the Sabbath on board the ship, true to their faith and godly convictions. On Monday, they resumed their explorations. From such foundational beliefs, America became one of the few nations worldwide to declare a National Day of Thanksgiving.

As we once again celebrate this season of thanks, the deeds of those who have gone before us should remind us of our need to humbly and frequently offer God our heartfelt thanks for the bountiful blessings he has heaped upon us. Perhaps it is the psalmist who best sounds the theme of the season with his timeless admonition to:

*Bless the Lord, O my soul, and all that is within* me
    *bless his holy name.*
*Bless the Lord, O my soul, and forget not all his*
    *benefits. (Psalms 103: 1,2)*

# Turn on the Light

Years ago, I read an article about a town in northern Norway where the sun never shines for the two months of December and January due to its location (two hundred miles north of the Arctic Circle). This community of forty thousand, called Tromsø, experiences eight weeks of continual darkness during mid-winter.

However, the reaction of the people who live through this time of gloom and darkness is even more fascinating than the constant darkness. As the article indicates, many persons who are emotionally healthy for the rest of the year may become unaccountably tense, restless, fearful, and preoccupied with thoughts of death. One psychologist from Oslo who has researched the Arctic was quoted as saying, "The polar night tends to bring out the least desirable elements in human behavior." Among those elements were envy, jealousy, suspicion, egotism, and general irritability.

Reading this article, I was struck by how similar this situation is to the general condition of the whole human race. Since the fall of man in the garden, darkness has been a part of our world. With the coming of sin, humanity also began to experience the darkness of sickness and death, evil, fear, hatred, greed, and deceit.

But God did not leave us in the darkness forever, and thank God for that. "The true light that enlightens every man was coming into the world." God desires that all men learn to walk in the Light. God sent his Son to dispel the darkness and to rid our lives of such elements as envy, suspicion, jealousy, and hatred. Jesus said, "I am the light of the world." And all who believe his words walk in the Light.

Epiphany's symbol is a star that recalls the star that led the Wise Men to Bethlehem. It also reminds us that the Light of the world has come to dispel the darkness of our lives and our world. As John has said, not everyone received the Light when it entered the world. "But to all who received him, who believed in his name, he gave the power to become the children of God." (1:12). This is the glorious truth upon which we base our lives today. The true and everlasting Light has come into our world. When we receive the Light, we become children of the Light.

# NEW YEAR

An old year ends and a new one begins. An old decade ends, and a new one begins. As Job reminds us, "How swifter than the weaver's shuttle are the days of our lives." As we ponder the theme of time in this new year, we realize that time is life and life is time, and both are gifts to us from God. In Psalm 31, we read: "Thou art my God, and my times are in thy hands." For the Christian, time is a gift and an opportunity for service and commitment. We mortals can fill our days with various activities; the fundamental question of our lives is which ones are pleasing to our Lord. To answer this question, the holy scriptures instruct us on how we are to live. The Law and the Prophets call us to love God with all our heart, soul, mind, and strength, and our neighbor as ourselves. Though an old standard, it is still an excellent guide and goal for daily living.

Some years ago, I saw an old grandfather's clock with a poem etched on the glass window, revealing the inner workings of that heirloom. This is the original version by Rev. Canon Henry Twells.

*When as a child I laughed and wept,*
*Time crept.*
*When as a youth I waxed more bold,*
*Time strolled.*
*When I became a full grown man,*
*Time RAN.*
*When older still I daily grew,*
*Time **flew**.*
*Soon I shall find, in passing on,*
*Time gone.*
*O Christ! wilt Thou have saved me then?*

If such a thought brings you up short, let us hear again from the source of permanence in an ever-changing world. "Jesus Christ is the same yesterday, today, and forever." (Heb. 13:8). "All flesh is grass... the grass withers, the flower fades, but the word of our God will stand forever." (Isaiah 40:8) If the prospect of the new year leaves us feeling fearful or inadequate, then hear again the words of Isaac Watts in his great hymn: Oh God, our help in ages past. Our hope for years to come. Be thou our guide while troubles last, and our eternal home.

# A WORD TO ALL YOUTH

When I was about your age (the teen years), I recall being told by a good friend of mine that I was now establishing some habits that would stay with me for the rest of my life. As I have grown older, I have come to understand the wisdom of his words. And one of the "habits" he spoke about had to do with giving, sharing, and generosity. So, I am writing to encourage you to develop this good habit and keep it always.

The Bible makes it clear that you and I (no matter what our age may be) are to return to God each week a portion of what he has first given to us. The Bible makes it very clear that you and I own nothing. We enter this world with nothing, and we leave it with nothing. (I Timothy 6:7) It all belongs to God. "The earth is the Lord's and the fullness thereof." (Psalm 19) But what you and I do between birth and death with the gifts that God has "loaned" to us is of vital importance.

Now I hear some of you saying, "Pastor, why are you writing to us teens? We don't have any money." I'm afraid I must disagree. Recently, I read that teenagers have the largest share of what is known as "discretionary spending" in the entire American economy. So, it could be argued that young people today have more expendable income than any other age group in our economy.

So, without apologizing, I am asking you to begin a great habit if you have not yet done so. I ask you to complete the enclosed pledge card and faithfully and diligently return that amount to your church weekly. And I can tell you this: God will bless you for your faithfulness. And you will also be doing yourself a big favor. Whenever we give to others, we win a small victory over that terrible enemy of all human beings: our own self-centeredness.

I want to share a true story. Years ago, a teen from our church came home with a paycheck of $406.00. The teen then asked his mother to deposit the check but retain $40.60. Naturally, the mother was curious about this odd amount and asked what it was for. At first, the teen didn't want to say what it was for. But when she asked again, he said he wanted to begin tithing his income to the church.

In other words, he wants to return 10% of all he earns to God. This story warmed my heart, not because of the money itself, but because of the strong faith this action revealed in this young man's life.

Please pray about this matter. Talk to your parents. Fill out the card with an amount you feel good about, then return it to the church. Mail it in or place it on the offering plate next time you worship with us. Faith in God and good stewardship go hand-in-hand. Let this be a time of commitment and enrichment for your young life. Pledge and start a great habit that will serve you for the rest of your life. And thank you for all the goodwill, support, and encouragement you give to the church of Jesus Christ. This work is more vital than any of us may ever know. Working in the Kingdom of God is the most significant work anyone can ever do. So, join us with your prayers, pledge, love, and youthful vitality. We need you, and we thank God for you.

# Section Three

## FAITH AND LIFE

# EVANGELISM

*This article was written in 1987*

The unholy war of the televangelists has died down a bit, so this may be an excellent time to comment on such events. As I see it, TV evangelism has serious dangers as we now know it.

First, vast amounts of money are involved (an estimated billion dollars annually) with practically no accountability. Such a situation can only lead to trouble. By contrast, in almost every "mainline" congregation, not a single dime is expended without the approval of some board or committee of objective and unbiased people.

Secondly, there is the constant danger of mixing worship and entertainment. The two are very different and should not be blurred or blended.

Third, the TV "church" is not the church of the New Testament. There is no observance of the sacraments, no congregation of people who care for one another, and no sacrificial call to do anything except give money to support the high cost of TV airtime.

Fourth, TV has two primary purposes: To sell you something or to entertain you. Therefore, it may not be a very appropriate forum for the church to utilize in the first place.

Five, there is always the temptation to worship the TV personality rather than God. This may also happen in a parish, but not nearly so easily.

Bottom line: TV gives us media idols whom we love to worship.

In 1980, independent underwriters studied some of the major TV ministries. These included Jerry Fawell, Pat Robertson (700 Club), Jim Baker (PTL Club), Rex Humbard, and Robert Schuller. By sharp contrast, our American Lutheran Church had a budget of about $32,000,000 that same year. With it, we established over forty-two new churches, supported four seminaries with an enrollment of over nine hundred students, eleven senior colleges and one junior college, twelve hospitals and two schools of nursing, one hundred and ninety-three full-time missionaries working in nineteen countries of the world, eighty-two youth and family camps across the nation, two major weekly radio programs, a chaplain Corp that is active in prisons and hospitals nation-wide, a campus ministry at hundreds of colleges and universities, almost two-hundred homes for the aged, and Social Service agencies that serve virtually every state in the union. In addition, we support publishing houses that produce vast amounts of Christian materials, and often, the ALC is the most prominent single supporter of the American Bible Society. And the list could go on and on.

The point is clear: The mainline churches of America do the most effective job with the financial resources given to them and should, therefore, never apologize for asking for responsible stewardship.

# WORSHIP

Pardon me, but I need to get something off my chest today. Some time ago, someone came to our late worship service, looked around, and then commented to one of our staff, "This isn't the kind of worship service I'm looking for," and promptly left the building. (It's doubtful this person found another service to attend that late in the morning).

But much more to the point is how we understand worship in to-day's society. I wonder if most of us realize how incredibly narcissistic our society has become. I am uninterested if something doesn't stimu-late, entertain, or thrill me. Our kids say it, their friends say it, and we adults say it, too. The criteria for measuring what we do with our time centers mostly on what someone or something will do for us.

But worship is in a very different category. The Greek word for worship is liturgia, which literally means "the work of the people." So, "worship" and "work" come from the same root derivation. I come to the church to literally work at my worship with God. The focus of wor-ship is not on the self but on God. I have heard well-meaning people say I don't go to church because I don't get anything out of it.

Frankly, this comment reveals an incredibly shallow understanding of the faith. The question is not how much I get from worship but how much I give to worship. Let's think about this. I come to worship to give all that I have to God. He asks for nothing less. The entire hour may be unfulfilling for me, but it may still be an excellent experience regarding what I have offered to God: my time, voice, and attention. My thanks, my prayers, my praise, my dollars, my repentance, my life. God doesn't show up to worship us. We show up to worship God. And to think oth-erwise is to display an arrested understanding of our proper relationship with God. Worship is one of the very few things we do in life that rescues us from those powerful innate tendencies toward self-centeredness.

Worship calls us to break out of the cocoon of self and offer ourselves totally and unconditionally to God and others. And it will be at this point that we begin to understand the whole meaning of worship. Someone has said that the Trinity of our lives is not the Father, Son, and Holy Spirit but Me, Myself, and I. Come to worship and give your all to God. Please find out how refreshing it is to have your life reoriented and realigned each week. And in the process, you will discover what true worship is all about. Don't go home (or stay home) because "this is not the kind of service I am looking for." Make the service your own by giving it your all.

# THE JOY OF STEWARDSHIP

It doesn't bother me a bit to talk forthrightly about stewardship. I believe it is part of the calling given to every pastor who is worth their salt. In the thirty-four recorded parables of Jesus in the New Testament, almost half instruct us on how to use our wealth and material possessions wisely.

My word to all of us who confess the name of Jesus is this: be sure you aren't cheating yourself, your Lord, and His Church. It amazes me how casual people are about giving to the church. Someone once asked me (quite sincerely) if I thought God cared what he put on the offering plate each week. My response was this: God cares a great deal about our offerings. If you doubt this, consider the story of Cain and Abel. Do you recall what happened to these two men? God asked for their offerings. Cain brought a few heads of grain from his field to the altar and tried to give as little as he could. Abel brought forward the finest sheep in his flock. He gave the very best of what he had to give. Cain gave his leftovers. Could the same be said of you and me? Then God honored Abel's gift but rejected Cain's gift.

I also think of the rich young ruler who came to Jesus and asked what he needed to do to be saved. Jesus told him to keep the commandments. He told Jesus he had from his youth. Then Jesus gave him one more test. Sell what you have, give it to people experiencing poverty, and then follow me. The man went away sorrowful because he loved his wealth more than God. One of the truest words Jesus ever spoke was this: "Where your treasure is, there will your heart be also."

Just where is your treasure today? Judging by what some people give to their Lord, their heart is somewhere else. To love and trust our wealth more than God is idolatrous and foolish. Let me tell you a little story. When Margaret and I were married many years ago, we tithed our income to our Lord. This is 10% of either our gross or net income. It was a decision we have never regretted. That first year, our weekly offering was $9.50. We lived on a small stipend from a hospital, where I worked as a chaplain while Margaret finished her education at the University of Minnesota. Over the years, I have learned that you can never outgive God. I have also learned the value of disciplined, weekly percentage giving. God deserves no less. Not many years ago, Margaret and I had a combined income of about $50,000. (Margaret works part-time for a social service agency that pays low wages, but she likes the work). It was the first time I was confronted with the reality of weekly giving to the church that reached three digits. I asked myself if it were possible to do so. All things are possible with God's help.

We started giving the three-digit amount and never looked back. Again, as my income has increased, so has my giving to my Lord. I would likely reduce my giving if my income went down, although that is not a foregone conclusion. It may interest you to know that some of the most responsible giving to the churches of America was done in the depths of the Great Depression. The reason for this? Tough times cause people to discard the frivolous and to see more clearly what in life is essential.

I do ask people to give generously to the church, knowing it is for their own good. The prevailing sickness of the human race is selfishness and self-centeredness. It was embodied in the crass remark of Ivan Boesky, who told America that "greed is a good thing." Our culture worships the "lifestyles of the rich and famous." We need to be rescued from such idolatry before God judges this nation. Generous and responsible giving of our wealth is one decisive way to combat the sickness of selfishness and to demonstrate before God that it is He whom we worship and trust above all else and not our wealth. Look carefully today at your assets. Unless you are making large gifts to charity outside the church, I believe with all my heart that God expects you to give weekly, generously, and proportionately.

Let me suggest another approach if tithing seems too big a challenge for you now. Give a dollar a week for each $1,000 of annual gross income. For example, if you make $30,000 a year, give $30 a week. If you make $50,000, give $50 a week. This is roughly equivalent to a half tithe and a worthy goal to strive for if you now give 1%, 2%, 3%, or 4% of your income.

Now, it could be that some of you are offended by what I have written. So, let me just close with this one thought. Someday, you and I and everyone on this planet will stand before our Lord face to face. Of course, he would not ask us what kind of house we lived in, how many cars we owned, or how thick our investment portfolio was. But he will likely ask this one question: "Of all the world's wealth that I entrusted to you in your lifetime, how much did you return to me, to my Church, and to the needy of the world?" How will you answer?

# The Existence of God

It seems today that many people in our land are questioning, as never before, the existence of God. Films like "Contact" add some fuel to the debate. The existence of God can never be proven using scientific methodologies, but neither has God left himself without witnesses. Popular author Jim Bishop, who died some years ago, wrote the following. I think you will find it worth your time.

There is no God? All of the wonders around us are accidental. No almighty hand made a thousand billion stars. They made themselves. No power keeps them on their steady course. The earth spins to keep the oceans from falling toward the sun. Infants teach themselves to cry when they are hungry or hurt. A small flower invented itself so that we could extract digitalis for sick hearts. The earth gave itself day and night, tilted itself so that we get seasons. Without the magnetic poles, man could not navigate the trackless oceans of water and air, but they just happened to be there.

How about the sugar "thermostat" in the pancreas? It maintains a level of sugar in the blood sufficient for energy. Without it, all of us would fall into a coma and die.

Why does snow sit on mountaintops waiting for the warm spring sun to melt at just the right time for the young crops in farms below to drink? A very lovely accident.

The human heart will beat for eighty or ninety years without faltering. How does it get sufficient rest between beats? A kidney will filter poison from the blood and leave good things alone. How does it know one from the other?

Who gave the human tongue the flexibility to form words and a brain to understand them but denied it to other animals? Who showed a womb how to take the love of two people and keep splitting a tiny ovum until, in time, a baby would have the proper number of fingers, eyes, ears, and hair in the right places and come into the world when it is strong enough to sustain life? The foolish person says in his heart, "There is no God." Psalm 14: 1

# HOW DO WE DEAL WITH THE
# TRAGEDY OF SUICIDE?

A few years ago, one of the members of our church lost a good friend when she took her life. Others in our fellowship have also tasted the bitterness of loss due to suicide. How can we understand this great sadness as Christians and as people of faith?

Let's begin by acknowledging that the church was not enlightened for centuries. It is believed that some of our thinking on this subject was filtered through the lens of Judas, who took his life after betraying Jesus. In some sad and ironic way, suicide became closely associated with the shame of Judas. It was an unfortunate association, to be sure. To be honest, the church has not always been very sensitive to either the survivors or the victims of suicide. Churches in the Middle Ages (and even very recently) often refused any kind of burial service for the deceased. Persons who took their own lives were usually buried outside the walls of the church cemeteries. To say that a stigma was attached to this painful event would be a gross understatement. In a sense, the church also reflected some of society's prevailing views in general. Undoubtedly, a lot of needless suffering was caused by a lack of knowledge, unfair stereotypes, bad theology, and cultural values that were often tenacious and very resistant to change.

Thankfully, things have changed over time. Today, we view this tragic event in very different terms. We know, for example, that the human body is incredibly complex and that certain hormones or other body chemicals can become seriously imbalanced. Sometimes, this condition eludes even the most perceptive doctors and therapists. When such imbalances occur, people may develop a deep and abiding depression over which they have little or no control. If this situation persists or goes undetected and untreated for any length of time, suicide may be the final result. It can be a devastating event for any family to experience. And its effects on their lives may remain for many years. Feelings of guilt, anger, frustration, and sorrow often haunt survivors of suicide. Yet, ironically, they most often deserve none of it. Suicide produces many unanswered questions and unfulfilled dreams—few happenings in life rival such grief and heartache.

But there is also a word of consolation for those who mourn. As I mentioned, the church today, as a rule, has developed a more enlightened understanding of suicide. It is my personal belief that when someone reaches such a state in life that they can override those powerful, inborn feelings of self-preservation; when life becomes so painful that the only viable option one sees is to conclude one's own life; when these and other factors come into play, then I believe that God, in his infinite wisdom, compassion, and mercy, does indeed receive these mortally wounded people into his eternal kingdom where they will never again have to do battle with whatever demons drove them to commit such a life-denying act.

There is an old saying in the AA organization that all alcoholics go to heaven because they have spent most of their lives in hell (as have most of their family members). I cannot say if this is true, but I mention it because it contains an element of truth. As I observe life, some people seem to wrestle with greater demons than others. Addictions, mental illness, chemical imbalances of the body, or certain physical afflictions sometimes cause people to become self-destructive. People, prayer, therapy, and medicine can intervene, but not always. We live in a deeply flawed and broken world, and when people deliberately harm themselves, we must place them in their Creator's loving and eternal arms.

When one of my professors at the seminary lost his daughter to suicide some years ago, he made this comment: "I will never understand why this had to happen, but there is comfort in knowing that God has now freed her from the inner turmoil that brought her to her death." There are mysteries of life we will never fully comprehend. In the meantime, we continue to affirm the gift of life, thank God for each new day that he gives us, and do all we can to help those around us carry their burdens down the road of life.

# A Word About the
## Book Series, *Left Behind*

Tim Lahaye is up to his old self again. His latest book, a novel entitled *Left Behind*, has already sold over three million copies. The public's growing fascination with the coming millennium is part of the book's success. Everybody wants to know what the year 2000 will bring: a whole new era of blessings or a time of judgment and the world's end. For those who are enthusiastic supporters of Lahaye, let me remind you of a couple of things.

In 1970, Hal Lindsey wrote a book called *The Late Great Planet Earth*. It was about a third fact, a third fiction, and a third foolishness. Some chapter titles should have given us a clue; one was entitled "Polishing Your Crystal Ball." (This hardly sounds like responsible theology.) Lahaye was convinced that Russia and godless Communism were part of the great anti-Christ mentioned in the Book of Revelation. He made more wild predictions than you can imagine. And by the way, whatever happened to that Russian beast that was to rise up and overrun the earth and usher in the end of the world?

Lahaye is simply a better writer than a theologian. He knows what sells and is good at tapping into people's fears. And he is getting very rich in the process. He also seems to enjoy what I call "manipulation evangelism," something Jesus never practiced.

Let's look at the facts from the perspective of scripture. Lahaye obviously delights in forecasting the coming rapture. The rapture is but one of several models set forth in scripture concerning the end of the world as we know it. For those who love to scare people into some kind of religious response, this is often their weapon of choice. The theory has it that God will rapture all faithful people into heaven while the rest are left in terrible pain for another thousand years. During this time, God will somehow cleanse the earth of all sin and ultimately defeat the Devil. The recent "Nightmare" production in Burnsville fits this thinking well. (A friend who saw these two presentations said the real "nightmare" was getting past the religious folk who encountered you after the program.) There may be a place for such an emphasis, but I am not inclined to promote it too enthusiastically. Jesus declared that you will not know the day or the hour. We should not even try to predict it. He also told us to take this world's needs and hurts very seriously. It is possible to be so heavenly-minded that you are no earthly good. When Luther was asked what he would do if he knew this was his last day on earth, he was said to have replied, "I would plant a tree." I like that emphasis. I have always taken great comfort in other "rapture" texts—for example, John. 5:24 quotes Jesus as saying. "Truly, I say to you, he who hears my word and believes in him who sent me has eternal life; he does not come into judgment but has already passed from death into life."

Remember, too, that whenever Jesus spoke of the end of the world and the ushering in of the Kingdom of God for his faithful people, he used images of a family reunion, a wedding banquet, or a time of great celebration. Indeed, there should be a sense of urgency in our lives, and we should be fully prepared for the return of our Lord. But let us not become so preoccupied with predicting the event that we forget our true calling: to love God with all our heart, soul, mind, and strength, and our neighbor as ourselves. If we do this, we shall be prepared to meet our Lord anytime. I encourage you not to get right behind *Left Behind.*

# THREE VERY IMPORTANT PHRASES

Focus on the Family is a global Christian ministry dedicated to helping families thrive. Their National Director, Dr. James Dobson, once said that three phrases should be spoken in every home in America every day. The first is THANK YOU. When spoken sincerely, two little words benefit the one who speaks and hears them. When I tell someone "Thank you," I declare my gratitude for some deed, word, or gift that very likely didn't have to be offered to me. Someone went out of their way to give me some form of assistance or encouragement, and I want to acknowledge their kindness to me. And the one who receives the thanks also benefits. They are affirmed, appreciated, and recognized for the good they have done. And they very likely wish to do more kind deeds, having discovered how helpful they are in this fast-paced, depersonalized world. So, let us never grow weary of thanking God for all of his gifts as well. Being able to thank another person in life is a true gift. What would our world be like without kind deeds and thankful people? I am not sure I would want to live in a world devoid of gratitude.

The second phrase is I LOVE YOU. Again, three very powerful words. It seems that God has made us in such a way that we need to hear them often. And even if our actions declare such love, speaking and hearing these words still seems vitally essential for all of us. If the primary characteristic of God is love, and if his will is that all humankind learns how to give and receive love, then who among us can say that this is not an important matter? In Romans 12:9, St. Paul tells us to "let our love be genuine." I assume he also thinks it should be expressed often, in both word and deed.

Third, I AM SORRY. I saved the toughest one for last. For many people, saying I am sorry sincerely is difficult. To say that I am sorry is an admission that I am not perfect and that I am capable of making mistakes. It is a declaration that I, too, am a fallible human being and that I, too, stand in need of the forgiveness of God and others around me. It may be that you grew up in a home where these words were seldom, if ever, spoken. Being wrong was the worst thing that could happen to a person. You became a master at blaming others and rationalizing your own faults and shortcomings. Over time, you begin to believe that you truly are always right and never wrong. This does happen to people, but it is a miserable way to live. If I am always right, I must proclaim my innocence, find fault in others, concoct excuses to justify my shortcomings, put on a false front, and live with the fear that I will be "found out." Worse yet, a person starts to believe that they are different from everyone else in the human race. They simply can do no wrong. Therefore, they never need to apologize to anyone.

The truth of the matter is that people who never apologize are very insecure. It takes a mature, secure person to admit their faults and to ask others for forgiveness. Such people live a much happier and more fulfilling life. They know they are not perfect. They know that they offend others sometimes. They know they make mistakes. They also know the benefit of asking for forgiveness and receiving it with grace and thankfulness. This is how relationships are healed. Mistakes happen tens of thousands of times a day. God's greatest gift to us is to know that we admit to an error, ask him and others for forgiveness, and then have it granted. It's one of the greatest feelings in the world. How sad for those who never allow themselves the luxury of being forgiven.

These are three little phrases but oh so very important to all. Speak them often, and everyone in your life will benefit.

# CREATIONISM OR EVOLUTION?
## OKAY, WHICH IS IT?

Every now and again, I get asked the question: what are we to believe as Christians about the ongoing debate between Creationism (the Biblical account of a seven-day creation) versus evolution (the belief that humankind evolved from micro-organisms over millions of years)?

In 1925, a famous event in Dayton, Tennessee, became known as the Scopes Monkey Trial. This trial was to settle the matter, but obviously, it did not. (If you want to learn more about the trial, rent the movie "Inherit the Wind" with Spencer Tracy; it's an absolute classic).

So, what to believe? Let me begin by noting that the Bible was never intended to be a book of science, as some seem to assert. It does not try to answer all the questions surrounding the world's creation and the universe's origin. The Bible is a book of faith and is often more interested in eternal truths than scientific facts. Truth and fact are not necessarily the same, although the Bible contains many important facts (such as the life, death, and resurrection of Jesus).

If we try to take the Bible too literally, we sometimes get into trouble. For example, if the sun, moon, and stars were not created until the fourth day of creation (as the Bible tells us), how long were those first three days? We simply don't know. Again, the Biblical writers seem much more interested in WHY God created the world rather than HOW he created the world.

When reading the Book of Genesis, stay focused on the main ideas: that God created a good world, he created humankind in his own image, sin came into the world through our disobedience, evil also makes its appearance, and God sets forth a plan to redeem his now damaged creation. These are some of the critical themes of Genesis.

Some thoughtful Christians might accept the idea of evolution with one essential provision: God did the creating. As long as we agree on this truth, it doesn't bother me how we got to where we are today.

But having said that, let me also state again the very important distinction between animals and humans. We are not the same. Humans have a free will, a soul, and a conscience. We fly airplanes, write letters, and build computers. Animals do none of these. Remember that natural laws govern nature (the physical world). The laws of instinct govern animals. And humans are governed by the laws of God.

Like it or not, we are free moral agents and are held to a level of accountability unlike anything seen in the animal kingdom. The Bible teaches that we are created in the image of God (the Imago Dei), and while we share some commonalities with animals, we are also profoundly different.

People ask where Adam and Eve's sons (Seth and Cain) find their wives who suddenly appear in the Genesis story. They seem to appear out of nowhere. But, again, remember that the writers of Genesis were not concerned about such "details." But as the story unfolds, it seems God somehow appointed Adam and Eve as "representative parents" of the human race, and their experiences soon become normative for all humankind.

There is an argument against evolution that I find quite persuasive. If life on this planet is evolving, how come we never see clear and direct evidence of this? While only on the planet for one hundred years or less, I know that our observation window is relatively small. But still, why do we not see some life forms transitioning to the next level? A mule is a biological cross between a horse and a donkey. I understand this. But why do we never seem to see other life forms that blend two species together, similar to the mule (which is a purely biological blending)?

On the contrary, when I look at the various species of life, I see them as being very separate and distinct and not at all in some state of transition or evolution. And in humans, when we surgically transplant common organs, there is a strong tendency toward rejection, even within the same species. Evolving life forms seem to be exceedingly rare, if not altogether nonexistent.

The debate will continue for a long time to come. The Bible and science can be quite compatible. We should not be afraid to ask the most probing questions and continue to seek answers concerning the universe's origin and life on this planet. Perhaps one day, we will find fewer theoretical answers and more that are solidly based on hardcore scientific evidence. Until then, the jury is still out. But any thoughts about a world created or evolving without God's almighty hand are, to me, foolish and dangerous. We cannot say how the world began, but we Christians do not believe it was some primordial "accident."

Edwin Conklin once noted that "the probability of life originating from an accident is comparable to the probability of the unabridged dictionary resulting from an explosion in a print shop." But, of course, such an idea is just ludicrous.

Life has a Creator, a purpose, and a point of culmination. To think of life on this planet as sheer happenstance would be the height of folly. We may not yet understand all the details of this world order, but there is great wisdom and comfort in the profoundly simple statement, "In the beginning, God created the heavens and earth..." (Genesis 1:1)

# DRUNKEN DRIVING

Ahead-on car crash killed an outstanding high school teacher. It turns out that the man who hit him was a drunk driver. Some time ago, a drunk driver hit a local high school youth. He had earlier hit another car in another intersection, left the scene, and was now driving at an estimated sixty mph without headlights. How the teen from our church escaped severe injury is a miracle. Her car was totaled, but she was saved by an airbag, a seatbelt, and likely the grace of God.

What makes my blood boil about this story is that the man who hit our teen friend has a history of DWIs as long as your arm, and to date, he has not even been charged. I can only ask why Minnesota allows such lunacy to continue. This man is armed and dangerous and will surely kill someone some time if we just wait long enough. He will kill you or me or someone we love. So, while we are allowing this sick man to drive, why don't we also give loaded firearms to small children, and why don't we also allow the public to play with matches and dynamite?

All three actions are ludicrous. Two of these we prohibit, and one we quietly tolerate. Why? As a long-time supporter of the MADD organization, we need much tighter controls over this deadly situation. An alcoholic person may need to drink but not be allowed to drive, especially when they endanger innocent lives. There are good ways to prevent the deaths of people like this outstanding teacher from Milaca. I have been told that in some Scandinavian countries, for example, if you are caught driving drunk, you lose your license for life on the first or second offense.

When I first wrote this, the Dakota County Attorney was working to enact new laws to get these killers off our highways faster and more effectively. Also, an excellent organization to donate to is MADD. A person may not be able to control their dependency on alcohol, but they cannot drive while under the influence. There is no place on our roads for lethal weapons. Too many people are dying needlessly. God calls us to be good stewards of life, and we need to restrain any who would destroy life for whatever reason.

# HOW THE BIBLE CAME TO BE

This may come as no surprise, but the Bible, while still an annual best-seller, has lost some of its clout in today's world. For some, this comes in the form of open hostility. But for most others, it's just a kind of benign neglect. It is a quaint old book that spoke meaningfully to our grandparents but much less so to us who live in this twenty-first century.

Whenever I encounter such sentiments (and there is a lot of skepticism in our world today), I always like to tell a story followed by a couple of questions. So here is a short course on how the Bible came to be. Suppose you and I were to start authoring a book today that would be completed twelve hundred years from now. Let us further suppose that it will be written in three different languages (Greek, Hebrew, and Aramaic), written on three different continents (Europe, Asia, and Africa), and be written by at least three dozen different authors. And finally, let's suppose it will include at least a dozen different literary styles, including poems, prayers, hymns, genealogies, parables, histories, sermons, letters, proverbs, short stories, psalms, etc. Now, my two questions. One, do you think our book would stand a chance of ever being finished? And two, if by some miracle it was finished (using all of the above criteria), do you think there is a chance in the world that it would make even a lick of sense? My answer is a resounding NO! And yet, this is the very criteria under which our Bible was written. Even a very cursory reading of the Bible will reveal an amazing unity with themes and threads that run from start to finish throughout these sixty-six amazing books. If this little story doesn't at least pique your imagination, check your pulse.

We call it by many names: A road map for our lives. A love letter from God. The owner's manual for our lives. Luther called it the cradle which holds the living Christ. The Psalmist calls it "a lamp unto my feet and a light unto my path." St. Paul said we are to use it to teach, to proclaim, to rebuke, to convince, and to exhort. And it is a truly unique book. It's not the story of humankind seeking after God (typical of so many world religions) but the story of God seeking after us and all of his creation. The stories of the Bible are of men and women disobeying God, ignoring God, rebelling against God, running away from God, or worshiping false gods. Still, God comes calling for us. His love knows no boundaries. Thank God for that!

# GATHERING AT THE ECUMENICAL TABLE

One advantage of getting a little older is having a more long-term perspective on the great events of life. And surely, one of those "great events" has been the ecumenical awakening of the Church over the past half-century.

Growing up as a boy in the 1950s in St. Louis, Missouri, there was a gulf between Lutherans and Catholics that looked much like the Grand Canyon. The fifteen kids who grew up on my street were either Protestant or Catholic. So even though we did not talk much about it, we sort of knew that our respective faith communities were not the least interested in overlapping, much less ever merging. And we undoubtedly had a lot of misperceptions about one another.

But some of that began to change in 1963 with the Second Vatican Council when Pope John XXIII decided that the Mass could be celebrated in English, that the word heretic should be used a lot less often in the church, and that it was okay for Catholics and Protestants to enter into extended dialogues to explore areas of commonality. It was a new and exciting time in the life of the Church after centuries of antagonism, distrust, and even persecution. It was as if we all got together, read the 17th chapter of John's Gospel, and decided we had better start living by the precepts of our Lord. And along the way, we seem to have discovered that (voila!) we had much more in common than we ever knew. I am happy to report that Christians of all denominations are probably closer to each other today than they have been in the past five hundred years. We have also discovered that we can have real unity in the Spirit without structural or ecclesiastical unity. One is not necessarily dependent upon the other.

But I do need to share one word of concern. I believe that some people in our Lutheran tradition still feel that we are some kind of "orphans" and will never be a legitimate church until we are again in the fold of Rome. Such unity may come about someday, but I suspect it will have more to do with the hand of God than with human hands.

The recent battle over the historic episcopate is a case in point. Some ranking Lutherans felt we needed to "legitimize" our very existence by fully endorsing the ordination rituals of the Episcopal Church and (by extension) the Catholic Church. I simply wish to remind readers that our history, our heritage, and our theology are rock solid and have been so for about five hundred years. As I recall, Martin Luther rediscovered and reclaimed the essence of the Gospel, and the entire Christian Church has benefited ever since. Then let us do away with this silly practice of self-denigration so that we might all come to the table of ecumenism as competent and confident partners. And may all of our dialogues grow out of a profound sense of mutual respect, parity, and goodwill.

# STEWARDS OF THE SOIL

I begin today with a disclaimer. I have never lived on a farm, nor have I lived in rural America. I was born and raised as a "city slicker" in five major metropolitan cities. But I was fortunate enough to marry into a large farm family, and from them, I have learned a lot about the land and these good "people of the soil."

My wife's grandfather went courting as a young man with a horse and buggy and lived to see men land on the moon. Probably no other generation in history has seen such technological advancements in one lifetime. My father-in-law started out as a young man harvesting corn by hand, and before he retired, he was driving one of those monster combines that allowed him to harvest up to one hundred or more acres a day. One of my brothers-in-law now farms about two thousand acres near Welcome, MN. He is averaging over two hundred bushels of corn per acre this year. One generation earlier, farmers would have been happy with fifty bushels an acre. With the help of some chemists, horticulturists, and agronomists, the American farmer is now three to four times more productive than just one generation ago. I read some years ago that one American farmer can feed up to eighty or ninety people. A Russian farmer, on average, was feeding only about eighteen people. The average farmer worldwide feeds only about five or six people.

Another article I read stated that if all the corn harvested in America in a recent year were placed in those jumbo railroad hopper cars, that train would run from L.A. to New York City not once but thirteen times. Obviously, American climate, soil, technology, and farming methods are among the best on the planet. Another brother-in-law now has two of those giant wind turbines on his farm, allowing him to produce electricity, while also growing grain and livestock. What a marvel. So, what can we say about all of this as the people of God? One, we should be forever thankful for the bounty of the land and the Lord God who makes it all possible. Never forget that the soil, the seed, the sun, and the rain are all gifts from his hand. Two, in our desire to increase productivity, may we do nothing to harm the land. Today, there are concerns about the overuse of fertilizers, herbicides, and pesticides, soil erosion, and the loss of precious wetlands. And finally, to always be asking, how can this productive land continue to feed both our nation and other parts of the world where starvation and malnutrition are a tragic part of daily life.

The Psalmist (24) tells us that the earth is the Lord's and the fullness thereof. It is his world, but we are always partners with him in caring for this amazing place we call Mother Earth. So let us all be careful and caring stewards of the land.

# You, God, and Your Money

It is common knowledge that a great many people (Christians included) have trouble managing their wealth and other kinds of physical possessions. With this in mind, let me share some general guidelines that may help you in your daily stewardship of the gifts God has entrusted you.

1. All that l have or ever will have belongs to God, so I should use his money wisely and always seek his guidance through prayer and studying his Word.

2. I should joyfully give my "first fruits" to God. Leftovers are an insult to God. My giving is one of the most apparent proofs that God is first in my life. Tithing is a great goal to move toward.

3. I should limit my use of credit, keep my finances as current as possible, and never become a slave to debt.

4. I should provide for the needs but not the greeds of my family.

5. I should work hard to get out of debt except for a home, car, cabin, etc. These significant life purchases most often require some mortgage or installment buying.

6. I should seek competent counsel before investing my wealth.

7. I should not speculate wildly but invest wisely to seek a fair return on my money.

8. I should avoid all "get rich quick" schemes, which are almost always too good to be true.

9. I should pay my taxes promptly, no more and no less as prescribed by law. Render to Caesar the things that are Caesar's.

10. I should avoid co-signing for a loan or other major purchase unless I know the persons well and trust them implicitly.

11. I should give to meet the needs of others. I should help those who cannot help themselves.

12. I should be prepared for decreases in my income. Saving for a "rainy day" is always a good idea.

13. Before purchasing some items, I should ask myself: is this a need or a greed? Is this the best value I can find for this item? Does this purchase reflect my Christian values? Can I afford to buy it without placing excessive financial pressure on me or my family?

14. I should establish a consistent program of saving and investing. I can store, but I should not hoard.

15. My checkbook ledger will reflect my Christian values and priorities. The Bible tells us that where your treasure is, there will be your heart also. Want to know what is essential in your life? Look at your checkbook ledger or credit card statement. This will tell you a lot.

Remember, God loves a cheerful (and gracious) giver.

# Essence of Christmas

S ome years ago, I found this little story by Norman Vincent Peale entitled "What If He Had Not Come." It really needs no further commentary.

## What If He Had Not Come
### by Norman Vincent Peale

On Christmas Eve, seven-year-old Bobby tacked his stocking to the mantel, kissed his mom and Dad goodnight, raced upstairs, and leaped into bed. It seemed that he hadn't been asleep any time at all when a voice shouted, "Get up!" He opened his eyes, blinking in the bright sunlight. Then he remembered what day it was. With a joyful shout, he bounded down the stairs.

On the bottom step, he suddenly stopped. No stockings hung from the mantel. The Christmas tree was gone, too. Then, the shrill whistle from the nearby factory made him jump. "The factory can't be open on Christmas Day," Bobby thought as he put on his coat and ran out of the house. The gatekeeper at the factory was his friend. He would tell Bobby why. "Clear out of here, kid," the gatekeeper shouted in a gruff voice. "No kids allowed." As Bobby slowly turned to go, he saw, to his amazement, that all the stores were open up and down the Street. "How can they be open on Christmas?" he asked a woman coming down the sidewalk. "Christmas?" the woman said blankly. "What is that?"

The hardware store, the bakery—everywhere it was the same. People were busy. They were irritated. And acted as though they had never heard of Christmas. "I know one place where they've heard of Christmas." cried Bobby, "at my church." He started to run. Here was the street. At least, he thought it was. But there was only a vacant lot overgrown with weeds. The steeple, the nativity scene, the stained-glass windows, there was nothing here at all. Bobby was beside himself.

Just then, from the tall grass near the side of the road, Bobby heard a moan. A man was lying on the cold ground. "A car struck me," he gasped, "never even stopped." "Help!" Bobby called to a man walking past, "This man is hurt!" The man jerked Bobby away. "Don't touch him! He doesn't live here. We don't know a thing about him." He hurried away. "I'll run to the hospital, mister," Bobby promised, "they'll send an ambulance." And off he ran down the street.

"St. Luke's Hospital," Bobby had often read the name over the archway at the entrance. But now, the stone wall ran around an empty field. Suddenly, Bobby ran home again as if his life depended on it. Last night, his father had read from the Bible. Maybe the Bible would tell him why everything had changed. The book was still lying on the table. Bobby snatched it up, but where the New Testament should have started, there were only blank pages. There was no Christmas story, no Jesus at all. Bobby flung himself on his bed and began to cry.

"Merry Christmas, Bobby!" It was his mother's voice from downstairs. "Aren't you going to get up this Christmas morning?" Bobby sprang out of bed and ran to the window. There was a wreath on the house across the street. And suddenly, the bells from the church tower began to ring out: Joy to the World! The Lord is Come! Let earth receive her King!

"Here I come, Mother," Bobby called. But he paused at the door and shut his eyes. "You came, Jesus." he whispered, "Thank you. Thank you for coming as our Lord, our Savior, and our Friend."

# FINDING HOLY GROUND

Welcome back to campus, one and all. We hope *you* had a good summer season. The new academic year is well underway, there is excitement in the air, chapel attendance has been strong, the student body is full of hope and enthusiasm, and the year before us is one of promise, discovery, and personal growth. May the Lord of all wisdom and goodness prosper us, each one, in all our endeavors. The theme for this year is "meeting each other again for the first time." That simple phrase brought to mind one of my favorite stories illustrating the surprising quality of love, be it the love of God or that of his people. This little parable comes from a book, *Stories for Telling,* edited by Pastor William White. I hope you enjoy it.

There once were two brothers who farmed together. They shared all of the work equally and split their profits evenly. Each had his own granary. One of the brothers was married and had a large family. The other brother was not married. One day, the unmarried brother said to himself, "It is not fair that we divide the grain evenly. My brother has many mouths to feed, while I have but one. I know what I will do. I will take a grain sack from my granary each evening and put it in my brothers." So, each night when it was dark, he quietly carried a sack of grain, placing it in his brother's barn.

Now, the married brother thought to himself, "It is not fair that we divide the grain evenly. I have many children to care for me in my old age, and my brother has none. So, I know what I'll do. I would take a grain sack from my granary each evening and put it in my brother's barn, and so he did.

Each morning, the brothers were amazed to discover that though they had removed a sack of grain the night before, they had just as much grain the next day. One night, the two brothers met each other in the moonlight halfway between their barns, each with a sack of grain on his shoulder. After a moment, they set their sacks on the ground and fondly embraced each other, with hardly a word spoken. There was little need for talk. The brothers realized again how deeply they loved each other. Together, they savored that wonderful moment for as long as they could. Legend states that God looked down on the two brothers and declared they were now standing on 'holy ground.'

For many, the Luther Seminary campus is also holy ground, where love is celebrated and practiced in a thousand different ways. I pray that you will also experience and share that love in many different ways this coming year.

# SOLO FLIGHT: NOT FOR GEESE
# OR FOR CHRISTIANS

One of the most majestic sights of the fall season is a flock of geese flying south for the winter. But have you ever wondered why geese consistently fly in their familiar "V" formation?

Some years ago, two scientists conducted a series of tests using a wind tunnel as their laboratory. First, they wanted to know why Canadian Geese almost invariably fly in formation. In time, they discovered that each goose, when flapping its wings, creates an upward lift, which greatly aids the following birds. In this way, they can travel two or three times further than they could if flying alone.

The scientists also found that the geese rotate their leadership because no one goose can stay in the point position for very long. So, if one goose falls back and begins to think he or she can go it alone, that goose immediately feels the strain of solo flight and will quickly speed up to get back into formation.

The spiritually alive congregation is for the Christian, what the "V" formation is for the goose. We need the uplift of fellow Christians to face life's temptations, discouragements, and frustrations. We need the uplift of fellow Christians to go the distance in giving, serving, and ministering in the name of Jesus, our Lord.

We have all seen people depart from the formation because they thought they could travel the whole way on their own and may have found that the load was too heavy alone. So, we, like the wise geese, should keep the formation—and the faith.

# WHAT IS THE REAL MEANING OF
## THE WORD LOVE?

One of the problems with our society today is that we do not have a workable and helpful understanding of the word love. A great deal of confusion surrounds this most basic element in our daily lives. When helping to prepare couples for marriage, I often ask them to tell me what they think love really is. The answers frequently focus on some kind of feelings that they have for each other. Popular music also seeks to perpetuate this notion of love as a feeling. But I find this answer less than satisfactory. Love and feelings are not the same. In fact, I think they are distant cousins at best. Building a lifelong relationship on feelings can be risky business. The problem, of course, is that we have little or no control over our feelings. They are so volatile. One day, I may feel in love; the next, I may feel nothing. And people tend to use their feelings as some kind of gauge or barometer to measure the worth of the relationship. This is a sad situation indeed.

We cannot control our feelings, but there is a part of our being over which we have a great deal of control, namely our will. You and I have a free will that, in fact, make us authentically human. We are not puppets, robots, or droids. We have a free will that allows us to make long-term commitments and keep them no matter our feelings. I can will myself to love another person even when they are very unlovable. I can will myself to care for another person. I can will myself to make sacrifices on behalf of another person. This is the kind of love that gives substance, strength, and continuity to the relationships of our lives.

It is also a very Biblical understanding of love. In St. Paul's great love chapter (I Corinthians 13), he tells us that love is patient and kind. It is not jealous or boastful. It is not arrogant or rude. It is not irritable or resentful. It does not insist on its own way. It does not rejoice in the wrong but only in the right. The word "feeling" never once appears in the entire chapter. Paul's understanding of love is very Christ-like: one based on servanthood and sacrifice. Yet, it is this kind of love that can endure for a lifetime.

I am quite sure that Mother Teresa, for example, did not relish going out every day into the streets of Calcutta to pick up some of the world's foulest, sickest, and most hurting people. She did not always feel like doing such difficult work, but she willed herself to do it. Likewise, the Marriage Encounter movement defines love very simply: love is a commitment of the will. It has little or nothing to do with our feelings. I have a very workable definition of love: love is what results when I become at least as concerned about the welfare of another person as I am about my own. It is a simple concept but profoundly important for all the relationships of our lives and especially our marriages.

On several occasions, Jesus told his followers to love one another as he first loved them: sacrificially, freely, and even recklessly. The word "feeling" does not seem to appear anywhere in his vocabulary. So, it shouldn't be a big part of ours, either. Of course, it is wonderful to fall in love with someone. But when the feelings fade, the love can surely remain because of a marvelous gift called free will.

## SOME THOUGHTS FOR A NEW YEAR

D o I have to go to church every Sunday? In a sense, this is the wrong question to be asking. First, it assumes a sort of legalism that God is checking off attendance on his heavenly class roster. This turns worship attendance into a sort of "good work" in the sense that we do it to stay on God's good side or in the hope that our worship attendance will yield some payoff. To be sure, participation in worship has its own intrinsic rewards. We might feel inspired or encouraged by it, and it forms us into the mind of Christ the more regularly we participate in it. But we have no promise that God will reward us with money, good fortune, or any other blessing merely because we worship regularly. By the same token, absenting ourselves from worship presents its own inherent hazards. I lose focus on who is first in my life. I miss out on God's counsel and Christ's presence in the Sacrament. It isn't that God will punish us with bad fortune if we are absent from worship, but when challenges come, we will be equipped to make some sense of them. So, what happens when we miss worship?

Nothing happens. That is the problem.

Second, this question reflects an immature attitude towards worship, that I go begrudgingly because it's my duty. To be honest, when I was a kid, I couldn't stand going to church. I grabbed hold of any opportunity to skip it. What happened that I should end up becoming a pastor? Quite simply, I grew up. As the Apostle Paul says, "When I became a man, I put away childish things." I admire the children in our congregation who want to be at worship on Sunday and are frustrated when their circumstances prevent that. I did not have spiritual maturity at their age. I wonder how many of us adults could learn a lesson from them? Part of coming into maturity in Christ is being gathered in worship, not out of a begrudging sense of duty, nor patting ourselves on the back for being such good churchgoers, but because we know that there is life here in God's Word and Christ's Sacraments and that participating in these awesome things is just a part of who we are. When we absent ourselves from the Church's worship, we are denying and depriving ourselves as a new creation in Christ.

Third, making worship a priority is a very necessary discipline in making Christ first in our lives. While we might not want to be legalistic about worship attendance, we must ask: if convenience, work, or laziness prevents my worship attendance, am I truly prepared to put Christ first in my life? The witness of the martyrs reminds us that we may be called upon to forsake much, even life itself, for the love of God. Can we possibly be prepared to do that if we can't make an hour of worship our first priority of the week?

Do you really want or need a "break" from Jesus? Do you really want a "break" from God's life-giving work? What will you put in place of that worship time, and will it give you any true refreshment that the Church's worship does not? Whether you're on vacation or at home, let us be mindful of planning our week to reflect our first priority as Christians, "not neglecting to meet together, as is the habit of many, but encouraging one another." (Hebrews 10:25)

I was glad when they said unto us, "Let us go up to the House of the Lord." Psalm 122: I

NOTE: This article was submitted anonymously by a close friend of Pastor Paul.

# Why Seminary, Anyway?

Why Luther Seminary? I am going with the short answer. Outstanding faculty, dedicated staff, and well-qualified students. It works for me, as they say. But let me broaden the question a bit more. Why any seminary? Why theological education? Why commit two, three, four, or more years of my life to this endeavor? This is a question worth pondering.

Let me set a bit of context. About five hundred years ago, theology, the disciplined study of the ways of God in the world as revealed through holy writ, was considered the queen of the sciences. There was no higher or holier calling in life. To give one's life to study, to the church, and to God was a sacred and honorable calling in life. There were debates as to just how many angels could dance on the head of a pin (apparently, some theologians had way too much time on their hands), but truth be told, there was serious work afoot. Important questions about life and death. Heaven and hell. Purgatory and limbo (ideas rejected by most of the Reformers.) Good and evil. Sin and grace. Truth and falsehood. Spirit and matter. God and Satan. Priestly and prophetic. Clergy and laity. Justice and injustice. And the list goes on. These were, and still are, the consuming questions of life, and we who study at seminaries are privileged to delve deeply into the sacred mysteries.

A seventeen-year-old woman from Fremont, California, did something that had never been done before. She got a perfect score of sixteen hundred on her Scholastic Aptitude Exam and another perfect score of eight thousand on the challenging University of California Acceptance Exam. Her name is Karen Cheng, and she is obviously a very bright young lady. But when asked this question by a newspaper reporter, "What do you think is the meaning of life?" she stated that she had absolutely no idea how to answer that question. She continued, "I don't know what meaning to give to my life or anyone else's for that matter." This rather direct comment speaks volumes to me about why we do theological education. There are lots of folks around today who are searching for meaning in life. Some are downright desperate for meaning. Yet, we who have been trained and entrusted with this holy gospel are also commissioned to go into the world and share the good news! And what a privilege it is to bring hope, forgiveness, peace, comfort, and healing to a significantly hurting world. So this is why we study at the seminary.

# ADULTERY—THE HURT AND THE HEALING

I watched a news piece on the television about top officers in our military who have been quietly dismissed within the last year or two. Some twenty officers were listed from all branches of the armed forces. What caught my attention was that seventeen of the twenty were dismissed for adultery.

As an ordained pastor for many years, I have worked with numerous couples who have experienced the deep pain that adultery brings to their damaged marriages. As a result, I often ask myself why people make such hurtful and destructive decisions. I understand that sex is a powerful and pervasive force in our lives. I understand that "forbidden fruit" can have an almost magnetic attraction. I realize that we are sinful, flawed, and imperfect human beings. I know that temptation and the Devil can be extremely subtle and cunning. I know that we humans often think more with our glands than with our brains. And I realize many people who get into an affair do not necessarily make a deliberate decision to do so.

But having said all of that, let me remind you that God did not create us to be puppets, droids, or robots. On the contrary, he gave us a marvelous gift that defines our very humanity in many ways: free will. He gave us a choice. He gave us the cognitive abilities to think seriously about our decisions before we act. And He gave us a conscience, that moral compass within each of us that allows us to critique and control our own behavior.

I am unsure if adultery is more prevalent today than at other times in history, but I do know that it never produces anything but heartache, betrayal, brokenness, and disillusionment. I can honestly say that I have yet to see anyone or any marriage benefit in any way from an affair. Obviously, God knew this when he gave us the 6th Commandment to protect the gift of marriage. But our society continues to throw this Commandment back into God's face. But in the end, the Commandment always has a way of demonstrating its truthfulness and its power.

Now for the big question: Can a marriage be salvaged after an affair? Yes, it can, but it will require some important steps to bring about healing:

1. There must be a complete and total disclosure of all that has happened regarding the affair. Both persons must be satisfied with the confession's depth and detail. It's a little like tooth decay. There is no point in putting in the new filling until all of the old decay is drilled out of the tooth.

2. There must be a total severing of any contact with "the third party." Anything less will preclude any hope of healing the relationship.

3. An apology needs to be made, open, honest, and as sincerely as any ever made.

4. A couple should count on in-depth marriage counseling for a year or two or more. Why did it happen? When did the trouble begin? Why weren't the causal factors addressed early on? What needs to be done now to bring about healing? What signs should a couple be looking for? In what sense were both husband and wife to blame for what happened? These are a few of dozens of important questions that need to be asked and answered.

5. A couple must learn to pray for each other, for patience, faith, hope, guidance, and most of all, forgiveness and reconciliation.

6. The process of building trust in a marriage is a slow one. And, even before love, there has to be trust. Have no illusions about a quick fix. Stabilizing and rehabilitating the relationship will likely take five or more years.

A final thought. A wise man once noted that whatever in life doesn't kill us will likely make us stronger. Couples do survive affairs. Sometimes, it catalyzes growth and maturity, though never without a price. God calls on us to forgive others as he has forgiven us, and I assume this applies to every area of our lives. Without the gift of for-giveness, life on this planet would be absolutely intolerable.

# DIVORCE AND WHAT THE
# BIBLE SAYS ABOUT IT

I preached a sermon using a portion of the Sermon on the Mount as a text. (Matthew 5:20 - 37) I don't mind telling you that it is one of the more difficult texts to preach on. In this passage, Jesus offers some rather stern-sounding words about murder, lust, adultery, lying, and divorce.

If you were present that morning, you might have noted that I did not say much about divorce. The omission was obvious enough to prompt more than a few of you to ask me to say more about this subject.

It might be helpful to give a historical context. In ancient times, a man could quickly dispose of a wife by signing a divorce certificate. (A Jewish woman could never divorce a man, as she had no legal rights.) Obviously, this practice could easily be abused, and it was. Marriages were dissolved at an alarming rate, and it was to this situation that Jesus was speaking. He harshly denounced those who would enter into divorce lightly and unthinkingly. Such counsel applies to our day as well. As a rule, the church opposes the dissolution of the "holy state of matrimony."

At the same time, the church also recognizes that we live in an imperfect and broken world. Because of the reality of sin, every area of our lives can be affected negatively, and marriage is no exception.

Centuries ago, Martin Luther wrote about this exact text concerning divorce. Jesus was once asked why, if God opposes divorce, did He allow Moses to permit divorce. Luther paraphrases Jesus' answer in this way:

For your hard hearts, Moses allowed you to divorce your wives. It is still not a good thing to do, but since you are such wicked and unmanageable people, it is better to grant you this much than to let you do worse by vexing or murdering each other or by living together in constant hate, discord, and hostility.

Then Luther goes on to say:

This same thing might even be advisable nowadays... that certain stubborn and obstinate people, who have no capacity for toleration and are not suited for married life at all, should be permitted to get a divorce. Since people are as evil as they are, any other way of governing is impossible. Something must be tolerated, even though it is not a good thing to do, to prevent something even worse from happening.

I think it safe to say that every faithful pastor wants to see all marriages thrive and prosper. Knowing this to be an impossibility, we strive to make the best of an otherwise fractured world. In my years of ministry, I have seldom found anyone who entered into divorce flippantly. Most people I have worked with have gone through gut-wrenching experiences involving months and often years of deep emotional pain before finally deciding to terminate a marriage.

While some may abuse divorce, many try all kinds of avenues before reluctantly concluding that their marriage must end. So often, these folks need and want the church's ministry at this sad and painful time in their lives.

Divorce is sometimes equated with death. Unfortunately, many of the same emotions that accompany death also accompany divorce. Indeed, this is not a time for the church to slam the door in the face of those experiencing such a disruptive and hurtful time in their lives. Let us keep in mind also that divorce may be the only sane decision in a marital situation that borders on the insane. A person living with a spouse who, for example, is alcoholic and physically abusive may try several avenues to seek a remedy for this sick situation. However, if the offending party has no intention of ever changing, for the sake of this person (and any children), a divorce may be the most humane and helpful course to follow. While our Lord asks us to do all within our power to save a marriage, he also does not ask us to spend our lives living in a hell of fear, abuse, shame, or drunken disruption.

Let us remember, too, the true nature of grace. Grace, defined as the mercy and compassion of God, offers us the opportunity to be forgiven, to pick up the pieces of our lives, and to start over again. Some of the wounds from the past may never wholly heal, but God is in the business of restoring and renewing His people. He desires that we live whole, healthy, and happy lives as far as is humanly possible. If we are to serve Him and others, we need to live in homes and families that are reasonably functional and affirming. A home filled with bickering, hatred, criticism, abuse, infidelity, alcohol, or shame is no honor to God.

When all avenues of help and healing have been utilized with no positive results, then perhaps divorce is the viable answer. Of course, pastors hope that no one will enter lightly into marriage and that no one will lightly exit a marriage. Each situation must be judged on its own merits. But when divorce is the only option left, let's be sure to apply a liberal measure of God's grace and mercy.

# CHARACTERISTICS OF A CULT

A As I write these lines, the Branch Davidians are still holding forth. We can only hope that it will all end peacefully. There has been enough blood spilled already.

This story reminds us that cults and cultists still flourish in the land. One newscast mentioned that there are over nine thousand such groups today in the US and likely many more that are unknown to us.

Some or all of the following usually characterize a cult:

1. A strong leader who claims divinity or, at the least, a special relationship with God. Such a leader often claims to receive special revelations directly from God.

2. Cult leaders (usually living) always demand absolute and unquestioning obedience. The leader is also the sole judge of a member's faith and commitment to the cause.

3. Members are often kept busy for long, exhausting hours with worship experiences, recruiting, fundraising, or menial tasks. (If members are kept busy and tired, they have little time to think for themselves.)

4. Communication with family members is sharply curtailed, and the cult itself becomes the members' new family.

5. The cult members are asked to put the cult's goals ahead of all other individual concerns, interests, career plans, etc.

6. Cults often use techniques designed to destroy the individual ego, transform the mind, and create dependence upon the cult.

7. The cult may hold members in a state of heightened suggestibility through changes in sleep and diet, intense spiritual exercises, constant indoctrination, and highly controlled group experiences.

8. Converts may display symptoms of extreme tension and stress, fear, guilt, lack of humor, regression in communication skills, logic skills, and reality testing.
9. Members of the cult are encouraged to live in isolation from the world. As a result, a "we" or "they" mentality quickly forms.
10. If the cult is threatened at all, it is seen as a verification that the leader's perception of the world as an evil place is accurate. If threatened enough, violence may result, and even serious talk of mass suicide.
11. All finances are consolidated under the control of one or two persons. Consequently, financial disclosures are rarely, if ever, made.
12. Though not always noticeable, a double standard often exists in a cult group. The leaders live by one set of rules, and the members must live by another.

I have often believed that the best defense is a good offense. The more we understand, appreciate, and practice the Christian faith, the less we need to worry about being pulled into a cultist group.

I want to add a word of clarification to the sermon I preached about the Islamic faith. As I said then, there are many devout Muslims who I believe seek to do God's will as they understand it. But unfortunately, Muslims are also often persecuted people. We need only look to Bosnia, India, Egypt, and other regions of the world as evidence.

However, I want to condemn again any who would use terrorist tactics to further their goals. Sadly, radical fundamentalism exists today in many religious and political movements. Wherever and whenever people take the law into their own hands (no matter how noble they think their cause), it is an affront to all humanity and usually produces disastrous consequences.

I often think of our Lord weeping as he looked out over the City of Jerusalem. His sad comment was this, "O Jerusalem, Jerusalem, would that you knew the things that make for peace." How slow we all are to learn this vital lesson.

# THE FOUR LAWS OF
# HUMAN BEHAVIOR

Every once in a while, someone will ask me about all the violence in the Old Testament. Men, women, children, livestock, and even whole cities are summarily destroyed, and some of it seems to be with the full blessing of God himself. What are we to make of these seemingly horrible events? My first answer is always to remember that the New Testament supersedes the Old Testament and, in many ways, seeks to show us a new and radically different way to live. "Love your enemy and do good to those who persecute you" or "You have heard that it was said, an eye for an eye and a tooth for a tooth, but now I say unto you..." How refreshingly different are the words of Jesus? Remember that some Old Testament writers may have given God's blessings to their warring ways when that was not necessarily true. If that sounds farfetched, consider the present war with Iraq. Some Americans are sure we are currently doing the will of God in that country, and others would strongly argue just the opposite. That debate will likely continue for a long time, and I suspect the same was true in ancient times.

But I have another answer to this violence issue that I hope will be helpful. I like to call it the Four Laws of Human Behavior.
And here they are.

First, the **Law of the Jungle.** For example, if you poke out my eye, I seek "justice" by killing your wife. This is a horrible way to live, though it has been around for a long time. It encourages chaos and societal anarchy.

Secondly, there is the **Law of Parity.** As strange as it may seem, this law was an improvement over the Law of the Jungle. And eye for an eye and a tooth for a tooth. Nothing more and nothing less. Gandhi once noted that if we choose to live this way, we will all end up blind and toothless. This law was written in ancient times on a stone pillar that contained what we now call the Code of Hammurabi, a Babylonian king who lived about seventeen hundred BC. As brutal as it may sound, it was a definite improvement in human behavioral codes of conduct.

Thirdly, there is **The Law of Conditional Love**. This is a teaching set forth by some world religions declaring that we should try to love our neighbors as we love ourselves. This code of ethics was a vast improvement over everything that had gone before, but it has been challenging for humanity to obey. We seem much more fulfilled when we are killing each other. Nonetheless, the bar had been lifted, and the human race began to try at least to live more sanely and civilly.

Fourthly, we have **The Law of Unconditional Love**. Along came Jesus in the New Testament, who asks us not only to love our neighbor but even to love our worst and most hated enemy. Now, the bar has been raised. No other religion in the world has ever emphasized such a radical idea. Was Jesus serious or not? Martin Luther King Jr. took Jesus at his absolute word. It may have cost him his life, but the world is undoubtedly a better place for King's nonviolent teachings and his powerful example to us.

There is the hope that one day, all nations will come to see the futility of war and seek to fulfill the prophecy of Isaiah (chapter two) that "nations shall beat their swords into plowshares, and their spears into pruning hooks; nation shall not lift up sword against nation, neither shall they learn of war anymore." Utopian? A silly dream? Perhaps. But it is a prophecy of the scriptures, and you never want to count God out of the picture. But by looking at these four levels of human behavior, we can at least begin to discern how far we have come as a human family and how far we have yet to go.

# Section Four

## FAITH AND LIFE

# BRINGING BACK PURITY AND FIDELITY

I have hesitated to write anything on this subject, but it seems to beg for some commentary. I hardly need to name them: several famous men and the notorious racist who paid an African American woman for decades to keep quiet about their "love child" daughter. Talk about hypocrisy.

A poll of four hundred married men found that 21% admit to wanting to cheat on their spouse while traveling on business and that 8% actually do. Perhaps this is nothing new. A portion of humanity has been misbehaving since the dawn of time.

As a somewhat cynical friend of mine likes to say: "Some men think more with their glands than with their brains." This might even be a bit comical except for all the hurt, anger, and disillusionment it leaves in its wake. Spouses feel betrayed, children watch the security of home and family disintegrate before their eyes, and trust, the foundation stone of any marriage, is shattered and scattered.

Sadly, our society is swimming in a sea of mixed messages about sex, many of which are sick and distorted. The airwaves broadcast programming that borders on the X-rated. Books and films portray sexual activity as one big game with little or no consequences. Talk shows have become ever more sensational to boost their ratings. Advertising literally drips with sexual imagery. And the promise of 'instant love' is given if you dial the correct number.

So, what do we say about all of this? Or, more appropriately, what does the church say about all of this? I would say what the church has been saying for two thousand years: Chastity (purity) before marriage and fidelity (faithfulness) during marriage. Such words today would sound naïve and archaic were they not the timeless truths of scripture.

These words of wisdom are immutable and given by a God who knows what is best for His creation.

Sometimes, the church doesn't say much on this subject because the facts seem to speak so loudly for themselves. Just look at society today. We have an epidemic of abortions, venereal diseases, shotgun weddings, extra-marital affairs, sexual addictions, sexual abuse, HIV infections, and unwanted pregnancies.

The toll illicit sex takes on the human family seems to know no boundaries. As self-centered, fragile human beings, we need guidelines. Without them, we tend to live only for the moment, giving little thought to the consequences of our actions. But practice these scriptural admonitions of purity and faithfulness, and we avoid so much of the pain that society is today inflicting upon itself. And remember, God gave his laws not because he is a killjoy but because he loves us and knows what is best for us. As someone once noted, it is not so much that we break the Commandments; it is just that the Commandments have a way of breaking us when we ignore them.

Live by the commands of God and discover the real joys of life. Centuries ago, St. Paul wrote: "Whatever is true, whatever is honorable, whatever is pure...think on these things." (Philippians 4:8)

These are words of wisdom then, now, and for all time.

# HAPPY HALLOWEEN?

**M**any people don't know it, but Halloween began as a religious observance. It was literally the Eve of All Hallows: the night before All Saints Day, when faithful Christians went to their churches to remember and, in some cases, to pray for deceased family members.

Later, this event became a children's celebration of candy, costumes, and cavities (if they failed to brush properly). But today, some adults have stolen this autumn holiday from the children. Masquerading (pardon the pun) as a community fundraiser, a local Twin City event called the Dungeon of Doom and Darkness features blood-soaked actors pretending to eat human flesh, dolls representing children getting their heads ripped off, placing others in cages in order to perform evil experiments on them, and many other ghoulish and bizarre scenes which any parent would be well-advised to keep their young children from ever seeing.

Don't our children already have enough neurosis, fears, and insecurities without exposing them to such weird and frightening behavior? So let the children enjoy a secure and fun-filled night of trick or treating without being scared half to death by some misguided adults. And then beat a path to your church on All Saints Day to give thanks for the saints of old. There, you will discover what this day is really all about.

# Beware the Power of Corporate Advertising

**M**any years ago, when I worked at the Chemical Dependency Unit of Abbot NW Hospital, its director warned about the dangers of America becoming a drug-dependent nation. I fear that his predictions may now be coming true. Let me share but one of many examples. Several years ago, a very subtle but effective ad aired on television. The ad did not try to sell you anything, only to inform (manipulate?) you. It told of a credible organization called the American Sleep Institute, which has supposedly been doing all kinds of research into the sleep habits of the average American. And guess what? Its findings declared that half of all Americans now suffer from severe sleep deprivation or sleep disorder. And then the ad ended with a half-transparent butterfly flitting around with the name of medication at the bottom of your TV screen. It was a reasonably convincing piece of work. And it was all designed to set you up for what was to follow.

What the ad did not tell you was that the American Sleep Institute was a bogus organization developed by a pharmaceutical company to create a problem they could solve with a new wonder drug. Talk about a slick way to create a problem, manipulate an enormous TV audience, and solve this "terrible problem" with a costly designer drug.

Now, please understand. There are some wonderful drugs on the market today, and they have greatly benefited many people. But creating a problem to exploit it is just unconscionable. (I understand that only a few nations worldwide will even allow this kind of mass TV advertising of drugs because they fear its effects on the general population.)

Here are a few statistics to ponder. Last year, the drug companies of America spent well over $300,000,000 on advertising. For their efforts, the American people spent over $2,000,000,000 on sleep aides. Americans spent over $250 billion last year on over-the-counter and prescription drugs. It would seem that such advertising has benefited these companies most handsomely.

Indeed, the American people are popping more pills today than ever before. Time Magazine recently reported that sleeping pill prescriptions filled in the US last year were up a whopping 60% since the year 2000. We now have a pill for everything you can imagine. And we wonder why our kids grow up and fall victim so quickly to the drug culture, legal or illegal. I recall again the words of my friend Phil. "If you can't sleep at night, get up and read a book, exercise, watch TV, write a letter. Eventually, you will get tired and go to sleep naturally, as God intended."

Bottom line: use drugs when necessary, but beware of the power of advertising and manipulation. Some forces at work in our lives today can subtly modify our behavior in ways that are not always in our best interests.

# Six Facts about the Elderly

I have two elderly parents who live in Waverly, Iowa. Dad is eighty-eight, and Mom is ninety-three. They have had full lives, enjoying much health and happiness. My brother and I thank God for each day we have together with our folks. Unfortunately, over the last three years, their health has begun to fail, as so often is the case. As marvelous as it is, the body wears out over time. It's a part of life. During this time, I have learned several things about dealing with older people, which I wish to share with you. These are not earth-shaking insights, but they may help any of you who also have (or one day will have) aging parents.

1. Older people move more slowly. We all know this, but it's good to be reminded that patience and kindness go a long way when helping older people. I recall my dad walking so fast as a young man that it often looked like he was running. My mother could never keep up. Now all that zip is gone. But that is okay. I need to know that it will take much longer to do even the simplest tasks when I am with my folks. I need to remember that they are not in a hurry because they have little to be in a hurry about. (Unless it's mealtime.) Remember to be patient and understanding.

2. Older people sometimes find their senses diminished. Taste, touch, and smell remain reasonably good. But sight and hearing are often casualties of the later years. Today, however, some modern technologies can be beneficial. Eyeglasses, hearing aids, clocks, phones with large numerals, speaker-enhanced phones, and scanners that pass over books and letters and then appear in large letters on a computer screen are just some of today's modern innovations. In addition, I recently saw a woman watching TV through a unique magnifying lens.

3. Older folks sometimes lose part of their short-term memory. Mom and Dad don't recall last week's events nearly as well as what happened forty years ago. On the other hand, sometimes it's just fun to sit and ask the folks about the good old days, and they will talk for hours with excellent memory recall. And there is a good reason for this. What happened yesterday isn't too important, but what happened to them during the prime of their lives is still very important. And by the way, if ever in this situation, take notes or get an audio or video recorder. This is family history; you can never regain it once it's gone. It's these kinds of stories that can help hold families together. Sharing old photos or scrapbooks can also stimulate great conversations about days gone by.

4. Older people tend to "mellow out" with age, which can be good. A stroke or Alzheimer's may produce a different personality, but not always. Older folks often become more patient, wise, gentle, and less volatile. It's just another one of life's passages.

5. Older people generally enjoy having visitors. Loneliness is the great enemy of life, but even more so for the elderly. So go and visit that senior citizen. You will benefit even more than they. You will know what I mean if you read *A Cup of Christmas Tea*.

6. Finally, older folks often become more religious. Indeed, this is not always true, but I think older people have more time to contemplate what is truly important in life. Or they have learned the great lessons of life over the decades. As a result, relationships, goodwill, trust, generosity, prayer, worship, the Bible, and the Church have become increasingly more important to many older adults. As the "flesh grows weaker," we fully understand our utter dependence upon our Creator God. Whatever the reason, it can be a time of wisdom, insight, and reflection for many older people.

# THE SKY IS FALLING! THE SKY IS FALLING! CHICKEN LITTLE

The popular book series, *Left Behind*, has now sold millions of copies. A second motion picture about the series is about to hit America. It will be entitled *World at War*. Once again, it plays upon the fears of our times while offering a very bogus interpretation of scripture.

One of the reasons these books sell so well is because of humanity's ongoing fascination with the future. Everybody wants to know what the future will bring: a new era of blessings, a time of judgment, or the world's end. So, for enthusiastic supporters of LaHaye and Jenkins, let me share a couple of thoughts.

Back in 1970, Hal Lindsey wrote a book called *The Late Great Planet Earth*. It sold eighteen million copies worldwide. It was about a third fact, a third fiction, and a third foolishness. One of the chapter titles was *Polishing Your Crystal Ball*. That doesn't sound like responsible theology to me. Lindsey was convinced that Russia and godless Communism were the great anti-Christ mentioned in the book of Revelation. There were many more wild predictions.

LaHaye and Jenkins are now carrying on the Lindsey legacy and making lots of money. The truth is these guys are good writers and lousy theologians. They seem to enjoy what I call "manipulation evangelism," something Jesus himself never practiced. Jesus stated that even he did not know the day or the hour concerning the end of time as we know it. (I have often thought if the end of the world is so near, why don't these guys give their millions to helping people experiencing poverty? They sure can't take it with them when they go.)

The entire "rapture theology" (the word rapture doesn't even appear in the Bible) is the creation of a British preacher named John Nelson Darby, whose ministry began in the 1840s. His entire end-times "dispensationalist theology" is based on three obscure verses in Daniel 9: 25 - 27. Most responsible Biblical scholars believe that the desolation described in these verses was an apparent reference, not to some future event, but to the desecration that tyrannical emperor Antiochus Ephipanes brought to Jerusalem in one hundred sixty-eight BC. Even more, neither Jesus nor any New Testament writers understood the Book of Daniel as encompassing some overarching plan for human history. Indeed, it contains no essential insights regarding the culmination of human history.

Furthermore, the Jewish community has never considered Daniel among the books of prophecy. Daniel is a book of Jewish history, nothing more or less. It is also helpful to understand the word prophecy in the Bible. The prophet did not try to predict the future. Instead, the prophets of the Bible called people to repentance. They advocated for the poor, the widows, and the orphans, and in general reminded people of the laws of God and their accountability before God. They were not fortune tellers or future tellers. I highly recommend Barbara Rossing's book The Rapture Exposed for anyone trying to make sense of all the sensationalism surrounding the Left Behind series of books and films. It is an excellent book that meticulously debunks this manufactured theology as nothing more than a complete sham.

With keen insight and solid Biblical study, Rossing exposes the hucksterism of the End Times movement and the Christian Zionists who exploit it. This is a "must" read for anyone seeking a deeper understanding of this popular but highly misleading trend of thought. Westview publishes Rossing's book, available at just about any bookstore in our area.

# THE UNSEEN PILOT

S ome years ago, while flying from Detroit to Hartford, Connecticut, I learned a lesson of faith that has remained with me ever since. About one-half hour before we were to land, our plane flew into a severe storm front. For what seemed like interminable minutes, flight fifty-six was buffeted about by turbulent winds as lightning flashed across the darkened sky and rain pounded ominously on the wings and fuselage. Claps of thunder, as I recall, could even be heard above the roar of the engines.

For those who have experienced such flights, one knows that a kind of deadly silence befalls the cabin, with perhaps the exception of a baby crying here or there. White knuckles gripped the armrests as the stewardess, trying to stand erect, instructed everyone to fasten their seat belts, return lap trays to upright positions, and ensure all small luggage items were tucked snugly under the seats.

The storm refused to abate as we proceeded ever closer to our destination. Finally, after several minutes, the plane's Pilot addressed the passengers via the intercom. I recall what he said as he spoke in a measured, confident tone. He first acknowledged that these were unusual flying conditions. He then informed us of our anticipated arrival time (modified somewhat by the storm), assured us that the weather conditions were being closely monitored, and even made a rather uncharacteristic comment about the airworthiness of the craft we were flying in. But most of all, I recall his calm, reassuring voice. A few minutes later, we made a bumpy but otherwise intact landing, which seemed to be accompanied by a general sigh of relief from all passengers and, I suspect, even a few crew members. As we entered the terminal, we were told that the airport was closed to further air traffic until the storm subsided.

Later that evening, as I climbed into bed at my sister-in-law's home (mighty glad to be on solid ground), I began to reflect on my experience. How like life that flight had been! Storms have a way of coming upon us much more frequently than we would ever like, and the scriptures never promise us immunity from the turbulence of life. Still, a word comes to us from an unseen Pilot. It is a word of hope and assurance. It is a word of comfort and direction. It is a word that enables me to believe that whatever storms come my way, my unseen Pilot can bring me home safely. Through his words, he tells me that he is with me always and will one day bring me to the eternal security of his heavenly home.

As I grow older, I am more convinced than ever that the key to life is to trust this unseen, but not unknown Pilot. I hear his voice through his words, which speak of peace, hope, and comfort even amid life's storms. How appropriate the old hymn, "Jesus, Savior, pilot me over (and through) life's tempestuous seas..." The life of faith is not a foolish life; it is the life for which we were created.

# ANATOMY OF AN AFFAIR

During five decades of parish ministry, I have worked with at least several dozen couples who have experienced firsthand the pain, betrayal, and angst accompanying an affair. What follows are some insights as to how and why affairs begin and what could be done in the future to prevent their reoccurrence.

An affair can begin anywhere, but many today start in the workplace. Men and women are brought together in close quarters by their careers and may even travel together professionally to distant cities and countries. And given the permissive nature of our society, there is often ample opportunity for men and women to discover some mutual attraction. Indeed, the so-called "one-night stand" has seemingly become a part of our culture and vocabulary.

One thing that interests me greatly is how affairs begin. There are stories of overly aggressive women, of course, but for the most part, it is still the male of the species who is the primary initiator and predator. Women, though willing participants, can also be seen as victims. Many women are naive about how men think and what motivates them. They may also be rather needy women looking for someone to lift up their low self-image. And men can be highly skillful in meeting such needs in exchange for a sexual relationship. The old line about men giving love to get sex and women giving sex to get love still has some validity. Many women have "sold themselves out" only to discover that their illicit relationship can never adequately give them what they seek inwardly. Affairs, by their very nature, can only end badly.

The motivation of the male is also interesting. He, too, may need his self-esteem boosted, though often his motivation is one of sexual and illicit pleasure. The thrill of the "hunt" and the "conquest" in the bedroom interests him above all else. Most importantly, it is crucial that both participants in an affair realize that genuine love was not part of the equation, much as they may want to believe this. An affair is never based on love but only lust. Think about it. They would resist the temptation to consummate their illicit relationship in the bedroom if they really loved each other. Such behavior becomes very counter-productive. Affairs often destroy one, if not both, marriages—a very high price to pay. Pain, sorrow, regret, disillusionment, betrayal, divorce (and wounded children, if there are any.)

This can never be called love. Love, as defined by the Bible, can never be involved with anything that results in pain, division, deceit, hurt, guilt, and the wounding of persons. This is a thing of the Devil; he alone rejoices over an affair. Yet, strangely, even after an affair is revealed, women often still cling to the notion "that he did love me." If he really loved you, the last thing he would have done is to initiate an affair. I am often reminded of that verse in the Bible that tells us that Satan can make evil look good and good look evil. Nowhere do we see this more clearly than in the aftermath of an affair.

# A HUGE LIE SOLD TO
# THE AMERICAN PUBLIC

The proliferation of "plastic money" (i.e., credit cards) in America is truly amazing. The reason that many of us get credit card applications in the mail every month is proof that these cards are an almost unbelievable gold mine for the companies that distribute them. The return on their investment is usually anywhere from 12% to 25%. I tell my children, "If you like making someone else wealthy, use your credit card irresponsibly." No one in their right mind would ever buy a home or a car at such rates as these, but millions of Americans carry a large debt and seem oblivious to the "robber rates" levied on their unpaid balances. A pastor friend recently told of a couple he was counseling with twenty-six cards and an outstanding debt of over $50,000. Talk about two people whose lives are out of control.

So, let me share a little advice with you. First of all, never again call it a credit card. It really is a debt card. The first time you fail to pay off a monthly balance in full, it is no longer a credit card. It is a debt card and should be referred to as nothing less. You are now a slave to your debt and your creditor is your unforgiving master. I don't believe this is how God intended for us to live; the Bible even warns about the dangers of excessive debt.

Solution? It's really very simple. Use just one well-recognized card as often as you must, but never fail to pay off the monthly balance. If you fall behind, stop using the card immediately and pay off the balance in full the next month. A mature person knows how to curb their appetite for material things and avoids impulse buying like the plague. If you can't control the urges that cause you to abuse your card, leave it at home and make your purchases with cash, debit card, or check only. Remember again the lie: this is not a credit card. It is really and truly a debt card.

One more thought. There are four essential things we can do with our money. Earn it, spend it, save it, and give it away. Americans do pretty well with the first two and quite badly with the last two. The 10/10/80 lifestyle of the Bible was given for your good and mine. But we are so slow to learn it. When you get a paycheck, pay God first, then pay yourself second, and all others come in third. But we Americans have it all backward. We pay others first, then some to ourselves, and perhaps a little to God. No wonder so many are in such an economic mess. When God is last in our lives, we are in a mess. Over one-half of all the families in America did not save even one penny last year. The teachings of the Bible are for our own good. But we won't believe it. This is sad indeed, but one positive step we can all initiate starting this very day is to control our debt card spending.

NOTE: US credit card debt is now well over one trillion dollars.

# BIRTH OF CHRIST, OUR LORD

O ver the years, I have collected a file full of notes and quotes regarding the birth of Christ, our Lord. I thought it might be of value to share some of them with you. So, as you read, stop and savor those that speak to the heart. Have a very blessed holy season.

*The great events of this world*
*are not battles and elections and*
*earthquakes and thunderbolts.*
*The great events are babies*
*for each child comes with the message*
*that God is not yet discouraged with humanity,*
*but is still expecting goodwill*
*to become incarnate*
*in each human life.*
~Anonymous

**God Sent Us A Savior**
*If our greatest need had been information*
*God would have sent us an educator.*
*If our greatest need had been technology*
*God would have sent us a scientist.*
*If our greatest need had been money*
*God would have sent us an economist*
*If our greatest need had been pleasure*
*God would have sent us an entertainer.*
*But our greatest need was forgiveness*
*So God sent us a Savior.*

*Christ was born in the first century but belongs to all centuries.*
*He was born a Jew, yet he belongs to all races.*
*He was born in Bethlehem, yet he belongs to all nations.*
~ George W. Truett

*What can I give Him*
*As poor as I am?*
*If I were a shepherd,*
*I would give a lamb.*
*If I were a wise man,*
*I would do my part.*
*Yet, what can I give him?*
*I will give him my heart.*
*(Old English Carol)*

*He was light*
    *coming into a world of darkness.*
*He was love*
    *coming into a world of hate.*
*He was life*
    *coming into a world of death.*
*He was peace*
    *coming into a world of strife.*
*He was bread*
    *coming into a world of hunger.*
*He was water*
    *coming into a world of thirst.*
*He was righteousness*
    *coming into a world of sin.*
*He was hope*
    *coming into a world of despair.*
*He was God*
    *coming into a world of humanity.*

He became what we are so that we could become what he is.

# The Birth of Twin Girls

Bill Lazareth reminds us that we are an Easter people living in a Good Friday world. Here is an Easter story that is one of my favorites.

There were two little girls conceived as twins who are still occupying the same womb.

Isn't it great that we were conceived? Isn't it wonderful to be alive? Oh yes, they both agree. Of course, it's great to be alive.

One day, while exploring their little world, they find a cord that gives each of them life in the womb. And somehow, they know this is their lifeline, at least for now.

As the weeks turn into months, they also discover that they are both changing, getting bigger with each passing day.

What does this mean? One of them asks.

It means our stay in this place is now coming to an end.

What?! Said the other twin. I don't want to leave this place. It's safe, warm, and familiar. I want to stay here forever.

Well, said the other twin, we have no choice. But I do wonder: Is there life after birth?

After all, how can we survive without this cord attached to us?

Won't we die without it? And what's it like out there?

No one has ever returned to the womb to tell us what's out there.

I wonder if we don't just die and that is the end of it. And the two little girls fell into a deep despair.

If life ends at birth, what is the purpose of life in the womb? What is the purpose of life at all, they wondered.

And maybe there is no Mother after all. Maybe this whole thing is just a cruel hoax, a prank, a lousy joke somebody made up.

Maybe it doesn't matter if we live or if we die.

And if there is a Mother, how come no one has ever seen her?

Maybe she is just a figment of our imaginations.

Maybe somebody made her up to make us all feel better.

Maybe it's all just a great big lie.

Should we believe in Mother or not?

So, their last days in the womb were filled with fear, anxiety, and uncertainty.

Finally, the day of their birth arrived. When the twins had passed out of their old world and into their new world, they opened their little eyes and were overjoyed as they were gently laid in their mother's and father's loving arms.

It has been said that you cried the day you were born, and the world rejoiced. And the day you die, the world will cry, and you will rejoice.

For the People of God, death has more to do with arrival than departure.

As St. Paul has written so eloquently, "no eye has seen, nor ear heard, nor the heart of man even begun to conceive what God has prepared for those who love him."

# A CASE FOR ABORTION

A black woman comes to the local Planned Parenthood clinic for an abortion. She is a solo mother of seven children whom she can barely now feed with the help of food stamps and the local food pantry. She is not employable and could never afford childcare. She was "raped" a few months ago by a boyfriend who came home one night in a drunken stupor and had his way with her. And, as is often the case, he offers her no financial support. She knows that the last thing in the world she needs is one more mouth to feed. She knows many other things as well. She knows that this child (the ultrasound says it's a boy) will grow up in a ghetto with few, if any, of the advantages that most of us were given by birth. He will live in substandard housing, have access to little healthcare, and attend a substandard school.

At some point, he will likely become a school dropout. He will learn very few life skills because there is no father in the home, and his mother is too exhausted at the end of the day to even think about reading to him or checking on his homework. Worry, anger, and frustration will dominate the home's mood because of poverty. He will spend lots of time on the streets looking for some "community," hang out with gangs, likely experiment with drugs, somehow acquire a handgun, and find himself primarily unemployable. Sooner or later, he will run afoul of the law and develop a "rap sheet" ranging from petty crimes to felonies. He will look at an affluent society around him and ask why he cannot share the wealth.

The temptation to steal will drive him to more reckless and unlawful behavior. Over time, he is arrested, convicted, and sent off to a prison system that is much more interested in punishment (the last thing he needs) and not genuinely interested in rehabilitation. He will now languish in a tiny jail cell for years, dealing with deep depression, abuse from other prisoners, some possible level of mental illness, and serious thoughts of suicide. His has been an almost totally wasted life. It might have been better had he never been born. Should he be lucky enough to return to society someday, he will find a world just as hostile and uncaring as the one he left before going to prison. And for many, adjusting to life back on the "outside" is nearly impossible.

Please know that this scenario is NOT an exception. What I have described here happens every day to tens of thousands of black, brown, Latino, and Native American (and even white) youth who are born into a life of poverty, hopelessness, discrimination, and societal barriers they know they will never be able to climb over. America now has the highest prison population in the world.

For example, our answer to mental illness is not treatment but prison. Instead of helping low-income families with such things as primary health care, some are now working overtime to demolish the ACA (Obamacare) with absolutely nothing to offer in its place except hollow promises and worthless words. Thinking about the tragedy of these wasted lives, perhaps abortion could be a blessing in some ways. For the youth I just described, his life has been one of pain, loss, sorrow, disillusionment, frustration, anger (rage?), depression, and injustice. Assuming this lost soul was and always will be in God's good graces, perhaps he would have opted never to have been born. Might it have been better for him to bypass this "veil of tears" and go directly to the heavenly realms we firmly believe in? For what does St. Paul tell us in Phil. 1:21? "For me to live is Christ, and to die is gain." I know the concept seems radical, but had this youth been given a choice, which do you think he would have opted for?

# A LIFE DEVOID OF GOD?

In recent years, I have noticed that many of our youth (high school and college age) seem to be struggling more and more with matters of faith. The questions come in different forms, but most ask, is there really a God? And if so, why is the world in such a mess?

The reasons for these questions seem to be driven by several factors. It may simply be the natural skepticism of youth. Or a lot of peer pressure or an influential teacher who questions everything. It may be a home without religious training or healthy models for godly living.

It could also be doubts about some chapters in church history, such as the Spanish Inquisition, the Salem "witch" trials, or the implicit endorsement of the African slave trade (all for which the church has long ago renounced and repented). And while some periods of doubting and uncertainty can often lead to an even deeper faith, one certainly hopes (and prays) that our youth would not "throw out the baby with the bath water." Finally, it may simply be a matter of helping our youth to hear another side of the story. They need to hear that, without a doubt, no other institution on this earth has done more for more people for more centuries than the Christian Church. Looking at Europe and America alone, we see that nearly every college and university was founded by some branch of the Christian church. (Some have now disconnected themselves from the church, but almost without exception, the church founded these schools of higher learning).

The church gave birth to the concept of hospitals, nursing homes, leprosariums, orphanages, halfway houses, and other social service agencies, all dedicated to helping, healing, and restoring broken bodies, minds, and spirits. In addition, the church has long been at the forefront of refugee resettlement, adoption services, and chaplain services for prisons, hospitals, universities, and all military branches. Furthermore, the church has played a significant role worldwide in disaster relief, food distribution for the starving, and medical services in some of the most remote parts of the globe. The church has also brokered peace treaties, fought diseases, promoted healthy lifestyles, and cared for some of the poorest and sickest people on the planet. Undoubtedly, the church has brought life, hope, and healing to millions over the past two thousand years.

And without the ministry of the Christian church, life becomes a one-dimensional experience devoid of meaning and purpose. Without the church and the Bible, the moral law would soon give way to a kind of relativism whereby any law could be contested, ignored, or circumvented altogether. Without the gospel of Jesus Christ and the church proclaiming that gospel, there would be no hope beyond the grave. And there would be no understanding of our role as God's people to be his agents of healing, reconciliation, and renewal in today's world.

In the end, everyone must decide for themselves what they believe. But I firmly believe I would not want to be a part of a world without God and his people (the church).

# GREAT GUILT AND GREATER GRACE!

On one particular Ash Wednesday, I preached a sermon on confession and repentance, for which I got a lot of feedback. I spoke about our ongoing need as human beings to hear again and again the good news of God's unconditional love for each of us. The sermon had two points. The first point was confession that causes us to acknowledge our true human condition: sinful, flawed, and broken. The second point is that confession also leads us to the remedy for our sinfulness. And that, of course, is Jesus, the sacrificial Lamb of God.

Martin Luther once observed that helping people to understand the difference between the Law and the Gospel is one of the most challenging tasks in the world. Nevertheless, the carnal man is convinced that he can indeed save himself. The Barna Research Group, a highly respected research institute, surveyed hundreds of people: "Can good people earn their way into Heaven?" Get this: 52% of Presbyterians said yes; Lutherans 54%; Episcopalians 58%; Mormons (Latter Day Saints) 76%; and Roman Catholics 82%. If these numbers are even partially accurate, they demonstrate a woeful lack of understanding, concerning the central message of the Bible. Let me state it as clearly as I can.

On God's green earth, you and I cannot earn our salvation. It is an impossibility. Our standard of holiness is a six-foot step ladder. And God's standard of holiness is the tallest skyscraper in the world. Get the picture? On our own, we don't have a wing or a prayer. The Bible states that our righteousness is like filthy rags. All have sinned and fallen short of the glory of God. (Romans 3:23) There is none righteous, not even one. (Romans 3:10)

This is not to say that we don't understand the Law. Indeed, we do. St. Paul says that the Law is written on our hearts, and we understand it rather well. But our pride wants to tell us that we are in control and can earn the favor of God. Unlike Christianity, the Islamic faith teaches that you can earn your way to heaven. Live an ethical life, follow all the laws, and you are in. But if this were so, why was the suffering and death of Jesus Christ a necessity? If we could save ourselves, Christ's death would have been for nothing. Our problem is that we think of sin as something we do. Sin isn't so much what we do as what we are. It is a disease. You and I have a fatal disease 100% of the time unless we find a cure.

We cannot cure ourselves and to think we can is sheer folly. But now for the good news. Your salvation is a gift, pure and simple. "For by grace you have been saved and this is not of your own doing, lest anyone should boast. It is a GIFT from God." (Ephesians 2:8-9) And all you need to do is to believe it. But it may be more complicated than you think because our pride doesn't want us to believe it. Our pride tells us we can save ourselves and don't need God's help. I love that old story about the guy who gets to heaven, and St. Peter asks for the password. The guy rattles off every religious word he has ever heard in his life. No luck. Finally, he turns to walk away and says, "Oh, I give up." St. Peter says, "What did you say?" "I give up," the man says again. "That's it," St. Peter says, "that is the password."

God isn't looking for activity but passivity on this matter of salvation. Just rest back in the everlasting arms of God and turn your life over to him. Submit your will to His will. But for some, this is easier said than done. Our pride does not want to acknowledge our utter dependence upon God. But when we heed his invitation, the world appears entirely different. As one of my professors used to say, "Now that you know that you don't have to do anything, don't you want to do something for God?" Yes, indeed. The whole motivation of your life changes from a big "I have to" to a big "I want to." I no longer have to worship God, I want to. I no longer have to worship God, I want to. I no longer have to help people experiencing poverty, I want to. I no longer have to forgive those who have offended me, I want to. When this change occurs, your life starts moving in a wonderful direction. God is no longer my judge and jury. He is my friend and companion who loves me more than I will ever know. Discover the great joy of trusting God in all things and the privilege of loving others as he first loved me. I discovered what St. Paul meant when he said, "Anyone who is in Christ is a new creation; the old has passed away, and the new has come forth!" (II Corinthians 5:17) The world tells us to hang in there baby. The gospel invites us to let go and to let God do his saving work. Let me close with some distinctions between Law and Gospel that I trust you will find helpful. Some of these ideas came from a book written by Pastor Lowell Erdahl.

**Gospel:**
- "The preaching of the Gospel does not demand a response of faith. On the contrary, it creates a response of faith."
- "The Gospel does not demand anything. It is not a demand but an invitation."
- "The preaching of the Gospel does not command me to be active for God. On the contrary, it invites me to be passive toward God and to let God act."
- "The Gospel does not tell me that God will love me if I repent and have faith. It tells me I can repent and have faith because God loves me."
- "The Gospel does not tell me how to get God to love me. It tells me that I can do nothing to get God to stop loving me."

**Law:**
- "The Law does not impose morality on me. On the contrary, it exposes immorality and mortality within me."
- "The Law does not strengthen my defenses. On the contrary, it breaks them down and exposes my need for grace."
- "The Law does not show me the way from me to God. It declares that there is no way from me to God on my own merits."

- "The Law does not contradict the Gospel. We preach the law in the context of the Gospel."
- "The preaching of the Law is not to condemn but to convict and to correct. Persons in Christ are free from the law's condemnation, but no one is free from its conviction and correction."

# BODY IMAGE

Years ago, I sat in a barbershop looking for reading material. Unfortunately, I could only find three magazines: *Glamour, Mademoiselle,* and *Seventeen.* I didn't get into any of them deeply, but I did notice something that has bothered me ever since. All three of these magazines continually stressed the idea of the perfect body. They suggested dozens of ways to develop or keep such a body if you already have one. Nowadays, the same thing can be said for social media. It seems to me that we have created a society that is fixated on physical appearances, and we have then created a multi-billion-dollar industry of diets, drugs, foods, cosmetics, exercise equipment, clothing, tanning booths, and even certain kinds of surgery that support this silly notion of the perfect body.

I could tolerate this, but what troubles me is the message such magazines and advertisements send to our youth and others. If you aren't slim and trim, if your facial features are not near perfect, if your skin isn't soft and blemish free, if your teeth aren't perfectly positioned, if your posture isn't statuesque, then you don't make the grade. You are second-rate. You aren't going to be listed among the world's so-called "beautiful people." What a shallow understanding of life. And how much pain it can cause. Youth have always been somewhat "body conscious," but we have pushed this idea to new and dangerous heights.

Youth may experience fear, ostracism, self-hatred, and great insecurity if they are not in the "in-crowd" or possess the perfect body. Growing up is tough enough, but this added pressure can push a person over the edge. I read not long ago that about 70% of the world's supermodels featured in so many magazines are themselves seriously anorexic. Sadly, the Barbie Doll has become the kind of icon that we worship fanatically. Ironically, a respected physician also tells us that if Barbie were a human being, she would not have enough body fat to have a normal menstrual cycle. So, just what is going on here anyway? Let me offer a few thoughts that, hopefully, counter some of this foolishness.

First, let's remember that the accurate measure of a person is not their physical beauty, which only lasts for a few years anyway, but the strength of their character. The lasting beauty we should look for is that found in the inner person. Look for traits like love, integrity, faith, maturity, and being able to give service to others. These are the true "beauty" marks of a person.

Second, remember to be thankful for a healthy body. Good health is a greater gift as a person ages than good looks.

Third, remember that your body is a gift from God and that God doesn't make junk. The Bible tells us we are made in the very image of God. The psalmist tells us that God fearfully and wonderfully made us. And when you start getting down on yourself for not being "attractive enough," remember that a few million people on this planet would likely trade bodies with you in a heartbeat. St. Paul tells us that our bodies are to be the very temple of the Holy Spirit, and as such, we have no right to demean them in any way.

Fourth, remember that we have been created with incredible diversity and variety. Thank God that we are not all alike. Maybe someday, with enough genetic engineering, we might create the perfect body and "program" all newborns to fit the model. What a dull world that would be.

Finally, take care of your body and never despise it. We should not abuse the body with unhealthy foods, excessive smoking, drinking, drugs, etc. We are to value this "earthly tent" that serves us so well for so many years. But please do not denigrate what God has given to you. How much better the world would be if we could more readily accept and celebrate our shape, color, features, and personality differences. Someday, when this mortal life concludes, we will be given a new body. But until that time, let's appreciate the one we have and thank God for it.

# THE JUDAS GOSPEL:
## HISTORY OR HERESY?

For some time now, we have been hearing a lot about the Gospel of Judas, a seventeen-hundred-year-old manuscript that has been restored, translated, and, in some ways, sensationalized by the media. What are we to make of this document, and does it in any way undermine our faith?

To begin with, we need to state that this "gospel" appears to be completely authentic. In the early centuries of the Christian era, there was an enormous amount of religious writing, as evidenced by many other books, letters, and gospels, including the Gospel of Mary, the Gospel of Thomas, the Gospel of Peter, and the Secret Book of James, to say nothing of the Apocryphal writings. This material, including much more recent findings such as the Nag Hammadi library discovered in Egypt in 1945 and the Qumran Dead Sea scrolls found in 1947, gives us a much fuller and richer understanding of the life and times of the early church. It was also a time in which several heresies were set forth. Indeed, it could be argued that all three of the major creeds of the church were written in response to a heresy of one kind or another. One of the most prevalent heresies of the early church was something called Gnosticism, which taught, among other things, that Jesus was not truly human, but more of a phantom or an emanation. If Jesus had walked down a dusty road, he would have left no footprints.

Gnosticism grew out of Greek thought, which tended to denigrate the body and elevate the spirit. Gnostics could never accept the notion of a holy god taking on all the weaknesses and frailties of human flesh. But holding firmly to the idea of a God who was both "true God and true Man," the early church worked hard to counter the influences of the

Gnostics. So, for example, John began his gospel with an explicit declaration that the Word had truly "become flesh and dwelt among us full of grace and truth" (l: 14). And when the early church fathers set about to codify the sixty-six books of the canonical scriptures, it only seems logical that they would reject that which they knew to be false. Jesus was human in every sense of the word, yet without sin. Like many other writings from the early centuries of the church, the Gospel of Judas was most likely rejected (if it had been considered at all) because it smacked of Gnosticism. Gnostics would have loved the notion that Judas was helping Jesus with his crucifixion so that Jesus might be liberated from his weak and frail human body to set his spirit free. But the New Testament will have none of this. Jesus, though transformed in some sense, is resurrected in bodily form. He eats a meal with the disciples at the seashore, Thomas touches his wounds and comes to faith, and he breaks bread with the Emmaus disciples on that first Easter evening. There is no question Jesus is both human and divine.

It should also be noted that the crucifixion of Jesus would have happened with or without Judas. After Jesus' triumphal entry into Jerusalem, the Sanhedrin and the Roman officials knew who Jesus was. It didn't take a kiss of betrayal to identify him. After cleansing the Temple, the Sanhedrin wanted Jesus dead. And the Romans weren't naive about identifying those whom they considered troublemakers. Jesus was a marked man with or without Judas.

Judas did betray Jesus for thirty pieces of silver. But perhaps this was not his greatest sin. His greatest sin was not believing that he could be forgiven. After all, despite Peter's thrice denial, there never was a word of retribution spoken by Jesus. On the contrary, Peter became one of the greatest of all apostles. The story of Judas might have had a similar and happier ending had he had a bit more faith in the power of God to forgive.

# WEEKLY WORSHIP—WHO NEEDS IT?

Margaret and I were visiting a friend who, in turn, introduced us to an acquaintance of his. When the acquaintance learned I was a pastor, he immediately told me about a bad experience with his church and how he had written off "organized religion" altogether. He went on to tell me that he believed in God but no longer needed the church. He and God would get along fine all by themselves, thank you very much.

I must tell you, this popular notion could not be further from the truth. Okay, perhaps *you* had a bad experience with the church. Then, find another church. Search for a church online. The internet is full of listings of churches. Ask a friend about their church. In the meantime, we all need to be reminded of the communal nature of faith. God does not encourage isolationism or narcissism. Look in your Bible. Almost without exception, God reveals himself among his people. We were created to live in communities of faith and churches, even if or precisely because they often demand something of us. Such is the life to which God calls us. Faith is always relational. Anything less is a joke, a farce, and a sham. Every reference to the church in the New Testament is relational: the vine and the branches. They cannot survive without each other. The hen and her brood, the shepherd and his flock, the teacher and his disciples, the temple of living stones, the people of God who gather, scatter, and then gather again on a weekly schedule to be fed and nourished by the Word and the Sacraments. Or St. Paul's marvelous picture of the human body with Christ as the head and all the other parts working together to accomplish the purposes of God on earth. Do you see anything that smacks of private religious experience or tells us that God thinks faith can be lived out in a vacuum? I don't think so.

Have you ever noticed how Jesus conducted his ministry? He almost always traveled in groups. He wanted their support, and they wanted his. There were twelve disciples, of course. There was also another group known as the seventy (Luke 10:1). Another group numbered about five hundred. So, it seems Jesus was constantly being followed by a multitude of one size or another. These numbers tell us something. They tell us that Christian ministry is intentionally done in a community with others. There is a lesson here for all of us.

I have always loved that old story about the fellow sitting by the fireplace one evening. He takes a pair of tongs and reaches into the fire to pull out one red-hot, glowing coal. He sets it by itself on the hearth only to discover it is black, cold, and dead a few minutes later. He picks it up again and tosses it back into the fire. A moment later, the coal is hot again, glowing. And very much alive. So, too, it is with you and faith. When we pull away from the church for whatever reason, we jeopardize our faith. Faith can and will die if left unattended. This is serious business, folks. Don't let the extreme narcissism of our present-day culture lull you into thinking God doesn't care if you show up or not for weekly worship. He does care, and there is even a commandment about it. Because God knows that your faith and mine will grow in the church, messed up as it may be at times. Away from that community of faith, our faith dies. So, I'll see you at worship this week and the week after. Trust me you need it, and so do I.

# Yours for Good Preaching

Dear Pastors,

One of the hallmarks of this congregation has been strong preaching, and I am glad you all continue to add to this tradition. Because I am always interested in improving my preaching and know that you, too, share this sentiment, let me offer a guide for sermon prep that has always been helpful to me and maybe for you too.

1. It seems to me there are three levels of preaching. The first is to tell your audience what you want them to know. This is an excellent place to start, and proclamations are undoubtedly a great place to begin. Tell me, for example, that God forgives me my sins. I need to be told this, and often. The trouble is, however, a lot of preaching never gets beyond this level. But good preaching will always lead to the second level.

2. After you have told me that God forgives me, I need for you also to show me his truth. This is a more difficult task. The way by which we "show" in public speaking is by illustrations and examples. I recall Professor Arndt Halvorson, who said that the most challenging thing a pastor does is find examples that quickly enlighten and stimulate the mind. Good examples are often rare but most necessary for good preaching. And they should not have to be explained. Halvorson noted that an excellent example should instantaneously light up the hearer's mind and imagination. If you need to explain an illustration, it is not a good illustration. Show me that God forgives my sin with such clarity that I will see and believe it almost without hesitation.

3.  But there is a third level that I think tests the mettle of every good speaker. Don't just show me. But move me. Move me to such an extent that when you finish your sermon, I will be ready to affirm and celebrate God's forgiveness of my sins and want to put it into practice in my own life immediately. This kind of preaching takes lots of hard work and prayerful study. But it is so worthwhile in the end. When a congregation is moved to this extent, they can accomplish anything. Putting my preaching to this three-level test may not be easy, but it can ultimately benefit both the preacher and the congregation.

The best quote I ever heard on public speaking was this: there are two kinds of speakers in the world, those who have to say something and those who have something to say. The difference between them is like a lightning bug and a lightning bolt.

# WHY WE WORSHIP

I want to say a good word for weekly worship. Worship is the lifeblood of the Christian Church. It is also the lifeblood of the individual Christian. Neglect worship for a long time, and your faith begins to wither and die. The Bible is one ongoing story of God revealing himself amid his people. While there are some stories of individual revelation, Biblical faith is most often lived out in the community of God's people. From the ancient Israelites of the Old Testament to the apostles and the early church of the New Testament, God comes to make himself known among his people. God promises you will not go home with an empty heart or head if you are faithful in worship.

Let me tell you about a parable Jesus once told. There was a man who gave a banquet and sent out many invitations. A number of those invited declined the invitation, offering such excuses as these: *"I just got married, I just bought some oxen, I just bought some land and need to go and appraise it."* Please note that while these are all excellent excuses, they are just excuses. And the banquet host makes it plain that these guests will never receive another invitation. Nevertheless, the point of the parable is obvious, and negligence has consequences.

I still like my friend's line. There are only two reasons for missing worship: *"You are sick or deceased."* All else comes off as nothing more than an excuse, which our Lord indicates is unacceptable. So, if you think missing worship is a harmless game you play with God, think again. This invitation may only be extended once.

I close with ten reasons why you and I need to worship at least once a week. I invite you to add your own to this listing:

1. In worship, we shift the focus of our lives off of self and on to God where it rightly belongs.

2. In worship, we hear God's word read, proclaimed, and applied to our lives.
3. In worship, we celebrate and receive the Sacraments.
4. In worship, we spend an essential hour together with family and friends.
5. In worship, we tell the world which side we are on. Jesus once declared that we are either for him or against him.
6. In worship, we fulfill the commandment to remember and keep the Sabbath day holy.
7. In worship, we have a marvelous opportunity to thank God for the blessings of life.
8. In worship (before, during, and after), we can comfort, support, and otherwise encourage one another in our journey through life.
9. In worship, we make an offering to God, a serious attempt to return to him a portion of what he has first given to us.
10. In worship, we make visible the body of Christ on earth today. When you are missing, the Body is not complete.

# WORSHIP—IT'S WHAT REALLY MATTERS!

Years ago, I read an article from USA Today entitled "Amen to a Church-Free Life." You can bet that headline got my attention! I still remember it vividly; the article told how some Americans today are forsaking the Church and finding their "spirituality" elsewhere. I hardly need to tell you that I was not impressed. Today, it is very fashionable for movie stars and many others to declare how spiritual they are apart from any identifiable faith community. To me, this is sheer nonsense. Let me state this as clearly as I can. The Christian faith has always been lived out in a community of believers. Nowhere in the Bible is there any encouragement to "go it alone."

On the contrary, the Bible teaches that "going it alone" is dangerous. The Bible is the story of God revealing himself to his people. Even those few stories of what seems like a private revelation, like the angel appearing to Mary, are set solidly within a living faith community. People who think they can live out the Christian faith apart from the church are only kidding themselves. It cannot be done successfully in isolation.

The church on earth is the Body of Christ. To reject the Church is also to reject the Body of Christ, and to reject the Body of Christ is to reject Christ himself. Christ calls the Church into being where we grow and mature in our faith. Here, we are baptized, fed, nurtured, taught, inspired, and commissioned by the Gospel of Jesus Christ. Apart from the Church, faith almost always withers and dies.

From ancient Israelites of the Old Testament to the apostles and early church of the New Testament, God comes to make himself known among his people. God promises you will not go home with an empty heart or head if you are faithful in weekly worship. Even Jesus went to the synagogue "as was His custom." (Luke 4:16)

Worship is not an option. It is the joyful and willing response of any faithful Christian. It is the lifeblood of the people of God. One day, we will all meet our Lord face to face. He won't carry an attendance book, but he may well ask why some of us thought worshiping him regularly when his people gathered around the Word and the Sacraments was not essential. I want to assure you that this matter of worship is no joke. It is truly a matter of life and death…yours and mine. I wonder if most of us realize how incredibly narcissistic our society has become. We are uninterested if something doesn't stimulate, entertain, or otherwise thrill us. Our kids say it, their friends say it, and we adults say it, too. The Greek word for worship is liturgia, which literally means "the work of the people." The words "worship and work" come from the same root derivation. I come to the church to literally work on my worship of God. Feeling entertained has nothing to do with it. The focus of worship is not on the self but on God.

Please find out how refreshing it is to have your life reoriented and realigned each week. And in the process, you will discover what true worship is all about.

# ON BECOMING UN-LOST

A s you may know, "Lost" was a very popular show for many years. I have to confess that I have never watched more than thirty minutes of the television show *Lost* since it first aired. But I want to share ways to become "un-lost" in today's wild world.

My wife and I watched the movie "Into the Wild" a few years ago. It's a true story about a young man named Christopher McCandless who grew up in a somewhat dysfunctional family, graduated from Emory University in Atlanta, was bound for Harvard Law School, and decided to chuck it all in an intense and even desperate search for freedom and meaning in his life. I admired his tenacity and willingness to make huge sacrifices for personal integrity. However, as the story unfolded, I realized that this fellow, who renames himself Alexander Supertramp, is on a self-centered journey. One realizes that McCandless lacks spiritual depth in his life. But, because he kept a detailed log of his adventures and thoughts, we obtain insight into what made him who he is. By the end of the story, he is beginning to realize the error of his ways and what he must do to get his life back on track. Sadly, his life comes to a premature end.

After viewing this film, I kept thinking of all the teachings of Jesus that clearly tell us where to find the purpose of life.

*Love God with all your heart, soul, mind, and strength, and your neighbor as yourself.*

*He who would keep his life will lose it, but he who loses his life for my sake shall surely find it.*

*And what will it profit a man if he should gain the whole world and yet lose his own soul?*

*If anyone would come after me, let him deny himself and take up his cross and follow me.*

Such straightforward yet profound words tell us exactly how to live so that we need not wander through life like this young man only to find the answers too late. There is a good reason why the Bible reads the way it does: so that we might indeed have life and have it in all its fullness. We once were lost but are now found. Thank God for the wisdom of his everlasting Word!

# CHAPEL WORSHIP

While serving as Campus Pastor, I noted many complaints and comments about our daily chapel services. While my office welcomes all forms of feedback (positive or negative), I want to encourage everyone to try harder to keep their eye on what is central to the Christian life.

Sometimes, I wonder if we realize how narcissistic our society has become. Over time, we hear comments like this: I don't attend chapel because it's not a welcoming place. Or the preachers seem to have some ax to grind. Or the language is too exclusive or too inclusive. (trust me, we have heard both comments). Or the room does not lend itself to meaningful worship. Or there is not enough time for prayer, meditation, or whatever. You get the point. And while all of the above likely contains some truth, it still begs the question, what is our daily worship of God all about?

In short, worship is the WORK of God's people. Worship has little or nothing to do with my needs, my wants, or my complaints. Although, as a former seminary president used to remind us, even if the entire worship experience is a disaster, we still have plenty of good reasons to be there, chief among them is to pause each day to thank God for the many blessings of life. Worship should be God-centered and not me-centered. We come to chapel to give God our prayers, our hymns, our meditations, our liturgies, our offerings, our time, our loyalties, and our very lives. Nothing less will do. Is every chapel experience memorable? Of course not. But every chapel experience somehow honors our Lord and Savior and likely feeds the soul.

There is an old story about a Lutheran pastor and a Catholic priest who served parishes in the same small town. One Sunday morning, there is a terrible blizzard, and not one worshipper shows up at either church. The Lutheran pastor locks up his church and goes home, but the Catholic priest stays in his sanctuary and offers the whole hour-long Mass even though there is not a single soul in the pews. And why? Because worship is God-centered. God was present that morning, even if only one person came for worship. We have a marvelous opportunity every morning at this seminary to pause for a few extraordinary moments to refocus our lives and to ask again for the blessings and guidance of God upon our lives. You need this daily discipline, and so do I. I hope to see you in chapel today, tomorrow, and the day after tomorrow.

# Section Five

## PERSONAL THOUGHTS

# LESSONS FROM EMILY, OUR CAT

Emily was our cat who died. Or, more accurately, we had her put to sleep at the veterinarian's office. Emily was a long-haired calico and had been a part of our family for sixteen years. She was old, not in good health, and had bladder control problems.

I have made some joking comments about Emily over the years from the pulpit, but I must tell you that saying goodbye to her was more difficult than I had anticipated. She had been an excellent house pet despite our original misgivings sixteen years ago when she was given to us by a friend. Her most endearing quality was an uncanny ability to sense whenever anyone in the family was sick, crying, or hurting. She was there immediately, lying on your chest or curled up in your lap, purring as if trying to communicate comfort and love. I now understand why pet therapy works so well in nursing homes and other facilities for older people.

So, we all got into the car, took her to the vet, said our farewells, and stood around wiping our eyes while a very kind and sympathetic vet did what we asked. She returned with Emily in a small box (she had been losing weight lately), and we drove home almost silently. We walked out to the garden in the backyard (now known as Emily's Garden) and laid her in the hole we had dug the day before.

We all took turns shoveling in the dirt and cried like we had lost a dear friend. I now realize that we had. We immediately left town for a couple of days, which was probably a good thing to do, though coming home to an "empty" house was also more difficult than we thought it would be. No one was there to greet us. In addition to saying goodbye to Emily, there was another level of learning for me. I kept thinking about the brevity of life and the frailty of our flesh, whether human or animal. The Bible teaches that we are very different from animals in some ways, yet we belong to the animal portion of creation. (we are not minerals or vegetables). Each day of our lives is a gift, and each day is precious. We've tried to live life in ways that are pleasing to God and beneficial to us and those around us. I hope and pray for long, healthy, happy lives.

But as with Emily, our days are also numbered, and we are foolish to think otherwise. The Psalmist tells us that all flesh is like grass. It withers, fades, and returns to the earth in due time. But thank God, through our Lord Jesus, that this is not the end of the story. From beginning to end, the Bible tells us that the grave is not the story's last chapter. If it were, then we should never stop grieving for our loved ones. A great shroud of death would cover the earth, and there would be no cause for hope whatsoever.

But, as St. Paul says, thanks be to God who has given us victory (over death) through our Lord, Jesus Christ. As one of my teachers used to say, this is either a great lie or the greatest truth. And sooner or later, we must all decide which we believe. I cannot believe that God is not good for his word. So, I grieve the loss of loved ones with a profound sense of hope and expectation. God invites us to do this.

A footnote. If there is a resurrection for humanity, might there be one also for animals? The Bible says nothing about this question, which every child who has ever lost a pet has asked. I recall a professor who once answered in this way: if your eternal happiness in heaven is somehow contingent on having your pet with you, then it shall be so. In time, we will know for sure. Peace and love to you all.

# THE WONDERS OF NATURE

1. A newborn fawn has no scent, making it very hard for predators to track and kill it.
2. Caterpillars, cocoons, chrysalis, butterflies, nature's version of life, death, and resurrection.
3. The Fairy Tern lives on the coast of the Indian Ocean. It's the only bird that lays a single egg high up on a tree branch without any nest.
4. The flying lizard can spread its folds of skin (like wings) and glide through the air for up to several hundred feet.
5. The Pufferfish can blow itself up so big that birds of prey cannot haul it away.
6. The Archerfish of India can spit a stream of water over two feet to knock insects and spiders off of low-hanging branches and into the water, where the fish eat them.
7. The Chameleon can change its color to blend in with its surroundings. It also has a long, sticky tongue that can catch an insect quickly. It also has eyes that simultaneously move in different directions to see forward and backward at the same time.
8. Many animals never see their young. These include turtles, frogs, and butterflies.
9. A black panther is an all-black leopard. As a result, it will often have babies that grow up with the same bright yellow spotted coats that most leopards have.
10. The European cuckoo lays her egg in the nest of some other bird. Then the cuckoo flies away while another bird sits on her egg and even hatches and cares for it.

11. The male and female Hornbills are the most unusual parents. They find a tree with a hollow in it, and the female climbs in. Then, together, they close the opening with a mud wall, leaving only a tiny hole for feeding. The female will stay in the dark hollow for up to four months, laying just one egg until it hatches. Then, she and the chick are fed when the male puts food through the hole in the mud wall. When the chick reaches a certain age, they knock down the mud wall so the female and chick can fly away as they please.

12. The Snowshoe hare goes from dark summer brown to pure winter white.

13. The human tongue has four major receptors: sweet, sour, salty, and acidic. It can also detect over a thousand different flavors.

14. There are about seven and a half billion people on this planet today and no two are exactly alike.

15. Almost half the bones in your body are in your feet with twenty-six in each foot along with thirty-two joints and a hundred ligaments.

16. The earth has spun on a twenty-three-degree axis around the sun with amazing precision. If we moved a quarter of a degree closer to the sun, we would all burn up. If we moved a quarter of a degree away from the sun the earth would turn into a block of ice.

17. The human body contains about sixty thousand miles of veins, arteries, capillaries, and vessels. Each of the seventy-five trillion cells in your body is connected to a blood source.

18. The human body gets a new skeleton about every ten years. And we get a brand-new stomach lining about every fifteen days.

19. The human heart pumps five quarts of blood every minute. It weighs about eleven ounces, beats two point seven trillion times in seventy-five years, and pumps one point six million gallons of blood per year without ever pausing to rest.

# LUTHERAN HUMOR

It may be time to laugh a little. Humor is a gift from God, and so far, as we know, we are the only creatures on earth that can laugh. (The hyena laughs but only by instinct.) So anyway, here is some humor (courtesy of Jeff Grant).

**You know you are a Lutheran when...**

...you carry silverware in your pocket to church just in case there's a potluck.

...you have an uncontrollable urge to sit in the back of any room.

...your house is a mess because you're "saved by grace and not by works."

You think an ELCA Lutheran bride and an LCMS groom make for a "mixed marriage."

...you're fifty-seven years old, and your parents still won't let you date a Catholic.

...you can't get into heaven without a casserole.

You think the 11th commandment is: If it's never been done that way before, don't try it now.

...you feel guilty about not feeling guilty.

...it's one hundred and ten degrees outside, and you still have hot coffee after services.

...the most mail you receive all year is from the Stewardship Committee.

...you win ten million in the lottery and decide to throw a party, so you rent the parish hall and ask all your friends to bring a hot dish, salad, or dessert.

...a fund drive is needed to finance the new one thousand-cup coffee urn.

...all of your casserole dishes have your name on the bottom.

…all your relatives graduated from a school named Concordia.

…you ask for "A Mighty Fortress" on the love song request line.

…you actually understand the folks from Lake Wobegon.

…as a teenager, you thought Martin Luther was a civil rights leader from the 1960s

# SOME WORDS OF WISDOM

Most Pastors keep a file of "quotable quotes" and wise sayings they have collected over the years. What follows are a few of my favorites. I hope you enjoy reading over them to see if one or more might apply to your life today.

- We are not put on the earth to see through one another but to see one another through.
- Talent is God-given. Be thankful.
- Fame is man-given. Be humble.
- Conceit is self-given. Be careful.
- No one ever collapsed under the weight of a single day's load. It is only when we pile on the load of more than one day that we get ourselves into unbearable situations.
- Yesterday is history, tomorrow is a mystery, and today is a gift. That's why we call it "the present."
- A friend is one to whom you can pour out all the content of your heart, chaff, and grain together, knowing that the gentlest of hands will take and sift it, keep what is worth keeping, and, with the breath of kindness, blow the rest away.
- Others will not care how much we know until they know how much we care.
- When my heavenly Father disciplines me, he reminds me that I am his son/daughter.
- The roots grow deep when the winds are strong.
- We are all faced with a series of great opportunities in life brilliantly disguised as impossible situations.
- Life is like a jigsaw puzzle with a variety of pieces. Our struggle to see it whole and finished never ceases. Some spend restless

hours asking, "Why?" and end in great confusion. Lord, help us realize it is only you who has the solution.

- When nothing seems to help, I go and look at a stonecutter hammering away at his rock perhaps a hundred times without as much as a crack showing in it. Yet at the hundred and first blow, it will split in two, and I know it was not that blow that did it but all the blows that had gone before.

Have a good day celebrating the
unconditional love of God in your life!

# Goodbye Dad, and
# Thanks for Everything

On Thanksgiving afternoon, I drove with my family to Iowa to visit my elderly parents. It was a one-hundred-and-sixty-nine-mile trip I had taken many times before. But this time was different. This trip was to say goodbye to my father for the last time.

When we arrived at the nursing home, Dad was already semi-comatose. Dad had eaten almost nothing for the past several days. He was, as they say, "shutting down." At ninety-two, perhaps he had simply lost the will to live. Or, as a nurse suggested, perhaps his dementia was now affecting that part of the brain that controls hunger, eating, and even swallowing. Or maybe it was a combination of the two. We will never know for sure.

What we do know is that Dad was getting ready to depart this life for a whole new dimension of existence. Yet, when his passing came early Sunday morning, it was peaceful, gentle, and holy. Two of the nursing staff stood by his bed and wept as though it was their own father who had just died. Such is the level of care given daily to the residents of the Bartels Home.

We gathered with the Chaplain to remember, to pray, and to comfort one another. In the midst of our tears, we also remembered the great promises of scripture: "I am the resurrection and the life," Jesus says. "He who believes in me, though he dies, yet shall he live. And whosoever lives and believes in me shall never die." Loss and victory, tears and laughter, joy and sorrow, despair and hope, life and death. It's all part of the human predicament and was so real as Dad drew his final breath of life.

Then came the stillness—no more breathing. There is no more color on his face. No movement of any kind. His body lay perfectly still. Dad had truly given up his spirit. This dad, whom I remember as being so strong, so alive, so vital, so full of energy, was now as still as stone. He had returned to his Creator, that One who had breathed life into his lungs some ninety-two years ago. And how good God had been to his servant John for all these many years—a good wife, children, grandchildren, great-grandchildren, education, health, employment, friends, freedom, travel, a zest for life, and a strong faith in the goodness and wisdom of God. What a full life it has been.

Summarizing a human life on one or even a hundred pages is impossible. But this son thinks back over his years to remember a dad who only wanted the best for him. He was a dad who offered advice, encouragement, support, and even discipline, but I always knew it came from a heart that cared deeply for each member of the family. A dad who, despite his own human imperfections, still managed to model a godly life and to give his son a profound appreciation for the importance of faith in God and the work of the Christian Church here on earth.

And now we entrust him to his Creator once more. Lowell Erdahl talks about our grief in his little book *The Lonely House.* "God lets us feel our loss. He does not fill the empty space right away, nor does he rush in to wipe away our tears or heal our broken hearts. And so that we, too, may pay tribute to the departed loved one, he lets us feel the pain of our loss. That pain is the price we pay for having loved and having been loved. But would we want it any other way? The pain of losing a loved one is a good measure of what that person meant to us. But beyond the pain is the healing, and we do hope for that day when God will wipe away all tears from our eyes and death shall be no more. But for now, we do experience grief. Neither broken bones nor broken hearts heal quickly. So, we give God time to do his healing work and seek neither to rush it nor prolong it."

So, Dad, I just want to say thanks for everything you ever did to get my life off to a good start. You mean more to your family than you will ever know, and we will never forget you. I only hope I have been as good a dad as you were. So, rest now from your earthly labors. You surely deserve it. You were always a faithful servant of your Lord, and I am absolutely certain that you are now enjoying the blessings, the rest, the peace, and the joy of God's eternal kingdom. And we look forward to that glorious day when we will see each other once again in a place where there will be no more sorrow, sickness, suffering, or death. And what a joyous day that will be for all of God's children.

Love always from your very grateful son, Paul.

# GOODBYE MOM,
## AND THANKS FOR EVERYTHING

I was putting the finishing touches on my sermon when the phone rang. It was my mother's healthcare facility in Waverly, Iowa, who would call from time to time to tell us how Mom was doing or if she had taken a recent tumble. But this call was different. In a soft and sad voice, the nurse told me my mother had just passed away. Mom had gotten up for breakfast, said she didn't feel too well, laid down for a nap, and never woke up again. It was the ending of a life and, in some ways, the ending of an era. One more of those "greatest generation" folk was now gone.

Mom was ninety-nine years old and had had a really good life, so you would think you were prepared for the day when that phone call came. But being prepared in your head is not the same as being prepared in your heart. This is, after all, your mother. The one who endured weeks of morning sickness while you developed in her womb and the one who likely experienced a fair amount of pain bringing you into the world. The one who nursed you, diapered you, and rocked you to sleep at all hours of the day and night. But it was her loving face that hovered over your crib or cradle and who made sure you had everything you needed to sustain your fragile little life.

And, of course, Mom's role changed as my needs changed. She taught me to be honest in all things, to be aware of the needs of others, to be generous with whatever I owned, and always to be thankful. She taught me to be kind to people. She showed me something about how to live a sacrificial life with her *own* simple yet gracious life. Most of all, Mom mentored me in the development of my most valued possession: my faith in God and my trust in his Son, my Lord and Savior. I recall going to sleep every night with Mom at my bedside. We would talk about the blessings and challenges of the day and how we could fall asleep knowing that we were resting back in the everlasting arms of God. "Now I lay me down to sleep. I pray the Lord, my soul to keep…" Mom very much enjoyed being a mother to her two boys.

Mom (and Dad) always taught Sunday School at every church we ever belonged to (they lived in eleven different cities for over fifty years). They were strong believers in the value of Christian education. Mom would say that we need to feed the mind, the body, and, most importantly, the soul; that part of our being designed for time and eternity, for now and forever. Mom lived her faith every day, no matter what. And for that, I will be forever grateful.

When Dad died nearly two years ago, it was tough on Mom. They didn't have a perfect marriage, but they deeply loved and respected each other. They were "joined at the hip" for some sixty-seven years, and you can never be quite the same after sustaining that kind of loss. Mom carried on so graciously as she always did, but time and age finally caught up to her. She loved her family so deeply, and we loved her. Her room at the nursing home was a literal "shrine" of family photos that lined all the walls. But it must have been time for her to move on. The day after Mom died was Dad's birthday, September 10. I think Mom wanted to join him for the party. She was tired of being alone. And most all of her generation was now gone.

Mom was laid to rest next to Dad at the old Luther Valley Cemetery near Orfordville, Wisconsin, which literally overlooks the farm where she grew up. Across the road is Luther Valley Church, a big white framed building where Mom was baptized, confirmed, and married. She is now at home again, having lived for ninety-nine good years. And Mom would be the first to say, "To God be the glory for blessing my life in so many ways." And I know, too, that Mom and Dad aren't really at the cemetery. Their earthly remains are there beneath the sod, but Mom and Dad are now sitting together at the feet of their Lord, whom they served all their lives. I miss them very much, but I know for a certainty that one day, we will all rejoice together at that great banquet table where there will be no more sickness, sorrow, pain, or death. And what a glorious day that shall be! For now, I just need to say, "Thanks, Mom, for everything." You gave me more than I could ever hope to repay. You were the best!

Love always, from your very grateful son, Paul.

# To Becca, on
# her Confirmation Day

Dear Becca,

Soon, you and eighty-two other youth from our congregation will publicly confess your faith in your Lord and Savior, Jesus Christ, and you will speak your confirmation vows. You will reaffirm the vows that your mother and I and your sponsors spoke at the baptismal font fifteen years ago. Where did the years go?

Your mother and I pray it will be one of your life's most important days. From the day of your birth, Becca, I have prayed for two things for you (and your sister and brother). I have asked God to give you a strong faith and good health. And frankly, if I ever had to choose between the two, I would opt for faith as l believe it is the most vital dimension in a person's life. Without it, life has no meaning and makes little sense.

We are very proud of you, Becca, and your whole class. Our church is blessed with so many wonderful young people. It has been a joy to have you as a daughter and to watch you grow physically, spiritually, and intellectually. You are a thoughtful and caring person, and you seem to be very sensitive to the needs of others. You and your class have so much potential and much to offer to a hurting and needy world. Some people just dwell on the world's problems (hate, drugs, violence, greed,) but a person of faith can also see God's activity in the world—his grace, power, kingdom, and ability to transform people and situations. With faith in God, life is an adventure and not an endurance contest.

Faith in Christ would be the most remarkable Confirmation gift I could give you, Becca, but I honestly can't give it to you. I can tell you what my faith in God means to me and demonstrate its importance. But no one rides into the Kingdom of God on the coattails of another person. You have to accept this gift in a very personal way. It's the one gift of life that never wears out or goes out of style. It benefits every area of life. And while it is a marvelous gift, it must also be nurtured and encouraged. This we do through weekly worship, prayer, reading the Bible, celebrating the sacraments, associating with other Christians, and sharing our faith with others. My prayer, Becca, is that you will continue to grow in your awareness of God's presence in your life. Serve, love, and obey him always. Put him above all others in your life. He will never let you down, and you will never regret it. On the day of your baptism, Becca, God promised you his unconditional love. On Confirmation Day, you will make some promises to God. I hope you will always keep them.

Becca, you were the first baby baptized at our church on Easter Sunday, 1981. We have come a long way together, and you will likely never know how much your mom and I love you. And remember, too, that many others from our church care about you and your entire class. Think of them as a cheering section pulling and praying for you. That is what's so great about being in the church. It is a wonderful support group; we all need one these days. So, keep the faith, Becca, and keep on trusting in God. It will be a personal joy to confirm you and your class. And it will be exciting to see where God leads your class as your young lives unfold. May God go with you today and always.

With much love,

Dad and Mom

*"Let no one despise your youth but set the believers an example in your speech and conduct, in love, in faith, and in purity. And do not neglect the gift you have, which was given to you when the elders laid their hands upon you."*

~The words of St. Paul to his young friend in Christ, Timothy

# SELF-CARE IN MINISTRY

Some of you might be interested to know that the notion of "self-care" in ministry is relatively new. I dare say that the phrase itself had little or no meaning just a few decades ago. In truth, many older pastors can no doubt recall how they, or some of their fellow clergy, spent so many hours a week doing "church work" that it seemed as though they were literally sacrificing themselves, and perhaps their families also, on the "altar table of the church." This was obviously not a healthy model for ministry and sometimes created bitterness and resentment in clergy families.

Part of the problem was likely a heavy dose of the old Protestant work ethic from years ago: "Idle hands are the devil's workshop." For others, it might have been a "Messiah complex" or some other form of work righteousness, or even an unhealthy way to gain recognition or sympathy: "Poor pastor; he works himself half to death."

So, in the wake of such unwise behavior, several books were published in the 1960s and 1970s promoting healthier lifestyles and a greater understanding of time management. Such a book was entitled *Ministry Burnout* by John Sanford. In his book, Sanford lists nine characteristics of parish ministry that can lead to fatigue, frustration, and burnout. He notes that the job has no boundaries unless you set them, it's often difficult to measure and quantify success in ministry, you are often dealing with people's expectations, some unrealistic, and working with hurting people can be very draining. Sometimes, you put on your "persona" and go and do the job just because it must be done. For example, you can't postpone a wedding, funeral, or baptism because you don't feel like doing one that day.

So, what is a professional church worker to do? Like most things in life, balance is a crucial concept. Finding the right balance between work and leisure, vocation and vacation, ritual and renewal, is critical. It is not always easy, but it is worth the effort. And don't be afraid to get some professional help if necessary.

One other thought. During fifty years of parish ministry, I discovered that those extraordinary New Testament paradoxes are true. In giving to others, I do receive. In losing myself for the gospel's sake, I find genuine fulfillment in ministry. And in becoming a servant, I discover a profound sense of freedom. Indeed, we ought not to work ourselves into an unhealthy dither for the sake of the parish. Yet, at the same time, I have always felt that as much as I gave, I most often also received in even fuller measure, and that made parish ministry one of the greatest joys of my life.

# Transitions: A Time of Both Hope and Anxiety

As the old saying goes, the one constant in life is change. We might as well get used to it, even though that can sometimes be difficult. Think of the changes happening right now. Spring soon turns to summer. The school year has come to a close. Some students are anticipating graduation and ordination. Internships are beginning or soon to end. Summer school or summer employment are on the horizon. Summer weddings. Perhaps a change in housing, if not a complete change of location. As the old Norwegians put it: Uffda!

But there is undoubtedly precedent for a "transitional lifestyle." Consider Noah and his floating zoo. Joseph joins a caravan hoping to see the Sphinx and the pyramids (well, not exactly). The Israelites ran around in the wilderness for years. Also, the Babylonian exile. The chosen twelve followed an itinerant preacher around for three years. Later on, all of them are sent out filled with missionary zeal. And did I mention the three big excursions of St. Paul? Indeed, God does not envision us to be sedentary people!

Many years ago, I sat in Gullixon Hall, and the professor gave an impassioned challenge to my class to leave Jerusalem (the Twin Cities) and go to Judea (Omaha?) and Samaria (Flagstaff) and the ends of the earth. Simply put, we are to get out of Dodge. A needy and hurting world is out there waiting to hear some good news. So, in 1972, I ended up in Pontiac, Michigan, vowing (to myself) to stay for just two years. We stayed for nine years and loved almost every minute of it. As Alvin Rogness used to say, "Just love your people, and over time, they will love you back, perhaps in greater measure." Last night, at supper time, my beloved sister-in-law made the most significant transition a person will ever make. She had fought an enemy called cancer for three years (throat cancer, never smoked) but would not win this battle. But if there was ever a "model" for dying, Janice was it. No complaints and no self-pity. She was not afraid to die (she had great faith in her saving Lord) but was very sad to leave her husband, children, and five beautiful grandchildren. We indeed grieve for Jan but never without the hope and the promise of the resurrection unto life everlasting. He is risen! And so shall we be. What an amazing word of comfort in an ever-changing world of transitions!

# A DISAPPOINTING FILM

Mel Gibson did a masterful job marketing his film, *The Passion of the Christ.* To the surprise of many in Hollywood, it has done very well at the box office and has earned Gibson a ton of money. (He put up millions of his own to make it.)

No one would deny that many scenes in the film are riveting and revealing, and Gibson should be thanked for undertaking such a project. But just how good is the movie altogether?

The hyper-violence on the screen does not square with the biblical narrative. Each of the four Gospels reports that Pilate ordered Jesus to be flogged (whipped), but this is all that is said. While crucifixion was undoubtedly a horrible way to die, the Bible contains no references to anything like the sadistic torture sessions the film depicts.

This film embellishes the story of Jesus' death with events that are not factual, not in the Gospels, and never in the Bible. And, when Gibson portrays the devil in the movie, why does he have him holding a devilish-looking dwarf in his arms?

The film is also devoid of any sense of joy or hope. The Resurrection does get twenty seconds on the screen, but even here, Jesus looks as if he is resentful, if not angry. Instead, the two hours are devoted to weeping, whipping, torture, bleeding, and pain. There is no sense that Jesus or his ministry had any life-giving qualities. Even the flashback scenes are all sad and depressing.

In the movie, Jesus is severely beaten, wrapped in chains, and thrown off a bridge. None of this appears in the Bible. The film gives viewers a twenty-minute scene of Jesus dragging his cross to the Calvary while repeatedly whipped and beaten.

Jesus was not thrown off a bridge. The Bible does not tell of a crow pecking out the eye of one of the robbers next to Jesus. Instead, the woman caught in adultery is seen as beaten and barely alive. In truth, this woman (in the Bible account) is not harmed because of Jesus' intervention.

The adult Jesus is made to look more like a zombie than a Messiah. His followers all look like they were brought there under duress. In the Last Supper scene, Jesus speaks in a monotone voice while the disciples look scared out of their wits. Gibson seems bent on making this story one long, painful, bloody event without any sign of hope, life, or salvation.

The Last Supper was likely a night of dining and mutual support among close friends. And, since there is no way to make the Resurrection depressing, it gets only a few seconds of screen time. I suspect that, for some, perhaps many, this film was helpful for their faith. But because there is so little character development, I found it hard to connect with the characters in the story. By the end of the film, I was more numb than empathetic.

It surprises me that some religious leaders have endorsed the film without reservations. I like this evaluation of "The Passion of the Christ," offered by one of our staff members: "If you want to get the right perspective, go home and read the four Gospels."

# A Father's Hard Work

Being a father is hard work. It is a great responsibility; it is also a high privilege. Realizing this, there are some things fathers can do to help their relationship with their children. At first glance, these suggestions may seem simple. Yet they can have lasting benefits for your family and help deepen your children's sense of being part of God's family.

1. Pray daily with your children. This "simple" action is not as simple as it first appears. If we are honest, most of us realize that we must work on our prayer lives. Finding time to teach our children to pray may be still more difficult.

   Then, too, fathers may not know how to pray with their children. Some may even be afraid to do so. Perhaps a devotional guide for children will be needed at first. Most bookstores that carry Christian literature have plenty from which to choose.

   Mealtime or just before bed is a good time for parents and children to pray together. But keep in mind that children don't require detailed prayer thoughts or beautifully structured sentences. Instead, a father and child can quietly share their faith with simply worded prayers.

   Initially, this may take some discipline, but it is well worth the effort. How sad for a child to grow past these formative years without having their faith shaped and strengthened by a father who takes the time to pray.

2. Tell your children you love them. Do it frequently. Feeling love for a child is essential, but expressing it verbally is likewise crucial. As with prayer, this can sound simple, but sharing such feelings through words may not be easy. Yet these little words,

when spoken sincerely, possess real healing power. Moreover, they are a good sign that the relationship between father and child is healthy and growing.

3. Give a definite segment of time to your children each day. Don't assume that just being home is enough. A prudent father will find some "prime time" each day and treat it as such.

When I was a young boy, my father gave me many things. Like most children in America, I never lacked food, clothing, shelter, toys, and the like. But what I recall most fondly from my childhood are those times when my father gave me himself. Sometimes, I was even privileged to "set the agenda." Such times are well remembered because Dad did not give me anything but himself and his time, two very precious gifts.

My own children now request my time as we read books, color, work on puzzles, and practice with the bat and ball. I know I have both an opportunity and responsibility during these times to impart to them many values, attitudes, and convictions that I hold dear and which I hope they, too, will share.

I know the day will come when they no longer ask for my time and attention. How important, then, that I take this chance to give myself to my children now while they still desire it. How fleeting and precious are these years of parenthood? When I consider these simple actions, I remember the life of Jesus. He taught his disciples to pray. He told his disciples of his great love for them. He gave himself entirely to his friends, even when this led to the cross. He set an example. Could a father find a better model after which to pattern his own life?

# ONE WHO MAKES THE DIFFERENCE

A friend of mine once asked me why I decided to enter the Christian ministry. While I pondered his question, many reasons came to my mind. But I soon realized that most of them fell into one general category: the desire to share the good news that has so impacted my life with others. This news is needed to live a happy and meaningful life in an otherwise fallen and broken world.

As I explained this to my friend, I told him I do not consider Christian ministry a job. But rather as an opportunity to share the good news full-time. I realize, of course, that all the people of God, no matter what they do, have the "full-time" privilege of sharing the good news.

In our society, I see people who are beaten, tired, fearful, frustrated, filled with anxiety or guilt, and too often find life an uphill battle. But this is not what God had in mind when he breathed life into the nostrils of humankind. Instead, life was given as a gift to be lived victoriously, joyously, and thankfully. Yet how is this possible in a world of hate, fear, sickness, corruption, and death?

There is a profoundly simple answer. It comes as God's gift of faith to us. He is the One who makes the difference in how we live because he adopts us as his own and invites us to live as his children.

A life of faith doesn't mean our problems will go away; our world is still a fallen world in need of redemption. But this life of faith does mean we do not have to face our problems alone.

I recently read Corrie Ten Boom's thrilling book, *The Hiding Place*. In it, she recounts her harrowing experiences in a Nazi concentration camp. As I read her story, I was struck that she continued to thank God for everything despite the horrible conditions surrounding her. She even thanked God for the lice that infested her dormitory; she later learned the lice kept the camp officers away, allowing her to continue her outlawed Bible studies and worship services throughout her imprisonment.

Corrie ten Boom discovered that even under the worst circumstances, praising and trusting God is possible because he is always faithful to us. Strange as it may seem, praise and trust can be the foundation stones of our lives no matter what happens. This can be so because God constantly upholds us with His love and keeps us in his grace.

# Twenty Truths to Live By

Sometimes truth, or at least great wisdom, can be found in a single thought or sentence. Below are twenty such "gems" that could well be hung on any refrigerator door for the great benefit of anyone who takes the time to ponder them.

1.  Faith is the ability to not panic.
2.  Blessed are the flexible, for they shall not be bent out of shape.
3.  Do the math. Count your blessings.
4.  God wants spiritual fruit, not religious nuts.
5.  Dear God: I have a problem. It's me.
6.  Laugh every day, it's like inner jogging.
7.  The most important things in your home are the people.
8.  Growing old is inevitable, growing up is optional.
9.  There is no key to happiness. The door is always open.
10. A grudge is a heavy thing to carry.
11. He who dies with the most toys is still dead.
12. We do not remember days, but moments. Life moves too fast, so enjoy your precious moments.
13. If you worry, you didn't pray. If you pray, you need not worry.
14. As a child of God, prayer is like calling home every day.
15. When we get tangled up in our problems, be still, so that God can untangle the knot.
16. The goals and dreams you're seeking require courage and risk-taking. Learn from the turtle who only makes progress when he sticks out his neck.
17. Greed, I've often regretted. Generosity—never.
18. You may give up on yourself, but God never will.

19. You will never forgive anyone more than God has forgiven you.
20. As much as you can, give thanks. God has already given us far more than we deserve!

# Section Six

## POLITICAL MUSINGS

# BLASPHEMY

Let's get something straight here. Blasphemy is NOT a crime in America. We have an amendment to our beloved Constitution that guarantees the right of free speech, no matter how offensive our "speech" may be to some people. If you are uncomfortable with this amendment, you should look for another nation where blasphemy is outlawed. But please know such nations are never progressive and most often are very punitive. Our founding fathers and mothers came to this great land seeking the kind of freedom that many in our world can only dream of. America is NOT a theocracy. It is a democracy where the rights of ALL citizens are protected. May it always be so.

# A Sad Story About Sugar

L et me tell you a story about America that is both sad and true. All during the 1940s and 1950s, the United States purchased as much sugar as it could from an island nation ninety miles from Key West, Florida, called Cuba. During those years, a greedy dictator named Juan Fulgencio Batista ruled that island and controlled about 90% of Cuba's wealth with several cronies. Without any middle class, Cuba was populated by poor peasants who kept the sugar cane industry going and earned pennies daily for their labor. It was a scenario that has been played out many times in history.

But the United States loved Batista because he was a strong dictator and sold us tons of sugar yearly at meager prices. American foreign policy was once again driven by multinational corporations that wanted to keep their stockholders happy and cared little about any moral or social obligations toward people experiencing poverty who created the wealth in the first place. As one might paraphrase the Golden Rule, he who has the gold makes the rules.

Then, one day in 1960, a fellow came out of the hills named Fidel Castro and told his people that he could offer them a better life under a system called Communism. So, when you are dirt poor, and your children are hungry and sick and lacking educational opportunities, you are so deprived that you have nothing to lose, why not try something different? So, a revolution followed: Batista was overthrown, Castro came to power, and many people in Washington, DC, stood around wringing their hands and asking themselves how this could have happened. How shortsighted we Americans can sometimes be. And to our surprise, many Cubans, even today, will tell you that they are better off with Fidel than they ever were with Batista.

While communism proved to be a very inept economic system worldwide, it did provide Cubans with some measure of health care, education, and hope for the future. For example, Fidel boosted his fellow citizens' literacy rates from less than 10% in 1961 to almost 98% in less than two decades. But this story is sad because it could have all been avoided. What might have happened if this very influential nation called America had said to Batista, "We want to buy all the sugar you can produce but with one important stipulation. For every dollar we give in exchange for your sugar, you keep sixty cents and then use the other forty cents for schools, low-income housing, clinics, parks, daycare centers, roads, job training, and a dozen other social services and projects, all designed to help the general populous of Cuba. Deal or no deal?" If Batista had said "no deal," we would go and find sugar elsewhere in the world. (It is not a particularly scarce commodity). And if he said" yes," even reluctantly, we as a nation would have scored a huge moral and social victory. Can you imagine how such a program would enhance our moral standing on the world stage? Instead of the greedy capitalists we are often perceived to be, we would strongly advocate for people with low incomes and those with no voice in any political process.

The United States has enormous economic clout worldwide, but we often don't use it to help those most in need. I am very aware that the boardrooms and stockholders of America would take a dim view of my proposal. But that is just my point. Instead of aligning ourselves with some of the worst dictators on the planet as we have often done in the past (Ferdinand Marcos, the Shah of Iran, and Saddam Hussein, to name just a few), we would become a strong voice for social justice and the alleviation of human suffering in all its ugly forms. I believe it would work. We have never even come close to trying such an arrangement, but now is the perfect time to do so.

# Go and VOTE

America is once again in one of those election cycles that never seems to end. It's not that it's so long; it's just that it's so contentious and, yes, downright deceptive. For example, a television station recently did a "fact check" analysis of one of the attack ads it ran for a particular candidate and found that all three claims about their opponent in the ad were bogus. Still, they kept running the ad! I could ask why, but I know the answer. Media outlets love campaign seasons. It's where they make tons of money.

I have often wondered how different our election cycles would be if candidates could only tout their accomplishments and credentials without so much as one negative word about their opponents. Of course, I know this could never happen because we so highly prize our First Amendment right of free speech, as indeed we should. Still, I seriously wonder if the framers of our beloved Constitution ever envisioned a day when political candidates would spend millions upon millions of dollars on ads that do little more than tell lies about their opponents. What possible good does this do for our nation?

But having said all of this, I am still highly optimistic about our republic and the election process. Compared to many nations in the world, we look rather virtuous. And I still have faith in the intelligence of the American people even as I pray that we never fall victim to the voices of extremism from either the far right or the far left. Some form of centrist government almost always best serves the citizens of this great land.

I recall a great quote from some wise soul who stated that a dictatorship survives because the people fear, and a monarchy survives because the people respect. A democracy survives because the people are virtuous. So, I pray we never lose our virtue as a nation.

So go and vote. Render to Caesar the things that are Caesar's. Engage the world that Christ died to redeem. Support candidates who are free of corruption and seek the greater good for all our citizens. Encourage those who speak for the people experiencing poverty, the children, the elderly, and people with disabilities. And in all that you do, do all for the glory of God!

# SOME OF THE WAYS
# WE COULD FIX AMERICA

1. Every piece of legislation in Congress is voted on separately—no more bundling (and therefore concealing) legislation.
2. All banks must hold their mortgages for at least five years. This simple law would have prevented much of the housing crisis of 2008.
3. We reinstate the Glass-Steagall Act (1935), which put a firewall between investment banks (Wall Street) and commercial (depository) banks; Robert Rubin, to his shame, dismantled this Act during the Clinton Administration.
4. No former Congressmen can work as lobbyists for at least ten years after leaving office. Our present system almost always works against the average American and favors special interest groups. (example Trent Lott)
5. That we reinstate the draft as a way to equalize both the burden and the horror of war. (result: fewer wars) Wealthy men often start wars, and poor men fight and die in those wars. Those still wishing to volunteer could do so.
6. Term limits in Congress. You are out after eighteen years (any combination of House and/or Senate). The founding fathers never envisioned career politicians. You serve your country for a defined period, and you are done.
7. Congress must equally abide by all the laws they impose upon the American people. Yet, until recently, it was legal for Congressmen to do insider trading.
8. Congress loses its current health care system and participates in the same health care systems as all other Americans. (Also, get rid of two different Social Security plans for Congressmen.)

9.  No corporate money is given to Super PACs. Corporations can now donate unlimited amounts of money anonymously to any candidate they choose through the PACs. Again, this is not what the founding fathers had in mind for this nation. Sadly, turning money into power and power back into money has become Washington's two primary industries. Big corporations and "bribed" politicians are now running this country. There are now over thirty-five thousand registered lobbyists in Washington, D.C. We have the best government money can buy.
10. That Native American casino profits be shared equally with all tribes across our nation and that casino profits be subject to the tax laws of their respective states.

# FIFTEEN THINGS THE UNITED STATES NEEDS TO KNOW ABOUT RADICAL ISLAM

1. The Muslim culture reached its zenith during the Middle Ages when it inspired breakthroughs in commerce, math, science, medicine, and philosophy. At that time, Islam was most open to the world and was enriched by the Christian, Greek, and Jewish communities with whom it co-existed. Sadly, Islam today is often closed, inward-directed, and resentful.

2. Many Muslims today see the US as shallow, arrogant, materialistic, and godless.

3. Some Muslims hate the US for three primary reasons: for backing Israel against the Palestinians, for propping up corrupt and bloated Arab governments with huge profits from our own thirst for oil, and for occupying sacred Arab lands with our "infidel" armies.

4. Today, a battle rages in many of the forty-one Islamic nations of the world. The question is this: will they be a regressive, medieval, fundamentalist state ruled by clerics and mullahs who endorse a strict interpretation of the Koran and Sharia law, or will they be a modern, forward-thinking state ruled by progressive laws and democratic principles? Remember that Islam seeks rigid control while democracy seeks liberation and free expression. The two can seldom live together peacefully.

5. Some Arab regimes, corrupt dictatorships afraid of their people, have made a devil's pact with the fundamentalists. They have allowed certain radical elements to move about quite freely (and have also funded them heavily) on the condition that they

themselves not be attacked. The House of Saud is particularly guilty of this agreement.

6. The Middle East is filled with schools that teach the Koran and hatred of the infidels (Jews, Americans, etc.) primarily. These schools are called madrasas. To give you an idea of how prolific they are, there were three thousand such schools in Pakistan in 1978. Today, there are over thirty-nine thousand. The same could be said of many other Arab states.

7. Some segments of Arab society can be fanatically religious. For example, we have witnessed young men and boys whipping themselves with chains to the point of shedding their own blood to honor the birth or death of some Islamic hero who lived centuries ago. Further, some radical Islamic clerics have enormous influence over the people and want nothing more than to dominate all Islamic nations. This struggle between hard-liners and reformists is played out daily in many Arab countries.

8. These are often very traditional people. Their religion is reactionary in almost every sense of the word and holds to teachings that do not fit well in the modern world. This, again, is a significant part of the problem.

9. Unemployment is rampant in many Muslim countries, creating a hotbed for frustration, poverty, ignorance, and anti-western feelings. This factor cannot be discounted in its importance. Yet, unfortunately, some governments quietly encourage anti-American sentiments to deflect criticism from their own inept regimes.

10. Radical Islam is a religion that seems to have precious little room for mercy or compassion. Whereas the ideas of grace, mercy, and forgiveness are central to Christian thought and doctrine, these are almost non-existent in the fundamentalist Islamic faith. An eye for an eye and a tooth for a tooth seems to be much more in keeping with radical Islam. And because there is so little flexibility or compromise, the West deals with a dangerous and entrenched enemy. Rigid self-righteousness is one of the worst

mindsets one may ever have to deal with. Further, some radical Muslims seem to love death more than they love life.

11. Add to this situation their belief that America is the Great Satan. We are seen as the infidels who have now contaminated their sacred lands and must be driven out in the name of Allah. Their position is uncompromising and relentlessly anti-Western. We should not be too surprised by their intense anger. After all, they remember the Crusades like they were yesterday, while many Americans have no idea what the Crusades were all about.

12. The last thing fundamentalists want is democracy. One renowned cleric recently stated that democracy is the enemy of the Muslim faith. The two really cannot live together in peace because their goals are so different. One seeks total control, while the other seeks to liberate.

13. While Christians often refer to God as "our Father," this thought is foreign to Muslims. No such intimacy with God is encouraged. Nowhere in the Koran does Allah demonstrate his love for humanity in any personal sense of the word. Allah is to be obeyed and nothing more. And if a person does not obey, the punishment can be severe, in this life or the next. A Muslim must live a life of strict conformity to Islamic law.

14. Islamic fundamentalists do not fight a war to win. The war itself is victory enough. War becomes a way of life and a reason for their existence. A man serves Allah best when he is fighting the infidel. This kind of thinking is foreign to most Americans. Worse yet, the war becomes a means by which young men become martyrs for Allah, guaranteeing life hereafter. Again, this is a foreign way of thinking for most Westerners.

15. Islam is the only major world religion founded with swords and armies. So those who choose to battle with Jihadist Islam should expect a long and bloody war. And no one should ever underestimate the determination of a group of fanatically religious zealots who have an abundance of weapons, money, and self-righteousness.

# FEAR NOT

Anyone who hasn't been asleep for the past year or so is keenly aware of all the bad news our favorite media personalities conveyed to us during this time. Unsettling news occurs almost daily in far-flung locations such as Lebanon, Israel, Iran, El Salvador, Ireland, Afghanistan, and even Lawrence, Kansas, "The *Day* After." If we wanted to become people paralyzed by fear, we could probably find enough good reasons to assume such a posture. But during this Holy Day season, I am again reminded of how often we read the words "fear not" the Christmas story.

We first meet Zachariah, serving in the temple. He is filled with terror at the appearance of an angel who tells him not to fear, for his prayer has been answered (Luke 1:13). Mary, the mother of our Lord, was also frightened by an angel who said, "Hail, oh Blessed one, the Lord is with you. Do not be afraid, Mary, for you have found favor with God." Joseph was troubled and gripped with fear when he learned that Mary was to become a mother. But again, a messenger of God came to him with the words, "Joseph, son of David, do not be afraid to take Mary as your wife." The shepherds must have also been scared out of their wits at the appearance of the heavenly light and the angelic chorus. After all, this was not an everyday happening, but the first words that fell on their ears were, fear not, for behold, I bring you good tidings of great joy."

Sometimes, we feel as if the causes for being fearful are striking us on every side like so many poison arrows. Then, it is worth recalling that God's "fear nots" are also for your benefit and mine. When the Christ of Christmas enters, his "perfect love casts out all fear" (I John 4:18). Great blessings come to us when we meditate on the Christmas message, which reassures us that God is still in charge, that his love for us is abiding, and that he sent his Son as our Savior. "Fear not" is the word for the Advent season; I bring you glad tidings of great joy. Your Savior is born!

# WHAT EXACTLY IS
# DEMOCRATIC SOCIALISM?

During our recent presidential campaign, some dire warnings were coming from certain politicians that America, if not careful, could quickly become a socialistic nation. Let's dig deeper to see if this warning has any merit.

The first argument I often hear is that socialist nations soon become communist nations. This is simply not true. About a dozen nations worldwide have had a socialist government for decades and have no intention of ever embracing communism. These nations, often called the happiest or most contented nations, include Sweden, Norway, Finland, Denmark, Germany, New Zealand, Ireland, Belgium, Canada, and the Netherlands. Interestingly enough, most of these nations have the highest standard of living in the world, especially the four Scandinavian countries.

Further, they are also the most generous nations on earth, giving away the largest percentage of their GDP (Gross Domestic Product) to the world's poorer nations. By contrast, as a percentage of our GDP, the US ranks about 19th in foreign aid to poor nations, though our politicians would have us believe otherwise.

Secondly, we are already a partially socialist nation by any definition. So, let's define some terms. (1) Pure communism is an economic system controlled entirely by some governmental entity. China and North Korea would be good examples. (2) Pure capitalism is an economic system that operates free of governmental constraints. (3) Socialism is a blending of free market capitalism and some governmental oversight, even including intervention in times of crisis.

A good example would be the 1930s when America was caught in the throes of the Great Depression. Over 25% of the American workforce was unemployed for months and even years. People stood in bread lines and soup lines for hours to get food for their families. We also had the Dirty Thirties (the Dust Bowl), when western farmers and ranchers lost everything under many feet of dust and dirt. Franklin Delano Roosevelt was elected in 1932, and many credible historians believe he saved America from total economic collapse. However, many Americans were saying that capitalism was a total failure and, at that moment in history, Communism in Russia and totalitarianism in Germany were both looking very viable and inviting. When you can't feed your family, you quickly become desperate and start looking for alternative forms of government.

Many believed the great "American experiment" had come to an end. Our democratic way of life was literally on life-support. I am not overstating the case in saying this. So, what was the solution? First, FDR took control of much of our economy with his now-famous programs, such as the CCC, the WPA, the REA, the TVA, and many others. He knew the federal government had to step in and find ways to get people back to work, even for meager wages. This was socialism at its best. The programs were not perfect, though they did a lot of good for the workers, their families, and the nation. (In Minnesota alone, the Works Progress Administration built twenty-eight thousand miles of roads, five hundred seventy-eight miles of sidewalks, one thousand four hundred and forty-three bridges, one thousand three hundred and twenty-four public buildings like the 4H building at the Fair Grounds, fifty-two stadiums, fifty-six sewage plants, three airports, one hundred and nineteen athletic fields, and six public swimming pools.) It finally took WW II to bring the nation back to full employment, but without these socialistic programs of the 1930s, America could not have survived as we know it today.

A few years ago, after giving a talk, I was verbally confronted by a man who thought I was a socialist. I assured him I was a devoted capitalist, with most of my retirement funds invested in the New York Stock Exchange. I also told him that he, like me, was also a socialist. He asked me to explain. I told him that most good governments levy and collect taxes for two reasons. One is to help redistribute wealth so that the divide between the haves and the have-nots doesn't grow to be too wide a divide. (Remember that throughout history, most revolutions began with a massive wealth disparity, i.e., France, Russia, Cuba, and countless banana republics). And two, I told him that good governments find ways, using public funds, to improve the quality of life for all its citizens. I then asked him if he received Social Security payments, Medicare, VA benefits, or farm subsidies (I knew he was an Iowa farmer) or if he had a child who attended a state-owned college or university. I think he got the point. He was as prominent a socialist as you would ever want to meet, but he seemed oblivious to this truth.

Just think about it. Fire and rescue, police protection, the US Postal Service, public libraries, roads, bridges, and highways, the National Weather Service, public health programs like the CDC and the NIH, sanitary sewers and waste treatment plants, airports and terminals, city, county, state, and national parks, national forests, wildlife refuges, public recreation areas, the county, state, district, and federal court system, all our public schools, ancillary services for children including counseling, health screenings, reduced or free breakfast and lunch programs, our national defense: Army, Navy, Air Force, Marines, Coast Guard, National Guard, the supply and distribution of the internet, electricity, natural gas, propane, and fuel oil, veterans hospitals and long term care facilities, crop insurance for farmers, price supports and land banks, worker's compensation, job training programs, low income public housing, regulation of our financial institutions, regulation of our utility rates, regulation of insurance and health care providers, the Food and Drug administration, disaster relief following floods, fires, hurricanes, etc., Head Start programs, Vista, Ameri Core, and the Peace Corp, the WIC program (food supplements for Women, Infants, and Children), Dept. of Homeland Security, emergency preparedness, FEMA, regulation of all gaming and gambling, public ground transportation of buses, trains, subways, light rail, the US Mint, US Bureau of Printing and Engraving (our money), the FDIC, regulation of our ports, canals, locks, and shipping lanes, the CIA, the FBI, the Federal Aviation Authority, the Security and Exchange Commission, the Dept. of Natural Resources, the EPA, the DOT, the Dept. of Economic Opportunity, the National Labor Relations Board, the National Transportation and Safety Board, the Treasury Dept., the Dept. of Agriculture, the State Dept., the Dept. of the Interior, the Dept. of Energy, the USDA, the US Forest Service, Title One schools, regulation of all our nuclear power plants, subsidies for wind and solar energy, the Interstate Highway system, storm sewers, signal lights, and street lights, and mosquito control! This is just a very partial listing of all goods and services that come to us via all levels of government: city, township, county, state, and federal. All of these programs and services are socialistic to one degree or another!

In a museum, I noticed two campaign-style buttons in a glass case. One of them read as follows: Say "No" to Socialism! Tell FDR no Social Security. The other button read as follows: Say "No" to Socialism! Tell LBJ no Medicare. And then this caption next to the two buttons: Remember fifty and seventy-five years ago when socialism destroyed our democracy and plunged America into irreversible ruin? How many of you would like to do away with one or both of these hard-won socialist programs?

I conclude with a story that may surprise you. It's about Fred and Donald Trump, and it's rather complimentary. In 1977, New York City was trying to improve the image of mid-town Manhattan, which looked a bit ragged at the time. The two-thousand-room Commodore Hotel on East 42nd Street was the center of this effort, first built in the 1920s. Fred and Donald Trump got wind of the cities' intentions and, with some real finagling and arm twisting, got the city of New York to offer them a personal forty-year, forty-million dollar tax abatement loan, which then allowed them to buy the hotel (in partnership with the Hyatt Corporation), make the needed renovations, and, in the process, make a ton of money. Donald Trump would never call this socialism, but that is precisely what it is by any practical definition. This engagement between the government and the private sector has also helped create an excellent American economy.

So, are we a capitalist nation? We surely are. And are we also a socialist nation in so many ways? Yes, we are that as well. By the way, did you appreciate getting your Covid shots and getting them at no cost? One more perfect example of socialism at its best.

# CHRISTIAN NATIONALISM, BLESSING, OR CURSE?

Recently, we have all heard the term "Christian Nationalism" thrown about in the political area, causing many to ask, just what is Christian Nationalism? Before I answer this question, let me share a bit of historical context.

When our founding fathers and mothers first came to the shores of America (some were native-born by the late 1700s), they or their parents had never known a nation that did not have a State Church and a Monarchy. When our founders set out to write the documents governing this new nation, they rejected both entities: they wanted no State Church and no Monarchy. (Some wanted George Washington to be called King George, but he pointed out that there was already a King George in England, and we did not need two.)

So, if there is no state church and no monarchy, what would this new government look like? And here we can be exceedingly thankful for a group of men whose genius and vision for the future was so brilliantly clear they created a set of documents that have stood the test of time for almost two and a half centuries. Among them were Thomas Jefferson, James Madison, John Adams, and Ben Franklin. They and their compatriots created the Articles of Confederation (early on), the Declaration of Independence, and the Constitution, which has been amended only twenty-seven times in our history and included the Ten Bill of Rights. And one of the most important principles in these documents stated or strongly implied, was the Separation of Church and State.

And why was this so especially important to our founders? Because they remembered all the religious wars back in the old country (mostly

Europe) involving the Church and State, and they wanted nothing to do with such conflicts. Such wars involved the ten major Crusades, the Spanish Inquisition, the very bloody Thirty Years War, and even the Peasant Revolt during the Reformation period. The Salem Witch Trials may have even influenced them on our own soil. Recall how King Henry the Eighth often begged the Pope to allow him to divorce some of his six wives because they could not give him a male heir to the throne. This the founders wanted to avoid at all costs.

And here is what many people are not aware of. In promoting this foundational concept of separation of church and state, Jefferson was not worried about protecting the church from the government but just the opposite! Instead, his concern was protecting the government from the church. In short, he said, "We don't want a Theocracy. We want a Democracy." We can only have this if we have a clear and lasting separation of these two potentially powerful entities. (By the way, if you want to experience a Theocracy today, spend some time in Iran, where a very repressive religious council led by the Ayatollah oversees every aspect of life in Iran. Let me assure you. It is a horrible place to live.)

So, back to the original question. Just what is Christian Nationalism? It is an attempt to Christianize most aspects of American life to the exclusion of all other religious groups. (Just the opposite of what the First Amendment is designed to guarantee.) CN is an effort to impose a particular religion upon an entire nation. CN seeks to blend Christian and American identities, distorting both the Christian faith and America's constitutional democracy with its promise of religious freedom for all its citizens. CN desires to be a state religion that excludes all other religions and often promotes some form of racial subjugation. Worst of all, CN is a political movement designed to gain power and control over society. Many symbols of CN were on display at the nation's Capital on January 6, 2021, including crosses, images of Jesus, prayers, a shaman, etc. This is NOT what the founders had in mind. And if you think I am overstating the case, consider this quote from Colorado House Representative Lauren Boebert, who recently stated, "The church is supposed to direct our government; the government is not supposed to direct the church. I am tired of all this separation of church and state junk." I assure you Thomas Jefferson would be spinning in his grave to hear a duly elected official of our government make such a misguided statement.

Christian Nationalism, in the extreme, can even inspire acts of violence and intimidation against those who don't look or believe the way we do. Rather than uniting people, CN works hard to divide people on the basis of race, creed, color, ethnicity, status, and even gender. CN may be nationalistic, but it is surely not Christian. When God looks upon his world, he sees no borders, no barriers, no boundaries, and no flags. For God so loved the whole world...and so should we who claim to be his people. Please watch for any number of manifestations of CN in the run-up to the 2024 presidential election and do all you can to educate people as to the perils and pitfalls of such a movement. We do not want to lose our democracy. We almost lost it on 1/6/2021.

# GUN VIOLENCE

First, find a group of marginalized youth who are not too mature, not emotionally healthy, and not very clear about what is right and wrong in life. Next, expose these "at risk" youth to a flood of violence on TV, in theaters, online, and in video games. Hollywood has been serving up graphic violence for so long that most of us are either repulsed or numb to it. Actors have all made massive fortunes trying to see who can shock their audiences the most. As a result, we have been desensitized to what may have shocked us even five or ten years ago. Then, add some video games, ever more graphic, violent, and interactive. Don't miss that last word: interactive. Now, one can "feel" what beating, maiming, or killing is like. But, of course, it's all make-believe. Or is it?

Now throw in a dysfunctional home, a youth whose life is almost devoid of a "support system" and add a sense of meaninglessness to which the child begins to understand how unimportant he is to those around him. Let's add some Beavis and Butthead for good measure, two fellows who are as morally depraved as any can be. Now, there is little we can do about the problems I have listed above. Hollywood, free speech, morality in the home, and attitudes toward life are tough to legislate. But there is one area where some level of control must be initiated, and it is this: we must find a way to remove such destructive weaponry from the hands of all who would do us harm. We must pass better laws to regulate a pistol or rifle's purchase, transfer, and discharge.

Want to know why we have these killings? It has a lot to do with legislation. We do not have to remove guns from good citizens, but we must find a way to keep them from irresponsible citizens. According to the National Institute for Justice, more than three hundred million guns exist in America. And about 16% *are* unlocked and loaded. Some experts are now proposing that the owner be held accountable if the gun falls into the wrong hands. If a bartender can be held responsible for serving alcohol to minors, why not someone who leaves deadly weapons lying around?

As Newsweek observed, "The argument that the easy availability of guns has nothing to do with the death toll is now patently absurd. Has anyone ever heard of a drive-by stabbing?" Is this a topic for the church to address? I think so. God is the author, giver, and sustainer of life, and the church needs to follow suit. We are here to promote, preserve, and protect life; better gun laws will achieve these ends. Then let us get on with it if we don't want to read about another killing field!

# ALF

## (Animal Liberation Front)

Years ago, a somewhat secretive organization known as ALF (Animal Liberation Front) broke into the laboratory campus of the University of Minnesota. Under darkness, they trashed the lab, destroyed several experiments, and stole over one hundred animals, primarily rats, mice, and pigeons. Their goal was to free the animals from inhumane treatment.

One of the members of our church asked me what I thought of this incident and if I would mind sharing my view in writing. So, I shall. I fully realize that some people are incredibly fond of animals. And love them so much that they are willing to break the law to set them free. However, I honestly think such people, though driven by what they consider noble motives, are pretty misguided. The Bible clearly shows that God gave humankind "dominion over the birds of the air, the beasts of the field, and fish of the sea."

We are not equal to animals; we are superior to animals. We have a free will and a conscience, while animals are driven almost entirely by instinct. We know right from wrong and are accountable to God in ways that animals are not. And we are free to use animals in ways that benefit us.

The Ten Commandments tell us it is wrong to kill another human being. However, no commandment tells us it is wrong to kill a cow. In India, for example, they might have far less starvation if they killed some of their cows for food rather than treating them as objects of worship. To illustrate how misguided people can be on this issue, even a religious sect in India known as the G'nish considers rats sacred.

Now, please understand what I am saying here. Do we, as Christians, care about animals? Of course, we do. We need to protect and manage our wildlife. Endangered species should be treated with the utmost care. But using certain animals to advance the cause of medicine is not wrong. The University studies were focused mainly on learning more about Alzheimer's disease. The lab animals were always sedated during experiments and kept from pain as much as possible. Most never suffered at all. Ironically, the ALF group freed all the animals, most of whom cannot survive in the wild.

As with many issues in life, the goal is to strike a balance. No sane person advocates animal cruelty. But indeed, some less advanced forms of life (like rats and mice), which also reproduce prolifically, can and should be used in controlled and relatively painless experiments. If such work enhances the quality of life on this planet, then I believe God is pleased, and our work is justified.

# What to Make of Islamic Extremism

Some of you know that from day one, I have been opposed to the war in Iraq. (I do think the Afghan incursion was justified because it was the home of the Taliban, Osama Bin Laden, and Al-Qaeda, and I certainly support our troops who are doing a difficult and dangerous job.) Preemptive wars based on faulty intelligence, hidden agendas, and personal vendettas are never a good idea. But having said that, I have not thought that our enemies should be taken lightly for a minute. While America has made many mistakes and often acted like the "big kid on the block," I believe the intensity of hatred coming from some parts of the Muslim world is largely unjustified.

So, how do we explain this current outpouring of venom? Sadly, much of it seems to find its origins in a belief system that is sometimes best characterized by authoritarianism, fanaticism, rigid conformity, and a deep devotion to a kind of legalism that is centuries old. And while this hatred comes from a tiny portion of the Islamic world, it is pretty disturbing. Born in the sands of the Arabian Desert in the seventh century, this religion leaves little room for diversity, liberty, or self-criticism. For the most part, 1.4 billion Muslims live in a black-and-white world of their own making.

Consider for a moment Salman Rushdie and his book Satanic Verses. To this day, he lives in fear of assassination. Or, when a Danish newspaper prints some cartoons depicting the prophet Mohammad in a less than flattering light, embassies are burned, hostages are taken, urban riots ensue, and a nun is killed. Or when the Pope makes an unfortunate reference to an obscure ruler from the Middle Ages, the Muslim world seethes in anger. While I do not deny that some offense was committed in each of these instances, I also believe the response was an overreaction based on hatred, vengeance, and blind indoctrination. After all, this religion has sometimes endorsed child marriages, honor killings, wife beatings, lethal stoning, and an almost homicidal loathing of homosexuals. Parts of this religion seem to be downright pernicious. Perhaps the saddest is a religion with little room for mercy, compassion, tolerance, or forgiveness. As is the case with all manufactured religions, it is a system of laws (Sharia being the most extreme) that creates either a sense of arrogance (I have earned my righteousness) or dread (I am doomed) among its adherents. This kind of religiosity is light years away from Jesus, who taught that we should first accept his love and then love our neighbor and even our most bitter enemy. Such reckless and sacrificial love is quite rare in the Islamic world.

Our new foe seems bent on an eye for an eye and tooth for a tooth philosophy of life. But this is a very primitive way to live. To paraphrase Gandhi, living this way will guarantee that we will all end up blind, toothless, and eventually dead. We are fighting an ideology, a theology, and a pathology, and the weapons of war will have limited value in this struggle.

Therefore, America must find a new, more effective way to engage this enemy. It will take all nations of goodwill working together to defeat this twenty-first-century menace called terrorism. And failing that, we should prepare ourselves for another hundred years of war. May God forbid.

# A Warning to
# A Blinded America

I watched a two-hour documentary on PBS called Frontline (one of the best award-winning programs on TV). The program was entitled *Lies, Politics, and Democracy.* If you missed it, you must find a way to view it. After watching that program, I am convinced of two essential facts.

The first fact is that Donald Trump is not going away, and his grip on the Republican Party is as firm as ever. I would go one step further. There now is no longer any Republican Party! There is only the Trump Party, and should you choose to cross him or challenge him in any way, he will squash you like a bug. He is hateful, vindictive, and power-hungry. And if you doubt me, look at how he dealt with Mark Sanford of South Carolina, Liz Cheney of Wyoming, Jeff Flake of Arizona, Alexander Vindman of the State Department, Marie Yovanovitch of Ukraine, and Mike Pence, after Mike prevented the forceful overthrow of our democracy on the night of January 6, 2021. And there are dozens more emasculated by this strongman who wishes to be a dictator and wants absolute loyalty and zero criticism.

The second fact is this: should he remain healthy, Trump will try again for the White House. His ego demands it, and his base is as strong as ever, if not stronger. Over 70% of Republicans believe the 2020 election was fraudulent, compromised, and stolen. (Nothing could be further from the truth!) It was one of the largest, most heavily scrutinized, validated, recounted, and cleanest elections in our nation's history, and anyone who tells you otherwise, like Alex Jones, Tucker Carlson, Sean Hannity, Maria Bartiromo, Steve Bannon, or Rudy Giuliani is a liar.

So be warned, America. This fight is not over yet. And Donald Trump is still a genuine threat to our beloved nation and democracy. And if you are still in any way a Trump supporter, please know that you are indeed on the wrong side of history and are supporting a man who wants nothing more than to be an unquestioned dictator and who will stop at nothing to attain that goal. He nearly destroyed our democratic form of government in 2020, and I am sure he will try it again if given even half a chance. But we dare not allow this perversion and corruption of our democracy. The stakes are way too high for that!

# AN ARGUMENT THAT
## DEFIES LOGIC

You have undoubtedly heard that old line from the NRA proclaiming that criminals don't abide by gun laws, so of what value are such laws? Well, if criminals often don't abide by these laws, what good are laws governing the use and ownership of guns in America? But if you follow the logic of such thinking, you must ask yourself this question: why do we have ANY laws at all?

If laws don't prevent gun violence, why do we have laws against murder, sexual assault, theft, drunk driving, and, more recently, the proper use of seat belts and cell phones? Don't people break these laws every day? Of course, they do, but no one is suggesting these laws are ineffective. They are very effective. In 1973, America passed a national speed limit law for most of our major highways, and guess what? Traffic deaths that year dropped a whopping 17%. When Mothers Against Drunk Driving (MADD) pressed lawmakers to pass better laws prohibiting drunk driving, deaths due to intoxication were cut almost in half. My point is quite simple. People break laws every day.

But they are still good laws that produce a LOT of good for our society. And the same is true for gun control laws. So, let's tell our legislators (and our president) to get off their collective butts and do something before we have another mass shooting, which will likely be tomorrow at a mall near you.

# PRAYER IN PUBLIC SCHOOLS

A n event in one of our southern states made the nightly news and grabbed a few headlines. It seems that a public-school principal was fired from his job for allowing students to read a specifically Christian prayer over the school's intercom during a period of several weeks. The prayer was no more than a minute in length. Following the firing, three students decided to boycott the school and accused those who fired the principal of being heathen and un-American. Who is right and who is wrong when it comes to prayer in public schools? My response may surprise you.

It has often been noted that the genius of America is partly due to the provision our forebears made in separating church and state. Many of them had come from nations where the state mandated religious practices, and they resented such oppression. And for good reason. Look at those European nations which until recently still had a state religion. As a result, the church is often constricted or nearly dead. By contrast, no American has to believe in God or pay dues or taxes to a church, mosque, or synagogue. And yet, the level of attendance at worship in the US far exceeds that of nearly any other nation in the Western Hemisphere.

Thanks to the carefully crafted opinions of our Supreme Court, no student is prohibited from exercising their right to pray silently or vocally at any time in the school so long as their praying does not disrupt educational activities. Our laws do not prohibit individuals from saying grace before lunch. They do not prohibit the study of religion as an important force in the development of our culture. However, the laws of our land (based on the First Amendment) correctly maintain that when the government (including our public schools) directs or sponsors the time, content, or manner of student prayer, it is clearly violating the Constitution. The First Amendment protects our right to practice religion without governmental interference and prohibits the government from establishing or promoting religion.

The point is that those advocating for formalized school prayer are wrong. Teaching children to pray is the task of the home and the church or synagogue. If we fail as parents or church members, let's blame ourselves, not the schools. I once saw a fascinating survey that indicated that many who advocate for public school prayer have little or no involvement with a Christian church. What hypocrisy. Is this another example of Mom and Dad conveniently passing off their God-given responsibilities to someone else? It is not the task of public school teachers to promote faith (though I suspect many exude Christian values and attitudes through their very lives, and this is as it should be). Teachers today have enough to do as it is. If the home and the church do a good job teaching the faith to our children, then the schools will likely take care of themselves.

Also, consider the practical problems that arise. For example, if someone formally offers a Christian prayer in the schools, someone else would have every right to offer a Hindu or Buddhist prayer. Or worse yet, someone would create a prayer so bland or unoffensive (one prayer fits all) that all religions would be trivialized and made meaningless.

While I sympathize in some ways with the fundamentalists who feel that America has somehow lost her soul, I do not believe the public schools are the proper arena to draw the battle lines. If anything, America's parents and churches must look long and hard at themselves. If we are doing a poor job (and I think we are), then let's clean up our own act and let the schools take care of themselves. Let me say it as clearly as I can: there is no task we have as parents that is more important than to teach our child(ren) to know the God of the Holy Scriptures and his Son, our Lord, Jesus Christ. If we do well in this regard, I promise you, a great many of our current social ills will quickly fade away.

# THANK GOD FOR TAXATION

### (No, that is not a typo)

"Render to Ceasar the things that are Ceasar's and to God the things are God's" (words of Jesus from Matthew 22:21). Over the last several years, some politicians from both sides of the aisle have criticized the notion of taxation to the point that I fear some Americans are now beginning to think of taxes as some horrible monster born in the depths of hell itself. Time out for a brief refresher course from Poly Sci 101.

Every civilized nation of the world has three essential obligations to its citizens. One, to provide for the national defense. Two, to write and pass laws that make daily life in society orderly, lawful, and reasonably predictable. And three, levy taxes that pay for goods and services that benefit society. Taxation is a form of wealth redistribution, and nations that fail to understand this are often poor and underdeveloped. The wealthy class in many poor nations feels no obligation to help the less fortunate or contribute to the common good. On the other hand, a nation like Sweden, which admittedly has high taxes, also has one of the world's highest standards of living, which benefits its entire citizenry.

We have all heard the mantra, "you can spend your money more wisely than the government." Frankly, that statement is not always true. Many governmental agencies spend money more wisely than citizens because "private money" is often spent selfishly. But "government money," in many cases, benefits a far greater number of people. While I realize there are many "pork barrel" projects in government (we do need to hold our elected officials much more accountable), I am also thankful for all the blessings good government brings to me through taxation. Without the government, we would have chaos and anarchy.

A partial list of services brought to you each day by your taxes follows.

Now, ask yourself how many you would want to do without.

- Fire protection
- Police protection
- The Postal Service
- The safe disposal of toxic wastes
- Libraries
- Street, bridge, and highway construction and repair
- National Weather Service
- Streetlights, traffic lights, sidewalks, and bike paths
- Social Security
- Financial help for people with disabilities, older people, and children in need
- Public health programs, including disease prevention.
- Sewage collection and treatment
- Water purification and distribution
- Construction and operation of our airports
- City, county, state, national parks, and wildlife refuges
- Public recreation areas and lake access
- Our court system, state, county, district, federal, supreme
- Public education for every child in America
- Higher education, state colleges, universities, and tech schools
- National defense, the entire military establishment Army, Navy, Air Force, Marines, and the Coast Guard
- Supply and distribution of electricity
- Keeping national reserves of specific petroleum resources
- Veteran's hospitals, nursing homes, and rehab facilities
- Building codes and inspectors

- Economic development for cities, counties, and states
- Worker's compensation programs
- Job training programs
- Public housing
- Regulation of all our financial institutions
- Regulation of all our utility rates and services
- Regulation of insurance providers and investment brokers
- Public parking facilities, such as park and rides
- Control of air, water, and earth pollution (EPA)
- Agricultural subsidies
- Disaster relief
- Mosquito control
- School lunch programs
- Head Start programs.
- Peace Corps, Vista,
- WIC Special Supplemental Nutrition Program for Women, Infants, and Children
- Emergency preparedness
- Homeland Security
- Alcoholic beverage regulation
- Drug, tobacco, and firearms
- Public transportation, buses, trains, subways
- The Food and Drug Administration
- The National Institute of Health
- The National Center for Disease Control
- The US Mint
- The FDIC Federal Deposit Insurance Corporation
- Medicare, Medicaid, and Medigap
- The SEC, the FBI, the CIA, the FAA

Are some tax dollars wasted? Yes. Should public officials be held accountable for the way they spend tax dollars? Of course. Is our current system of taxation corrupt? I don't believe so. There are very few items in the above listing that I would want to do without. Especially mosquito control!

For more insight on this subject, see Romans, chapter thirteen.

# WHAT WOULD HAVE BEEN A TRULY CHRIST-LIKE RESPONSE TO 9/11/01?

*The article was written in 2002.*

Let's put aside the flag-waving, bravado, and deep-seated desire for revenge for a few minutes. We have all seen this countless times in the annuals of human history. And let's ask a straight-forward question: as citizens of Christ's kingdom, how could we have responded differently to the events of 9/11/01? This answer may seem radical, daring, and even foolish in the eyes of some. Yet, it is precisely this kind of response to hatred that has most often and most dramatically changed the world for the better.

1.   We refrain from any form of counterattack. We return no evil for evil. It is difficult to believe that the death, suffering, and carnage we have created in Iraq and Afghanistan have anything to do with Christ's plan for his world. Thousands of civilians have died in these two countries. Several million people have been made refugees. The civilians that have been severely wounded number in the thousands. US military casualties now number in the thousands, with tens of thousands more wounded, to say nothing of this being America's first trillion-dollar war, which we will be paying for many decades from now. While a carnal man almost always seeks vengeance, Christ calls us to turn the other cheek and remove the sword. "Vengeance is mine, says the Lord, and I will repay." (Romans 12:19). Our task is to love our enemies and do good to those who persecute us. And I hardly need to mention that every premise for this war has proven false or fabricated. There were no WMDs, no yellow

cake uranium from Zaire, we were not welcomed as liberators, Saddam Hussein had nothing to do with 9/11/01, or as Mr. Cheney promised, "it will all be over a matter of a few months."

2. We swear off Persian Gulf oil. But unfortunately, our foreign policy and our nation's car culture have been driven by our insatiable thirst for oil. Let no one tell you that our invasion of Iraq had nothing to do with oil. There is good evidence of more oil in Iraq than in Saudi Arabia. The Arab states have us over a barrel (literally) as we annually send more than seven hundred billion "petrol" dollars overseas. Every time we fill up our tanks, we contribute in some way to world instability.

3. We reassess our relationship with Israel, a nation now practicing apartheid, much like South Africa three decades ago. Yet, in the Muslim world, the US and Israel are seen as one entity, and until we change that perception, Arab hatred of America will continue unabated.

4. By weaning ourselves off of foreign oil and conserving more at home, we can stop supporting any number of bloated and corrupt Middle Eastern governments, some of whom are more than willing to redirect the anger and frustration of their own citizens onto America.

5. We withdraw most of our troops from Arab soil as soon as possible. We are seen as the infidel, the Great Satan, who defiles their sacred soil with our presence. The wisest thing we can do is drastically lower our military profile on the Arabian Peninsula. As long as we are there, we give the radical jihadists more and more reason to hate us and stifle any moderate voices that would speak out on our behalf. Several credible sources believe that the morning after 9/11, there were no more than a couple thousand hardcore jihadists in the world. Today, their number is thought to be over a quarter of a million.

6. We launch a massive public relations campaign to show the world that the US still has integrity and competence in foreign affairs. Instead of billions for bombs and rockets, how about

seriously addressing some of our world's acute humanitarian needs, starting with the Palestinians, many of whom have spent the past half-century living in the squalor of a refugee camp? Seeing these places with my own eyes, I know how much hatred is born of these nearly intolerable conditions where Palestinians look out upon homes and land that were once rightfully theirs. Instead, these camps are hotbeds of hatred perpetuating itself generation after generation. At one time in history, the Palestinians owned more than seventy percent of the lands in Israel.

7. We stop calling this a "war on terrorism." 9/11 was a crime against humanity. We are not fighting a nation or an army. If you are interested in this subject, read the book *Leaderless Jihad* by Marc Sageman. We are fighting an ideology, a theology, and a pathology. This struggle between two cultures will be won, not with a meat ax but a scalpel.

8. We have come to recognize that this part of the world has never known democracy and does not seem to want it. Their centuries-old form of government has been tribal, ruled by regional warlords who know nothing of democracy. The dominant Muslim faith in this part of the world is all about control and conformity. Democracy is all about liberty and diversity. The two cannot peacefully co-exist because they are as different as night and day. It is doubtful that a democracy and a theocracy can ever be compatible.

9. We come to recognize that this war is not going to be won militarily. Take note of how other nations deal with this menace through solid investigative techniques, intensive surveillance, comprehensive intelligence gathering, advanced technology, greater cooperation between governments of goodwill, and even some racial profiling. Before boarding those planes, the shoe and underwear bombers should have set off alarm bells. We must become more innovative and sophisticated than we have been in the past.

Jesus often spoke of loving your enemies and not demonizing them. This kind of love is risky but no riskier than the insanity we see today. Perhaps a good dose of love, humility, and diplomacy could go a long way in changing the tenor of our times. Jesus once said, "Be wise as serpents and innocent as doves."

Thomas Jefferson once noted that we must never confuse dissent with disloyalty. Many Americans are intensely loyal to this nation, and our Armed Services, but wish to denounce these costly wars while continuing to honor all those in uniform. We are learning once again that starting a war is a thousand times easier than ending one. This could still be one of America's finest hours, but we must act soon to change our tactics and find a new course of action based solidly upon the teachings and example of our Lord. Short of such a change, this "war" will continue, and our nation will remain in peril for years to come.

# YOU DON'T GO TO
# WAR ON A HUNCH!

I heard on the news, 53% of Americans now believe that our wars in Iraq and Afghanistan "were not worth" all the blood and treasure we have invested in them. I have to ask sincerely why it has taken us so long to arrive at this obvious conclusion. My heart goes out to the thousands of military personnel who died for this misbegotten cause and the tens of thousands who will now suffer serious life-long injuries of mind, body, and spirit.

For the sake of that other 47% of Americans who may still be supportive of these two wars, let me remind you of some harrowing facts. First comes the run-up to the Iraq war. Do you recall that the Chief United Nations Weapons Inspector Hans Blix was on the ground in Iraq with a team of over two hundred other inspectors before the start of this misadventure? Saddam was finally giving them the freedom they wanted to move about his country as inspectors. And had we given Blix and his team a few more months, even a few weeks, it is almost a certainty that we would have discovered that there were no weapons of mass destruction. But, oh no, George W. Bush and his team, comprised of Dick Cheney, Condoleezza Rice, Donald Rumsfeld, and Paul Wolfowitz, could not wait to begin the invasion. Remember all that arrogant talk of shock and awe? And George Tenet, then head of the CIA, said that the presence of WMDs in Iraq was a "slam dunk." He later said those were the two dumbest words he ever spoke.

And there were so many other falsehoods put forth. Dick Cheney said the war would "be over in months." Not so. He said we would be welcomed as liberators. Not so. He said that Iraqi oil would help pay for some of the costs of the war. Not so.

And then there was that total fabrication set forth by the president in a State of the Union address that Niger, Africa, was shipping weapons grade yellow cake uranium to Saddam Hussein for his WMDs. Shortly after, New York Times reporter Joe Wilson went to Niger to discover the truth. Nothing of any military value was being shipped from Niger to Iraq. When he wrote about it in a *NY Times* article, the White House retaliated by outing his wife, Valerie Plame, an undercover agent for the CIA. To do so is a federal offense, and when the investigation got too close to the office of Dick Cheney, his assistant, "Scooter Libby," took the fall and went to prison for a very short stay. His sentence was quietly commuted late on a Friday night and hardly noticed by the press. This is government at its worst.

But the biggest lie was the one the Bush administration repeatedly purported, which claimed a strong relationship between Saddam Hussein and the events of September 11, 2001. There never was ANY correlation. It was all a big lie to justify this unnecessary war in Iraq. It is no understatement to say that you could stick in a thimble what the Bush administration knew about Iraq before the invasion: its history, its culture, its ethnicity, politics, and religion. The ignorance of this administration in going off to war was exceeded only by its arrogance. The negative consequences of America's first trillion-dollar war, financed partly by the Chinese, will be with us for many decades.

I have always said that we should move the Vietnam War Memorial and place it right outside the Oval Office so that every day, every American president sits and stares at fifty-eight thousand names of soldiers who died in another misguided adventure. A friend who works for the Veterans Administration told me recently that we could have another Vietnam War Memorial of fifty-eight thousand soldiers who have all died by suicide since that war ended in the early 1970s—a double tragedy, to be sure. Vietnam was a civil war between the North and the South. We should never have been there in the first place.

So, what have we accomplished in these two wars? Sadly, precious little. What we didn't understand, among many things, was that it took a ruthless thug like Saddam to hold the lid on all this hatred and religious fanaticism. Once we "took him out," all heck broke loose, and we destabilized the entire region. Iraq had long been a counterbalance to Iran, but no one in the Bush White House knew about any of this.

I often reflect on that old folk song, *Where Have All the Flowers Gone?* And then that mournful refrain, "When will they ever learn? When will they ever learn?" Yes, when indeed?

As for the Afghanistan war, here are the facts. We were there for some twenty years and four presidents: G.W. Bush, Obama, Trump, and Biden. We spent about two and a half trillion dollars fighting that war. There were over two thousand American casualties and another twenty thousand wounded soldiers, to say nothing of the thousands of civilian casualties. And here is the bottom line: the Taliban were in charge the day we arrived, and they were in charge the day we left! So, you must ask yourself just how misguided and fruitless was this war? Tragic indeed!

# Eleven Reasons Why Hillary Clinton Lost The 2016 Election

1. Sexism. Voters who could never accept a woman president.
2. Racism. A backlash against a black Democratic president.
3. Hillary's failure to visit key states like Michigan, Wisconsin, and Pennsylvania during the campaign. Big mistake!
4. Pollsters led the nation into believing that Hillary was a shoo-in. I think tens of thousands of Americans were kicking themselves the following day for not voting. Hopefully, they have now learned their lesson. Every vote counts!
5. The Bernie Sanders backlash. When Wiki-Leaks revealed that the DNC was working for Hillary and against Bernie, many young voters just checked out and did not vote to protest "the DNC system." This was a HUGE blunder on our part.
6. FBI Director James Comey's letter to Congress ten days before the election claiming new emails had been found on Anthony Wiener's wife's (Huma Abedin) computer. They were few, and they were not new. But the damage had been done. If Wiener had not been "sexting," nothing would have happened. Also, Comey broke a time-honored rule for the FBI—never make ANY public comment on an ongoing investigation.
7. Wiki-Leaks emails coming from Russia cast Hillary in an unfavorable light. One such "dump" came just two hours after Trump's crude Access Hollywood bus comments and how he viewed women. Data dumping was highly orchestrated, and the media sadly bought these lies about Hillary "hook, line, and sinker." Worse yet, it took the spotlight off Trump for his crass and despicable comments.

8. Voter apathy and voter disgust. One-half of all eligible voters in America did not bother to vote. Are we still considered a democracy with numbers this low?

9. The constant bashing of Hillary by Steve Bannon, Glenn Beck, Sean Hannity, Rush Limbaugh, Alex Jones, etc. This drumbeat of negativity has taken its toll on the entire nation and the American soul. And in the process, they have generated so much distrust in the apparatus of our American government.

10. Too many Americans voted with their emotions and not with their brains. They saw President Obama as weak and ineffective while he was one of our more competent Presidents.

11. Mark Zuckerberg's eleventh-hour confession was that he sold Facebook space to the Russians, who used that space to bash Hillary. There should be a law that no foreign government ever be allowed to influence our national elections. And should one of our citizens help to make such outside influence possible, they are tried and sentenced ASAP.

This kind of activity tears at the very fabric of our democratic system. Add your reason(s) for Trump's very narrow victory. Maybe we need to get rid of the Electoral College. It was likely needed in colonial times, but those days are long gone.

# An Under-Rated President

When Harry Truman left office in 1953, his approval ratings were among the lowest ever seen by an outgoing President. However, as the years passed and historians looked closer at what he accomplished in the White House, we now see him as one of our greatest presidents.

Here are fifteen reasons why:

1. He ended WWII in Europe and the Pacific with two atom bombs that saved tens of thousands of American lives. A very monumental decision.
2. He helped to reshape much of Europe at the Yalta Conference following WWII.
3. He confronted Stalin forcefully when he sought to take over Greece and Turkey.
4. He oversaw much of the enormous postwar European refugee crisis.
5. He established the Truman Doctrine as the UK relinquished much of its power and influence on the world stage.
6. He established the Marshall Plan, which helped twenty-two nations rebuild after WWII.
7. He helped form NATO, which has been critical to world peace for some seventy-five years.
8. He orchestrated the Berlin Air Lift, thus saving thousands of lives in Germany immediately following the war.
9. One of the first nations on earth to recognize the State of Israel in 1948.
10. He fired the greatly admired General Douglas McArthur for insubordination.

11. He integrated the US Military, a very courageous and controversial thing to do then.
12. He dealt with mentally ill (and alcoholic) Senator Joe McCarthy from Wisconsin, whose phony Red Scare had some Americans believing there was a "Commie under every bed" in America. (Edward R. Murrow also helped Truman "neutralize" McCarthy.
13. Barely defeating Wendell Wilke when very few thought he could win in 1948.
14. He renovated and gutted the White House in 1949 with a steel and concrete infrastructure. It was long overdue.
15. He helped to establish and strengthen the United Nations in New York City.

# Where Christianity and Capitalism Collide

Let me be clear from the start: I am a capitalist. My father began investing in the markets in the 1950s, and that relationship served him and millions of other Americans well throughout his life. Looking around the world at other economic systems, one must conclude that part of the wealth and prosperity of America is solidly linked to our free markets and free enterprise system.

But we also know that everything good can be pushed to excess, and capitalism is no exception. Capitalism is a great blessing to a point, and that point is greed. America has just lived through two full years of deep recession, much of which was caused by arrogance, shoddy oversight, and a woeful lack of regulation that led to levels of greed and avarice seldom seen before in our nation's history.

Emmanuel Saez, professor of economics at the University of California Berkeley, calculates that from 2002 to 2007, the wealthiest 1% of American families accounted for 65% of all income growth. Former Secretary of Labor Robert Reich says, "It is estimated that 20% of all Americans now control over 85% of our nation's wealth."

CEOs of the most prominent American companies earned forty-two times as much as the average worker in 1980 but five hundred and thirty-one times as much in 2001. And those numbers are still climbing in some sectors of our economy.

Perhaps the most astounding statistic is this: From 1980 to 2005, more than four-fifths of the total increase in American incomes went to the wealthiest 1%. As Timothy Noah of Slate Magazine noted in his excellent series on economic inequality, "The United States now arguably has a larger unequal distribution of wealth than traditional banana republics like Nicaragua, Venezuela, and Guyana." This does not bode well for our nation.

I find all this quite disturbing as a loyal American and devout Christian. Have we sold our souls to the god of personal again? Has pursuing wealth closed our eyes to what is truly important in life? Do we no longer care about the greater good of the masses? And what would Amos or Jesus say about these obvious inequities?

The Bible says much about nations driven solely by greed and selfishness. The parable of the Rich Man and Lazarus has sobering implications for our lives. Jesus soundly rebuked the Rich Man for his total lack of concern for people with low incomes. There is no mercy offered anywhere in the story.

Similarly, the man who built bigger barns to hold his wealth was given a real wake-up call: "This very night shall your soul be required of you!" The steward who buried his master's wealth in the ground is also shown no mercy.

And it is the Good Samaritan who freely gives of his wealth to care for a man he would have despised. I have often wished that this parable ended with this line, "and when the Inn Keeper saw the generosity of the Samaritan, he too was moved to charge the poor man nothing for his services." Of course, it didn't happen that way, but it is beautiful to see when Christianity trumps capitalism and self-interest.

As a nation, we must be reminded of some fundamental biblical truths. One, you and I own nothing; it all belongs to God. "The earth is the Lord's and the fullness thereof." (Psalm 24)

Two, we are only managers or caretakers of our wealth, even for a relatively short period. We enter this world with nothing and leave it with nothing: the only thing that matters is what we do with that wealth in the meantime.

And three, we can be good managers or bad managers. A friend likes to say that good stewardship isn't about how much I will return to God but how much I will be stealing from him! It's all his, to begin with.

I want our nation to remain healthy, which can only happen when wealth is distributed more evenly. We never want to lose our middle class, which is the key to maintaining a democracy. Lose your middle class, and you are soon ripe for revolution, as we have seen many times in other nations.

Christianity, emphasizing a radical generosity that grows out of a genuinely thankful heart, is the best antidote to counter the obscene greed we have witnessed in recent years in this nation. Christianity and capitalism are good for each other when both seek to serve all people's greater good. Anything less is not acceptable.

# ON THE PEACEFUL TRANSFER OF POWER

*This article was written on 1/5/21.*

Trump took an oath to protect and defend the Constitution, including the peaceful transfer of power after an incumbent lost a national election. Yet, Trump is unwilling to concede and openly calls for rebellion and rioting in the nation's capital. This is despicable and unprecedented. It is what Third World countries do, NOT what America does! It is a deliberate and demonic attempt to destroy our democracy that has served us so well for over two hundred and forty years. Even though our Constitution sets the date in stone, Trump has even floated the idea of delaying Mr. Biden's inauguration. Further, Trump met with former adviser Michael Flynn, who has publicly urged him to declare martial law and then "rerun" the election in the states he clearly lost.

Trump's erratic behavior has so alarmed military commanders who fear he might try to use troops to stay in the White House that every living former defense secretary, including two that he appointed himself, issued a warning against the armed forces becoming involved in any way. Never have we seen such unlawful and undemocratic behavior by any sitting president. I believe Trump's ego is so massive and fragile that he simply cannot tolerate the idea that about half this nation did not vote for him. He would rather compromise our entire democratic system than admit that he somehow lost an election.

Further, all these deranged politicians were quickly drawn into Trump's web of lies, hate, and corruption. Their loyalty to Trump is idolatrous. Are they not aware that democracies are very fragile and what they are doing is undermining the very foundation of this beloved nation? May God judge them all for their stupidity, blindness, and idolatry.

Note: This piece was written the day before the storming of the capital by some of the most misguided and blinded people on the planet. This event will forever be a dark stain on our nation's history, which I will never forget. At this time, the world desperately needs to hear the Bible's central message: God gave his Son so that we might all be reborn to a new life of love and service, not hate, lies, and vengeance.

# SICK THEOLOGY

S omeone has noted that "man-made religion" can be a dangerous thing. I could not agree more. Perhaps even more dangerous is religion, which borrows words and ideas from the Bible and presents them without regard for their true meaning and purpose. Two glaring examples come to mind immediately.

The first involves the radical Islamic factions based in several Arab countries of the Mideast. I realize that genuine injustices have been done to the Palestinian people in recent decades, but these cannot be used to justify wholesale bloodshed and murder. I refer to certain suicide bombers who kill or injure dozens of innocent people each year. The "theology" behind such deeds teaches that if a person intentionally kills himself while also destroying "the enemies of God," (in this case, infidels, western imperialists, Jews, etc.), then they will, upon death, immediately ascend to heaven for the selfless deed they have done. This is sick theology at its worst! What twisted mind could conceive of a God who rewards those who kill or maim innocent people? It is scary to think that people can miss one of the Bible's central themes: love God with all your heart and your neighbor as yourself. If the Koran or any other book should call for the death of another person, for whatever reason, then we must stand with one voice and declare that God does not reward murderous and cowardly acts. Those who subscribe to such deeds may never see the heavenly realms and should genuinely fear for their very souls.

More recently, we have seen sick theology in our own nation. So-called separatists, secretive militia groups, and other ultra-right-wing fanatics quote the Bible freely to justify their hate-filled deeds and words. What a pollution of scripture. To depict the federal government as "some enemy of God that must be destroyed to save our nation" is absolute lunacy. How God must despair when his name and his words are employed in such a twisted and corrupted manner. The world desperately needs to hear the Bible's central message: God gave his Son so that we might all be reborn to a new life of love and service, not hate and vengeance. Any other teaching is false and heretical and can only lead to further pain, sorrow, and loss of life. Jesus once warned that not everyone who says, "Lord, Lord," will see the kingdom of heaven. Indeed, today, more than ever, we must be prudent, prayerful, and clear-minded in applying the real message of the scriptures to our daily lives.

# A Blessed Nation

*The article was written in 1996.*

The nation will celebrate its two hundred and twentieth birthday in a few days. By any standard of measurement, we are an incredibly blessed nation. But just what are our greatest blessings? Indeed, our many freedoms, our apparent prosperity, our rich natural resources, the stability of our government, and the fact that no foreign power has ever waged serious war within our borders. We are a blessed people.

But there is one more blessing that we must always seek. The Psalmist (33:12) tells us, "Blessed is the nation whose God is the Lord!" But when I look at our land today, I often wonder if we haven't forgotten God amidst all our materialism and affluence. Edward Gibbon lists five reasons great civilization withered and died in his monumental work, *The Decline and Fall of the Roman Empire*. Give these some thought:

1. Undermining the dignity and sanctity of the home, which is still the basis of any healthy society.
2. Higher taxes and the spending of public money for free bread and circuses for the populace. An insatiable need to be constantly entertained.
3. An absolute craze for pleasure while sports are becoming ever more exciting, brutal, and consuming.
4. The building of great armaments while the real enemy is the decay of individual responsibility.
5. The decline of religious faith fades into mere form, losing touch with real life and losing the power to guide and change people.

Another great historian, Arnold Toynbee, reminds us that the average age of most of the world's great civilizations has been about two hundred years. There also seems to be a pattern that has inevitably characterized all great nations: they have gone from bondage to spiritual faith, from spiritual faith to courage, from courage to liberty, from liberty to abundance, from abundance to self-centeredness, from self-centeredness to complacency; from complacency to dependence; from dependence back to bondage. I don't believe the cycle is inevitable, but it may be good for each of us to ask ourselves where we think we are as a nation?

As we again celebrate a national birthday, let us pray earnestly for this republic that we might once more be a cleansed, pure, and righteous nation in the eyes of almighty God. "If my people, who are called by my name, will humble themselves and pray and seek my face and turn from their wicked ways, then I will hear from the heavens, and I will forgive their sins, and I will heal their land." (II Chronicles 7: 14)

*So shall our prayers arise, To God above the skies, on whom we wait. Thou who art ever nigh, guarding with watchful eye, To Thee aloud we cry, God save the state!* (LBW #569)

# A HUMBLE REFLECTION ON THE DEATH

## OF OSAMA BIN LADEN

I will reflect on a situation from years ago when the major television networks were interrupted by a special announcement from the President. Osama bin Laden had been located and killed. A nearly decade-old search had finally ended. Yet, as I heard the news, I found my reaction conflicted in some ways. I did not feel like rejoicing. Instead, I thought about how we might have apprehended bin Laden ten years ago when he was at Tora Bora, and instead, our army was told, in essence, to stop, turn around, and head for Iraq. And what a costly mess that has become with thousands of US soldiers dead, not to mention civilian casualties in the tens of thousands. This will indeed become America's first trillion-dollar war.

I saw people standing near the White House chanting "USA, USA, USA," and I hoped that the world, especially the Arab world, would not think we were gloating, though I am sure some were. There is a place for patriotism, but it carries the risk of becoming idolatrous. We would do well to remember that when God looks at his world, he sees no boundaries, borders, or flags. I thought about how this killing might change our so-called "war on terror," if at all. I wondered what kind of retaliation might now be in the planning by our enemies. I wondered if bin Laden's death might now bring some closure to the families who lost loved ones on 9/11/01. I wondered if more bin Ladens were waiting in the wings to carry on his evil intentions. And perhaps, most of all, I thought about what a genuinely Christian response to this event might be. And here is where it gets sticky for those of us who call ourselves Christians and seek to honor our Lord's words. Should we join in the celebration or not? And what did Jesus mean when he asked us to love our enemies and do good to those who persecute us? Do these words still apply in an age of mass destruction, such as The World Trade Center Twin Towers and mass murder. How can we understand such radical forgiveness, much less apply it meaningfully to our lives? And there are so many other similar passages. Go, sell all you have, give it to people experiencing poverty, and come, follow me. Who is taking that message seriously today? Or welcome the stranger and the foreigner with open arms. If that is good advice, why is there a massive debate over immigration in our land? Or remember the Sabbath day and keep it holy. Or do not profane the Lord's name. Or do not commit adultery. Do not distort the truth about your neighbor. And do not covet his property. How well are these commandments going down these days? I think it fair to say that being a Christian today has its share of dilemmas. And it always has. Do we go to war or not? Do we love our worst enemies or not? Do we share our wealth with low-income people, even if we think they may be lazy? Do we forgive those who have grievously offended us or not? Does the Sermon on the Mount still have relevance to the twenty-first century?

The answer, of course, is Yes! The scriptures will always have relevance. And the great joy, the great challenge, and sometimes, the great dilemma of our existence is figuring out just HOW to live out these words. We do this as individuals and corporately as a church, and even as a nation. We pray, struggle, and seek God's wisdom, guidance, and discernment. We likely never get it exactly right. God is always in the mix as we seek to be light, salt, and leaven in his world. And we know the words of Micah by heart. But they are ever timely: always seek to do justice, love mercy, and walk humbly with your God.

# CREATING A CULTURE OF
# GUN VIOLENCE IN AMERICA

Many Americans have been asking how America has become such a violent place. The kind of violence we see today was almost unheard of just one generation ago. So, what has changed? As with many kinds of societal problems, there is no single answer. In this case, there are several contributing factors.

One, Hollywood movies today are more graphic and more violent than ever. Not long ago, a national talk show host listed over twenty films with "revenge" or "vengeance" in their titles. The plot lines are pretty simple. First, something horrible is done to our hero or his family (or some perceived injustice), and the rest of the film plots and eventually gets the revenge they seek. Such movies can be cathartic for the viewer. Still, the messages they send can be destructive to people who may be mentally unbalanced, have been the victims of bullying, and strongly identify with the "offended" hero. They then are tempted to act out their anger and seek revenge, usually with lethal consequences.

Two, television. It is estimated that a child growing up in America today will have seen well over one hundred thousand murders on TV by the time they graduate from high school. Think about this for a moment. Is it not true that most programs like Criminal Minds, Blue Bloods, SWAT, FBI Most Wanted, and a dozen more, almost always conclude with some kind of a shoot-out? The message is clear to all: the best way to resolve your differences is with a gun. How tragic is that?

Three, violent video games. They're young "gamers" today who play video games to the point of six or more hours a day. Worse yet, many of these games, which can be violent (Grand Theft Auto), can cause the gamer's mind to sometimes blur the line between reality and fantasy. When you have been killing people all day (with very realistic graphics), how hard is it to replicate this same violent behavior in the real world? In my opinion, it is a very short leap.

Fourth, tragically, our media sources know that violence "sells," so when there are disturbing images to broadcast, they gladly do so because they know human nature. (Why do we all slow down to observe a car crash on the highway?) The old saying states, "If it bleeds, it leads." So, when something horrible happens, they show it over and over and over again. This should not be the case. I am all for our First Amendment rights, but I strongly object when the media sensationalizes and profits from violence.

Five, the National Rifle Association. No other organization in America has done more to block the passage of sensible gun laws than the NRA. The NRA is one of Washington, DC's most influential and well-funded lobbies. The NRA also constantly promotes the lie that the "government is coming to get your guns." Nothing could be more untrue, but this kind of propaganda always boosts the sale of guns and ammo. It also increases NRA memberships and revenue. Almost all of our recent mass shootings in America have involved the AR-15 military-grade assault rifle, which can discharge over sixty rounds a minute. This weapon is close to the M-16 rifle our combat troops use in the field. Why any civilian in America should have this gun is beyond all logic. This gun is unsuitable for target shooting and even less for hunting game. Its sole purpose is to kill massively, methodically, and rapidly. We must find a way to ban this gun once and for all. We did have a ban on assault weapons during the Clinton years, but sadly, George W. Bush and his friends foolishly let it expire.

There are no easy answers to this ongoing problem, but if we don't want our beloved nation to become little more than a Wild West shooting gallery, we must take some corrective actions, and the sooner, the better.

# WHAT HAPPENED TO
# CIVILITY IN AMERICA?

The President of the United States sets the tone for our nation more profoundly than most people realize. Over four or eight years, our nation, in some rather subtle ways at first, begins to mimic the very personality traits of the president himself. Donald Trump is a powerful case in point. Trump can best be described as crude, defensive, arrogant, divisive, hateful, vindictive, insulting, demeaning of others, incredibly narcissistic, and lacking in any genuine empathy for others.

Many Americans find this behavior repulsive, disgraceful, and downright disgusting. But sadly, for many other Americans, it is as if Trump has given them permission to throw off all forms of civility as they increasingly imitate his sick, vulgar, rude, and criminal behavior. Trump has poisoned the veins of our formerly civil society (I have lived through fourteen different presidencies, and never have I seen anything quite like this), and we are still in a kind of national recovery mode. After four or five years of gross bigotry, lies, bullying, and hatred of others, it will take some time for us to get our equilibrium back to anything that resembles normalcy, respect for others, and common decency.

May God grant us the necessary resources for this critically important healing process and restoring our national psyche.

# Seven Ways Good
# Gun Laws Make a Difference

1. In 1934, the Mafia in America was using the Thompson sub-machine gun so effectively they were soon outgunning the police departments in some of our cities. So, Congress voted (almost unanimously) to outlaw the sale, transport, or manufacture of this lethal weapon, and it soon disappeared from our cities.
2. After the Christ Church, New Zealand, massacre in March of 2019, which took the lives of fifty-one people and wounded over forty others in a Mosque, their Parliament moved swiftly to outlaw any assault weapon. Since then, there has not been one incident involving an assault rifle.
3. In 1995, there was a school shooting in the UK. Parliament acted quickly with new laws restricting gun ownership, and there have not been more than one or two mass additional shootings in the past twenty-seven years.
4. Twenty-six years ago, there was a mass killing in Tasmania, Australia, which took the lives of thirty-five people. Two weeks later, the then Prime Minister passed some sensible gun laws, including banning all automatic and semiautomatic weapons. There was also a "buy back" program and voluntary surrender of weapons, which eventually netted thousand of guns. Since then, there has only been one other mass shooting.
5. During the Obama administration, an Executive Order restricted mentally ill people who wanted to purchase firearms. However, one of the first things Trump did after taking office was to rescind this policy. He then had the gall to stand before the nation after the Marjorie Stoneman Douglas High School massacre and tell us how sorry he felt about this horrible tragedy.
6. In recent months, some thirty or more candidates seeking office across America have run campaign ads (including posters,

flyers, and even Christmas cards) featuring them holding a gun, loading a gun, or even firing a gun at targets that could be construed as their opponents. What kind of a message does this type of behavior send to persons who are mentally unstable or imbalanced?

7. Texas and one or two other states now allow for the purchase of a gun without a permit, without any training, without any background checks, and even without any age restrictions at some gun shows. We still have a lot of work to do to end this epidemic of gun violence.

# THE MOST SHAMEFUL DAY
# IN AMERICAN HISTORY

As many of you know, the horrific and despicable storming of our Nation's Capitol was not a one-day event. In truth, it all began months earlier when Donald Trump began to realize he was trailing in the polls and that there was a distinct possibility that he would lose the November 3rd presidential election. (Many now believe that Trump lost the election due to his inept handling of the Covid crisis.) Because Trump has such a massive and highly fragile ego, he immediately set the stage for the January 6 insurrection in Washington, D.C., which resulted in the deaths of five people and wounding one hundred forty Capitol police and D.C. police. Some of these heroes have been wounded for life, including several suicides.

The first sign of trouble came when Trump started claiming that the only way they could lose this election was if it was a rigged election. A few days later, when questioned by a reporter, Trump refused to commit to the peaceful transfer of power should the election not go his way. (Every four or eight years, this event lies at the heart of our democracy; lose faith in the integrity of your elections, and your democracy will soon disappear.) These comments were repeated many times over right up to Election Day. There were also substantial red flags signaling a president willing to do anything, legal or illegal, to hold on to his power. And sadly, these words began to take root in the minds of a lot of people. The foundation stones for the January 6th insurrection were now being laid. November 3rd came and went, with Joseph Biden winning with a margin of over seven million votes. Trump's ego, of course, could not accept these validated results. And thus began his most devious plan to retain the power of the presidency. First of all, he came to us with the

Big Lie. While baseless and without evidence, he repeatedly told us that he had "won the election by a landslide" and that the election had been stolen from him. It is estimated that Fox News, Trump's favorite bullhorn, stated over five thousand times in ten weeks that the election was rigged and stolen. The Big Lie was running and spreading like cancer across the land.

Never before has America seen such corrupted behavior coming from a sitting president. Along with the Big Lie, Trump had other strategies to retain power. He first called for a stoppage of all ballot counting in states where he lost. He did this within hours of the closed polls, unaware he had no such power. Ballot counting authority belongs to each state, county, city, or precinct. Then, frustrated with a lack of cooperation in perpetuating his Big Lie, he began sending out chilling threats to any who would not comply with his wishes to overturn the valid election results. As the recent House Select Committee hearings have so graphically illustrated, Trump and his minions initiated severe threats of bodily harm to state legislators, local poll workers, and even state officials across America. Many of Trump's supporters picked up on all his talk of intimidation and fearmongering by literally extending death threats to some of their local election officials. The FBI went so far as to place some in their protective custody.

Next, Trump called on his legal team to issue lawsuits claiming that there had been massive voter fraud, lost ballots, corrupt polling officials, and even voting machines wired to double count Biden's votes and discount Trump's votes. There were over sixty such lawsuits, and all but one was immediately thrown out as totally baseless and often by the very judges whom Trump appointed. States like Georgia had their votes counted three different times, which ultimately gave a handful more votes to Biden. There was NO fraud, vote stealing, or corruption in our 2020 presidential election! On the contrary, some have said it was one of the cleanest and most closely scrutinized elections in our nation's history.

Still not deterred, Trump began calling Secretaries of State and other local state officials, pressuring them to "find me more votes."

Such behavior is not just outrageous; it's completely illegal. Trump has shown us over and over again that he lacks any morals, ethics, scruples, or boundaries. Additionally disturbing is the complete unwillingness of most GOP members of Congress even to begin to challenge the Big Lie. Worse yet, either verbally or by their silence, they are also now complicit in keeping the Big Lie alive, which was the driving force behind the January 6 insurrection. It is hard to believe that one hundred forty-seven of our lawmakers voted to overturn the election results even in the wake of the January 6, 2021, insurrection. Trump originated the Big Lie but it could never have flourished without dozens of horribly misguided allies on Capitol Hill.

Trump tried another illegal tactic. He and Rudy Giuliani sought to replace legitimate Electors from each state (who would then cast their ballots on January 6) with imposter Electors throwing the election in Trump's favor. Never before has America seen such a brazen and corrupt attempt to undermine the results of a valid presidential election. By now, Trump is getting desperate. His next tactic is to place enormous pressure on his lapdog and most loyal supporter, Mike Pence, to stand before Congress and overturn the election, declaring Trump the winner and Biden the loser. One can only imagine the intensely conflicted feelings Pence was experiencing when Trump asked him to do something he knew was fraudulent, deceitful, and damaging to our nation and its future. Thank God Pence had the backbone to not buckle under Trump's twisted request. But Trump had one more trick up his sleeve. Rapidly running out of non-violent options and knowing that his fragile ego could never admit to a legitimate loss at the polls, Trump now opted for a violent solution. For almost ten weeks following the election, Trump had been rallying a sick, deluded, and conspiracy-loving group of followers who believed the Big Lie. This group included Q-Anon, the Oath Keepers, the Three Percenters, the Proud Boys, the Boogaloo Boys, and a sprinkling of Neo-Nazis, the KKK, local militias, and various white supremacists. And, because social media today is so pervasive and so persuasive, over eight thousand of their members came to D.C. on the very day that Congress was scheduled to vote to certify the results of the Electoral College. And rally they did. But their intent was not just to disrupt the vote but to kidnap and even kill certain elected officials like Mike Pence, Nancy Pelosi, Chuck Schumer, Liz Cheney, and anyone else they thought stood in the way of Trump retaining his power. The mob was the dynamite, and Trump lit the fuse. The mob was the haystack, and Trump tossed in a lighted match. If our founding fathers and mothers were with us today, they would not believe what we witnessed on January 6.

Folks, there is only one cure for the Big Lie: for our elected representatives (all of them!) to tell the Truth about this election and renounce their loyalty to Trump. Politicians who do not tell the Truth perpetuate the Big Lie by furthering a false narrative, supporting baseless conspiracies, weakening our democracy, and very likely fomenting violence more severe than what we witnessed on January 6, 2021.

Since that day of bloody insurrection (and near coup), we have heard many of our leaders tell us this is not who we are as Americans. I beg to differ. I think that misguided mob now represents many Americans, including many of the seventy-one million who voted for Trump. And they have no clue how close we came to losing our two-hundred-and-forty-five-year-old system of laws and governance. Donald Trump wanted nothing more that day than to overthrow our democratic institutions and declare himself the apparent winner of the 2020 election. Had he and his mob prevailed, it would have been the darkest day in our nation's history.

It is a sobering thought that many of those who have testified before the House Select Committee believe that Trump and his blinded followers are still a very "clear and present threat" to our democracy. We must all remain vigilant and do what we can to stamp out the utterly false narrative of a stolen election and the many bogus conspiracy theories that keep it alive.

Note: All states vote independently when we host a national presidential election. All counties vote independently. All townships vote independently. All cities and precincts vote independently. So, to have some massive vote fraud across all fifty states, there would have to be a coordination of tens of thousands of poll workers, ALL willing to lie about the totals they were tallying. The very idea is ludicrous! It defies all logic. Also, vote totals are closely scrutinized at the polls by members of all political parties, making voter fraud even more impossible and implausible! The notion that Trump's election was somehow stolen is just pure nonsense! It's a damnable lie, and it must be stamped out before it does any more harm to our beloved nation!

# THE COST OF TAKING
## THE EASY WAY OUT

During the recent season of political campaigning, the issue of military spending once again came to the fore. Some candidates—often the challengers—try to "outdo" their opponents by showing more resolve and promising ever more spending "to keep America safe."

Other candidates may try to rein in military spending, knowing that they risk looking weak in the eyes of some voters. Perhaps some examination of the facts would be helpful at this time. Depending on what is included as part of the military budget, the US is spending about $975 million a day, or about $11,000 per second, for all expenditures related to maintaining its military. By way of example, the Navy now has thirteen carrier' "battle groups," each one made up of an aircraft carrier, an Aegis cruiser (capable of knocking down incoming missiles), several frigates and destroyers, one or more submarines, and several attending supply ships. Until recently, no other country had even one battle group of such size and firepower. In his book *Washington Rules: America's Path to Permanent War,* Andrew Bacevich notes how some politicians, as well as some Pentagon leaders, love redundancies. He cites the Strategic Air Command (SAC) as an example. During the Cold War, the US had land and sea-based missiles aplenty. Did the US also need bomber-based weapons, which came with an enormous price tag? (The missile gap during the Cold War favored the US, not the Soviet Union.)

Americans need to consider much more carefully how and why to go to war. Iraq is a glaring example. Factoring in the cost of caring for wounded vets for decades to come (as well as we should), this will be America's first trillion-dollar war, much of it financed by China. (The decision to enter two foreign wars and, at the same time, cut taxes will have implications on the budget deficit for generations.) Worse yet, every rationale offered for the Iraq War proved false. There were no weapons of mass destruction, and Saddam Hussein, while a nasty character, had nothing to do with September 11. No nation should ever go to war on a hunch. Today, wars are fought differently. Is it possible we don't need all this manpower and costly equipment? (Keeping one combat-ready soldier on foreign soil now costs about $1.2 million annually.)

Today, warfare is high-tech, with drone missiles whose operators are on airbases in Arizona or New Mexico. Wars should be fought with a scalpel, not a meat ax, if needed. Boots on the ground will always be necessary, but what is the point of waste and overkill? Finally, how should the US deal with its enemies? John Paul II once declared that war was the most brutal and least effective way of resolving conflict.

Another commentator declared, "War is the coward's escape from the challenges of peacemaking." Think of the billions of dollars wasted. This money could be better spent on addressing poverty, illiteracy, substandard housing, better schools, health care, and disease at home and abroad. Known for caring for the world's hurting people, this may make us a safer nation than all the bombs and rockets that can be built. As always, our Lord offered great insight when he declared, "Would that even today you knew the things that make for peace." (Luke 19:42)

# WHICH MORALITY?

When Bill Clinton's sexual indiscretions with Monica Lewinsky became public, the Christian Right in America became unglued. The venting of their righteous indignation knew almost no boundaries. Mr. Clinton had desecrated the White House and, by extension, all of America. A pox on him forever! We need a moral president to run this nation.

But wait a minute. I seem to recall some other presidents who had sexual affairs in or out of office, men who are now held in high regard. For starters, there is Thomas Jefferson, Franklin D. Roosevelt, Grover Cleveland, Warren G. Harding, Bill Clinton, and John F. Kennedy. Some of these men are now thought of as having been good—or even great presidents.

So, what is my point? Am I endorsing lecherous presidents? Certainly not. But I also reject all this nonsense about wanting my president to be some great paragon of moral virtue.

- I hope our president will demonstrate sexual/ethical decency in his private life. But most of all, I want a president who is a statesman.
- I want a person who does not cater to corporate giants who line his pockets with legal or illegal campaign contributions.
- I want a person who listens, really listens, to the cries of people experiencing poverty.
- I want a person who makes decisions that are in the best interest of every American, no matter what race, creed, or color.
- I want a courageous person who affirms human rights and embraces the time-honored Geneva Conventions.
- I want a person who sees himself as a servant of all the citizens of this land.

- I want a person who understands the horrors of war and would never rush our troops into needless battles.
- I want a person who would resist the temptation to declare to the world, "Either you are with us, or you are against us," as if we were the only genuinely virtuous nation on earth.
- I want a person who values the goodwill and cooperation of other nations in addressing the ills of this world.
- I want someone who understands and works diligently to protect our environment's fragility.
- I want a person not driven by a narrow ideology that benefits only the rich and the powerful.

In summary, I want a president with intellect, compassion, and integrity—a person who wants most of all to see all Americans move forward with their lives, enjoying the fruits of freedom and good government while also caring for the elderly, the poor, the sick, and the disabled.

Both moralities are important. However, the one I value the most at this hour is more public than private.

# MAGA

## Making America Great Again

Over the past few years, I have often asked myself this question: Why did the MAGA motto of Donald Trump resonate so effectively with Trump followers? (That motto did nothing for me as I believe that America has always been great, and we did not need Trump to somehow "save" America.) But his followers heard their new-found hero promise to return America to a safe and simpler time, something like the 1950s…

1. when African Americans knew that "rightful place" in society,
2. when gays and lesbians were still locked securely in the closet,
3. when white supremacy was the order of the day, and no one questioned it.
4. when no one dared to propose reasonable gun laws.
5. when Christian prayers were offered up exclusively in our public schools.
6. when Jim Crow laws were still enforced in many parts of the South.
7. when no one ever questioned the "qualified immunity clause" that often excused and tolerated police brutality.
8. when women were still second-class citizens in the workplace and elsewhere,
9. when the coal industry was still in its "glory days" with seventy-five thousand miners,
10. when Native Americans, Hispanics, and Asians also knew their "rightful place in American society."
11. when you could honor the Confederate flag and all types of Civil War statuary

12. when the USA was the unquestioned superpower of the day (post-WWII)
13. when a woman was seldom believed when accusing a man of raping her
14. when immigration at our borders was strictly regulated (truthfully, it never was)

This, in many ways, is what Trump was promising his followers. A very conservative, regressive, and, in some ways, punitive picture of America from days long ago. For those threatened by change, it is a charming picture of the "good old days." But it is not realistic, nor is it in any way healthy for America. In the end it was all just a bunch of empty promises.

# IS DONALD TRUMP A RACIST?
## YOU BE THE JUDGE

1. For two years, Trump spread the outrageous lie that Barack Obama was born in Kenya, and tens of thousands of unsuspecting people believed this lie.

2. Over the years, dozens of lawsuits have been filed against Trump for blocking minorities from renting units in his apartments and other rental properties. These suits were brought by the city of New York, several counties, and even the State of New York. Trump was flagrantly violating the explicit provisions of the 1968 Fair Housing Act. The Trump administration is currently working hard to get this act repealed.

3. Trump began his campaign by announcing that thousands of Mexicans were coming to America as "rapists and drug dealers." However, credible studies show that very often, there is a lower crime rate in immigrant communities in America than among the general population. And this is still true today.

4. After a race riot in Charlottesville in 2017, Trump said there were "good people on both sides," including the KKK, Neo-Nazis, the Proud Boys, Oath Keepers, etc. Just another lie.

5. Trump frequently refers to African nations as "s---thole" countries.

6. Trump has appointed over two dozen District and Appellate Court judges in the last three years. All are young, white males. Not a single minority anywhere. Also, Ben Carson is the one token black man in the entire Trump administration.

7. Trump initially chose Jeff Sessions as his Attorney General. But unfortunately, Sessions has a reputation as one of the worst racists in the South. Mitch McConnell would be a close second.

8. One of Trump's closest advisors is Stephen Miller, whose stated goal for America is almost zero immigration, especially people of color. He and Steve Bannon would like to slow immigration to a trickle. Miller is a bigot and racist of the first order, and Trump loves him.

9. Since Trump took office, there has been a noticeable and disturbing spike in hate crimes. His hateful, inflammatory rhetoric is despicable. And sadly, he appeals to a segment of our population that needs little prompting to commit acts of hate and violence. For example, Trump sent condolences when the Notre Dame Cathedral burned. Yet, three black churches were torched in the South that same month, and not one word of support was offered for these black communities.

10. Recently in a speech, Trump referred to two black woman as "monkeys."

11. In the 1980s Trump took out full page ads in four of New York's major newspapers falsely accusing five young black men for raping a white woman in Central Park. These ads were so inflammatory that the young men spent ten years in prison before they were totally exonerated when the real rapist came forward with his confession. Trump is a racist of the first order and he would never offer anything close to an apology. Once asked if he ever sought forgiveness from God he replied, "I don't ask for forgiveness because I have never done anything wrong."

# Re-establishment of
# the State of Israel

D onald Trump declared Jerusalem Israel's capital city, thus reversing an American foreign policy that lasted almost seven decades. But unfortunately, he may have tossed a lighted match into a haystack. Not one other capital in the world endorsed this decision, except for Tel Aviv itself. This action also appears to be a concession to Trump's far-right, conservative religious base.

For some time now, there has been a popular notion that the re-establishment of the state of Israel is a sure sign that the end of the world is near and, therefore, the fulfillment of some great biblical prophecy. Unfortunately, the highly over-rated *Left Behind* book series also feeds this misguided thinking. (Note: people of faith are not here to escape the world but to engage it.)

In addition, some high-profile television preachers like Robert Jeffress and Pat Robertson have asked their viewers for contributions to help Jews immigrate to Israel and, thereby (it is believed) hasten what is sometimes called "the second coming of Christ." Re-build the temple and hasten the return of Christ. But is it not the epitome of arrogance to think that we mortals can somehow manipulate God's timetable?

One enduring myth that seems to be driving this whole movement asserts that God gave what we call the "Holy Land" to the Jews and that, at one time, they owned and occupied all of it. This is utter nonsense. A careful reading of the Old Testament makes it clear that Palestine was never exclusively owned by anyone. Even at the height of their power, the ancient Israelites shared this land with other tribes like the Amalekites, Jebusites, Hittites, Philistines, and Canaanites. Some of these are the ancestors of the Arab people who reside on the land to this very day.

Further, while the Arabs have lived on this land for centuries, most Jews left their homeland in the Diaspora (the scattering) after the Romans' destruction of Jerusalem and its temple in 70 AD. The Jews began to return following World War II after having been absent from the land of Israel for some nineteen hundred years. And while the Jews have some right to a portion of this ancient land, it is not theirs alone. The three million Palestinians who currently reside there have as much right to the land as anyone. Do these conservative Christians who want only Israel to possess the land think God has no love for the Palestinians? Have the Palestinians no right to the homeland which they never left? Recall that the promise of God to Abraham was to his seed and his posterity, which surely included Ishmael and Isaac. (Genesis 17:8 and Genesis 21: 13 & 18)

Let's be clear: the re-establishment of the state of Israel has nothing to do with the second coming of Christ or the fulfillment of some long-lost biblical prophecy. The Israel of the Old Testament has almost nothing in common with today's Israel. And I assure you that God is not into real estate. He owns it all, anyway. (The earth is the Lord's and the fullness thereof, the world and those who dwell therein. Psalm 24:1). When God looks at his world, he sees no boundaries, barriers, borders, or flags. So, God doesn't care anymore (or any less) for the state of Israel than he does the state of Montana or the state of Arkansas.

Of course, there are holy sites in Israel like the Wailing Wall, the Temple Mount, and the Dome of the Rock. But such places are no more important to God than any other part of his creation. Worse yet, these places have become idolatrous creations, making all this bloodshed tragic. So, does the city of Jerusalem have historical value? Of course. And so does the cabin where Abraham Lincoln was born. But no one should have to die fighting over it. Do you recall the words of Jesus to the woman at the well in Samaria? (John 4:21) "Woman," he said, "the hour is coming when neither on this mountain nor in Jerusalem will you worship the Father." Jesus was trying to tell this woman that God was now to be worshipped "in spirit and truth" (vs. 24) and that a particular ancient "holy site" should no longer be of any real significance.

How pathetic and provincial we humans can be. Jesus stated clearly that his kingdom was not a territorial kingdom. It is not a military kingdom. It is not a political kingdom. It is not a geographical kingdom. It is not even an ecclesiastical kingdom. But it IS a spiritual kingdom that exists in our hearts and minds, and if it doesn't exist there, it doesn't exist anywhere. It is a kingdom based upon justice, mercy, and truth. This kingdom calls upon all people to practice the fruits of the Spirit: love, joy, peace, patience, kindness, gentleness, faithfulness, and self-control. None of this has anything to do with some piece of real estate in the Middle East.

Jesus spent much of his ministry trying to convince his followers that this coming kingdom was unlike any other kingdom the world had ever seen. Recall what he said, "I will destroy this temple, and in three days, I will raise it up again." (Matt. 26:61). The temple He spoke of was his body and not some pile of stone. Indeed, God must weep over our silly and idolatrous ways. What God most desires is changed hearts and minds. Everything else—including land—is incidental. How badly we all need to learn this lesson before any more blood is needlessly shed.

# WHERE IS THE MERCY?

This man had a burned-out taillight. This man failed to dim his headlights. This man walked through a home that was under construction. This man fell asleep in his car. This man stole a couple of cigars. This man wore a hoody and looked "suspicious." This man allegedly tried to pass a fake $20 bill. This man was trying to sell cigarettes on the sidewalk. A few minutes later, ALL eight men were either choked to death or shot dead. Have we lost our minds? When doing police training, does anyone ever talk about the difference between the Letter of the law and the Spirit of the law? Is the fine art of de-escalation being taught anywhere these days?

Committing a felony demands one kind of response. Committing a minor infraction of the law demands a different response. I realize that policing today is very difficult, but none of these men deserved to die. What if the police in Atlanta had allowed this man to walk home alone as he had peacefully requested after getting out of his car? End of story. Or get your taillight fixed this weekend—end of the story. Or, next time, dim your headlights—end of the story. The prophet Micah asks us to do justice, show MERCY to others, and walk humbly with God. Ancient words that are still so relevant and needed today.

# We Can Fix This if We Want To

America has a severe problem that is tearing apart our society's fabric. Never in my lifetime did I think I would go to a mall or a theater and wonder if there was an active shooter somewhere in the building. According to the Washington Post, over two hundred and fifty mass shootings in America occurred during the first half of 2022. For the record, a mass shooting is defined as four or more people being shot, not including the shooter.

Many of these shootings have involved the AR-15 assault rifle, which is very similar to the M-16 rifle used by our military on the battlefield. The AR-15 is a military-grade weapon designed to kill mercilessly and massively. It has no value whatsoever for hunting games or target shooting. Given a high-capacity magazine, this rifle can fire sixty or more rounds a minute. It is a deadly weapon. And no civilian in America has any need for one.

So, why do we tolerate this tragic development for even one day? Because a group of Republican senators have sold their souls to the gun lobbies of America, including the NRA. And they will never approve the restoration of the ban on assault weapons we had in place during the Clinton administration. (G. W. Bush foolishly allowed the ban to expire.) And this, even though well over 60% of all Americans now favor this ban.

Fortunately, there is a solution to this ongoing tragedy. We must pass laws to ban the sale, manufacture, transport, and use of these weapons. In 1934, the Mafia in America used the Thompson submachine gun so effectively that they outgunned our police. So, Congress passed a law (almost unanimously) prohibiting the sale and manufacture of this gun.

And guess what? Problem solved! These guns quickly disappeared from our streets.

Assault rifle violence in America must stop. People are being slaughtered like so much livestock. America is being held hostage by several Republican senators (and a few Democrats) who are directly responsible for this orgy of death that plays itself out almost daily in America. Take away these extremely lethal guns lawfully (it can be done!) and end this bloody and senseless cycle of suffering, dying, and grieving. I assure you this kind of blood bath is not what the Founders envisioned when drafting the Second Amendment.

# Section Seven

## SOCIAL JUSTICE

# CHARITY AND JUSTICE ARE
# NOT THE SAME THINGS!

In recent years, certain voices in Washington have called upon churches and Americans, in general, to become more charitable toward people experiencing poverty and the disenfranchised. A noble challenge indeed. But not if it comes as a cheap substitute for Justice. Charity and justice are not the same thing.

Charity is a matter of personal generosity. Justice is a matter of public policy. Charity seeks to alleviate the immediacy of human suffering. Justice seeks to eliminate its deep-seated causes. Charity does not challenge the status quo. Justice does. Justice always leads to political confrontation. Justice seeks to reframe the social order, usually with a strong prophetic voice.

So, it was Moses who called upon the pharaoh to "let my people go." It was Nathan confronting the sins of King David concerning Uriah and Bathsheba. It was Elijah thundering against Ahab and Jezebel. It was M.L. King calling upon America to become genuinely color-blind. It was Gandhi who brought about the end of British rule in India. It was Bonhoeffer who so clearly saw the evils of Nazism. And none of this could have happened through charity alone. Justice involves a painful examination of the status quo and a deep desire to change it. And God is always seeking to alter the status quo because his world needs redemption.

This is why we pray, "Thy kingdom come." This is why Isaiah tells us that the people perish without a vision (for change). This is why the prophets of Israel, who loved their nation, also railed against it. They knew the status quo was not acceptable to God. Sometimes, the status quo can even be deadly. Today, we hear about traditional values and family values. But these speak of a personal morality and not a social morality. The prophet did not say, "Let charity roll down like mighty waters." Instead, he said to "let justice roll down…"

Indeed, we must feed the hungry, clothe the naked, and shelter the homeless. But also, the answer to homelessness is homes, not overnight shelters. The answer to hunger is good jobs and not food pantries. Our treatment of the symptom is commendable, but only to a point. We must also treat the cause, as William Sloan Coffin stated, "What the poor and downtrodden need is not piecemeal charity but wholesale justice." And to this end, we need to hold our elected leaders more accountable.

# Concentrate on Justice,
## Not Wealth

When I was in college, I took an introductory course in economics. I recall the professor drawing a diamond on the board, pointing out that this is a healthy national economy with some rich people at the top, some poor people at the bottom, and a very sizeable middle class in between. This distribution of wealth, he said, is what sustains a democracy.

He then put a second drawing on the board of a pyramid. He said this is the shape of a "banana republic" with some rich folks at the top and everyone else living in poverty or near poverty. These countries, the professor noted, are constantly agitating for revolution because they have no middle class to support and sustain a democracy. I have never forgotten that lesson, even though it was many years ago.

Over the past couple of decades, Americans have had several politicians and captains of industry who have made greedy and shortsighted decisions that have placed enormous pressure on the American middle class. In case you haven't noticed, the rich in America are getting richer, and the poor are getting poorer, while the middle class is under more stress than ever.

In recent years, changing economic realities have reduced the size and aspirations of the middle class. For example, the number of Americans living in middle-class neighborhoods in the one hundred seventeen most significant metropolitan areas has declined significantly. In 1970, these citizens comprised more than 65% of the population; today, that number is 44%. Over the past forty-three years, Americans living in poor neighborhoods grew from 15% of residents to over 30%, while Americans living in wealthier neighborhoods grew from 7% to 14%.

The extremes of wealth and poverty have grown at the expense of the middle class.

Robert Reich, a former Secretary of the Treasury, recently stated that about four hundred Americans control more wealth than one hundred and fifty million other Americans. That number should give us all some pause.

Since the early signs of the end of the Great Recession in 2009, the top 1% of Americans have taken in 59% of all income gains. I find this another frightening statistic.

The question, of course, is how this great division of wealth came about in the first place, and the answer is, as usual, multi-faceted. Let's start with the banks.

During the Clinton presidential years, then-secretary of the Treasury Robert Rubin fought hard and foolishly to dismantle the time-tested Glass-Steagall Act of 1933, which placed a firewall between the Wall Street investment banks and hometown commercial lending banks. President Franklin D. Roosevelt supported this reform during the Great Depression because he knew that banks would soon act more like casinos without such a safeguard. And that is precisely what happened in the run-up to the meltdown of early 2008. Some argue that this fateful decision led directly to our recent Great Recession.

At the time, banks used to be the servants of American business and commerce. Now, they act more like the masters. Today, America's eight largest financial institutions control nearly fifteen trillion dollars worth of assets, or about 90% of the nation's Gross Domestic Product.

Banks are now the second-largest corporate special interests group (healthcare conglomerates continue as number one), spending about one-half billion dollars a year on lobbying, according to the non-profit, nonpartisan Center for Responsive Politics. And all this lobbying has now turned the recent Dodd-Frank banking reform bill into something that looks like Swiss cheese.

Last year, the nation's seven largest publicly traded fast-food companies netted $7.4 billion in profits while paying their top executives $53 million in salaries. Yet, at the same time, these companies' corporate executives resist efforts to require that they pay their workers a living wage.

More than one-half of the nation's 1.8 million "core" fast-food workers rely on the federal safety net to make ends meet. In other words, these corporations are getting wealthier by forcing their workers to seek public assistance to keep their heads above water. At the same time, American corporations are now sitting on more than $1.3 trillion while paying their CEOs hundreds of times that of an average worker.

There may be no easy solutions to this "new normal" in America. But we need to find one fast. I so often reflect on the parable of the rich man and Lazarus. Jesus condemned the rich man and showed him not an iota of mercy, not for what he did but for what he didn't do. He just never took notice of the poor man sitting at his gate. "He who has ears to hear..."

# WHAT IS THE TASK OF THE
# CHURCH IN THE WORLD TODAY?
# THE ANSWER MAY SURPRISE YOU

B ack in my seminary days, I recall a lecture by one of my professors focusing on the church's work in the world today. To be faithful to its calling, he stated that the church must always practice two different forms of ministry: the Priestly (or pastoral) and the Prophetic. Both are vital, and neither can be ignored. Allow me to elaborate.

The first form of ministry, the Priestly, is the easiest of the two to understand and most apparent. The Priestly ministry involves the general pastoral work of the church: public worship, counseling, teaching, preaching, baptizing, evangelizing, befriending the lonely, giving hope to the despairing, comforting the sick, praying with the dying, and in general, proclaiming the life-giving message of Jesus Christ to the world.

Equally important, the second form of ministry is of a different kind. The prophetic work of the church may sometimes cause controversy and be altogether unwelcome. This form of ministry is not vertical in nature but horizontal. It calls upon Christians of all denominations to take a long, hard look at the world around them and ask how it can be changed for the better. I often think of the parable of the Good Samaritan as a classic example. As long as the Samaritan stops daily to help a robbery victim in the ditch, no one objects. We applaud his selfless efforts. But the Prophetic ministry begins when the Samaritan asks some hard questions. What are the conditions that spawn this kind of criminal behavior? Why isn't there better police protection on this road? Can we find a safer system of transportation for our citizens? What are the systemic power structures in our society that allow for and perhaps even foster this kind of criminal behavior? These are not easy questions to answer, but they cry out for an answer. Unfortunately, there are hundreds of similar examples in everyday society.

The Prophetic ministry of the church can be difficult and even dangerous. I think of those who paid with their lives for taking a prophetic stand against the status quo: Deitrich Bonhoeffer (Nazi Germany), Steven Biko (South Africa), Mohandas Gandhi (a Hindu in India), Martin Luther King, Jr. (USA), Polycarp (early Christian martyr), Roald Wallenberg (rescuing Jews), and of course, Jesus himself. Unfortunately, the world sometimes hates what the church has to say. Resistance to the gospel message can be very stiff indeed.

So, what are the questions of our day? Here are a few: Why do we still have homeless people in a land of abundance? Why do some forty-two million Americans not have any form of health insurance? How can we do a better job of both feeding and employing people experiencing poverty? Is spending billions on military hardware a good idea when social programs often go begging? Why do teachers in some inner-city schools have up to thirty-five children in a single classroom? When is war necessary, and when is it not? Do we care when the top 1% of the wealthiest people in America own 40% of our nation's wealth while the bottom 45% of the population own only 1% of the nation's wealth? Why do we still find blatant examples of racism and sexism in our society? Is it suitable for America, which represents less than 6% of the world's population, to own or control over 40% of the world's wealth when so many in the world today have so little? What if the church condemned the self-righteousness that leads to cutting programs like WIC and Head Start while protecting our pet projects?

Do these questions make you feel a little uncomfortable? They should. I, too, would like to sweep them under the carpet and hope they disappear. But this is not our calling as the people of God. It is part of our work to ask the hard questions of life. The church is, in some sense of the word, the conscience of the world. If we don't ask, if we don't at least raise the issue, who will? The discomfort we may feel comes from the very fact that the values of the Kingdom of God are not the same as the values of this world order. They are different and, in some cases, very different. We need to feel this tension. We need to be counter-cultural. We are not the church if we don't feel this tension. Perhaps we have made an easy peace with the world. We may seek a comfortable lie rather than a painful truth.

If you think I am overstating the case, read the Beatitudes from Matthew, chapter five again. Better yet, read the entire *Sermon on the Mount,* Matthew, chapters five, six, and seven. In part, Jesus was put to death because he challenged the values and structures of the world around him. There is a genuine sense in which you and I are called to do the same.

# HEARING THE CRIES OF THE POOR

A few years ago, I read Barbara Ehrenreich's book *Nickel and Dimed*, the true story of a woman who lived in three different cities in Florida, Maine, and Minnesota and tried to survive on minimum wage jobs such as a server, hotel cleaner, nursing home aide, and retail salesperson. She soon discovered that you need two or three jobs to live indoors. A sizable segment of our society is now slipping out of the middle class and into the ranks of low-income people.

In the past years, there has been a group of politicians whose mantra has become "no new taxes" or "let's cut every tax we can." I question the long-term validity of such policies. For some, this is nothing more than a smoke screen for the rich to become more prosperous and avoid, as much as possible, any obligation to the poor.

Listen, friends, despite what some politicians may tell you, taxes are not all bad. I paid mine last year (state, federal, property, sales) and will pay this year. And in return, I got over one hundred goods and services that make living in America a pretty good deal. The fact of the matter is that Christian and civic charity, no matter how generous, cannot run public schools, pay medical bills for the poor, provide fire and police protection, build highways, maintain prisons, support a judicial system, library system, park system, airport system, social security system, and a hundred other essential pieces of our communal lives. Many of the pressures we now face result from this "no taxes" mantra. It's bogus, and if carried too far, it will severely damage the social fabric of America. Martin Luther King once noted that you could judge the health of a nation by how well it cares for people experiencing poverty. Caring for the oppressed is still the legitimate task of government, and it should not seek to shirk its duty.

Let me close with a story. A rich man and a poor man were sitting at the gate to his house. Nothing in the story suggests that the rich man had gotten his wealth by stealth or deceit. On the contrary, he was likely a very upstanding community member and highly esteemed by his peers. But he made one major mistake. He ignored the cry of the poor man at his gate. Not a sin of commission but of omission. And Jesus, much known for his great mercy, quickly dispatches the rich man to the hottest fires of hell. There isn't even a hint of mercy here. This story should give us all pause. If one constant theme runs through the Holy Bible, it is this: take good care of the poor. In progressive societies that resist the temptation to become self-centered, taxation is often the most effective medium for accomplishing this task. Not billions for bombs and rockets, but money for the programs that truly help the needy and the oppressed. Let's not forget that in the judgment scenes of Matthew 25, Jesus is most interested in those who feed the hungry, clothe the naked, and heal the sick. One of the primary roles of any good government is to collect taxes and redistribute wealth for the good of the entire community.

That idea may surprise some, but historically, this vital role of government has made America great. In the current political climate, let's not lose sight of what has made America such a gracious and caring nation for over two centuries.

# WHICH CARDS WERE YOU DEALT

Anotion that runs deep in American society goes something like this: Work hard, be ambitious, and you will succeed in just about anything you attempt. I grew up with this notion and still believe it's true. But *only* to a point. It is genuinely commendable when people pull themselves up with their bootstraps. But what about those who have no boots to begin with?

That idea was driven home dramatically in a comment made by Warren Buffett. Buffett is one of the wealthiest men in the world and one who gives generously from his abundance. Here is what Buffett said to an after-dinner audience a few years ago: "Congratulations! You have all won the Ovarian Lottery! What, you ask, is the Ovarian Lottery?"

Buffett went on to explain. "You were born white. You were born in America. You were born healthy. You were born with a reasonably high IQ. You were born into a home that placed some value on education. And you were born into a home that promoted a work ethic.

"Now," Buffett said, "don't you dare take credit for any of that! It was all a gift from God or perhaps an accident of fate. But, whichever, you were granted six gifts of great worth. Change any one or two of these factors, and your life could be the opposite of what it is now. After all, these gifts most likely enabled you to get whatever wealth you possess."

You could have been born in a rice paddy in Bangladesh, a mud hut in Tanzania, or a slum in Brazil. Was our birthplace and birth home a gift from God or just dumb luck?

We may never know for sure, but in either case, most of us won the Ovarian Lottery, and we ought never to look critically at those who were not so lucky. We could easily have been given a low IQ, poor health, a dysfunctional family, or even dark skin, which, in some parts of the world, is still a "handicap" because of an ugly reality called racism. I am unsure what message Buffett hoped to convey, but it reminded me that life is like a card game.

Some folks are dealt high cards, some low cards, and some no cards at all. At the very least, we should all be more thankful, generous, empathic, and less critical of those around us.

# Root Causes of Poverty

In my lifetime, I have been privileged to visit four places in the world that could well be described as being very poor. These included Tanzania (Africa), Juarez (Mexico), Indonesia, and some Palestinian sectors of Israel. It is difficult to witness such poverty up close and not be changed somehow. Yet, I often ask myself, how was I lucky enough to be born into a time of relative peace and prosperity in the wealthiest nation on earth? And, as a Christian, what are my responsibilities to the world's poor people?

As I look at our world today, I realize how great is the gulf between rich and not-so-wealthy nations. And I ask myself how this all came to be. How does such an enormous disparity exist between varying nations on this planet? Let me briefly outline some causes of national poverty and then look at possible solutions. I have discovered at least seven root causes of poverty.

1. In some countries, there have been decades, even centuries, of systematic greed and corruption at all levels of government. Thank God that we Americans have had comparatively little of this in our land. For example, Boris Yeltsin and other high-ranking members of his government are suspected of siphoning millions of foreign aid dollars for their personal bank accounts. Marcos did the same in the Philippines. Mobuto was said to have taken forty million dollars, left Zaire, and died six weeks later of cancer. Somoza, Suharto, Menghistu and DuValier all did the same thing. They took millions of dollars that never got to the people they were supposed to help. It was incredible selfishness and corruption at the apparent expense of their own respective countries. Remember Imelda Marcos and her four

thousand pairs of shoes? As long as this condition exists, a nation can never move forward.

2. Sadly, some nations have few natural resources, so they cannot compete in the world market.

3. Colonialism. Tanzania is a good example. At least three nations have occupied and exploited this nation in the last one hundred fifty years. It is difficult for any nation to recover from such foreign domination.

4. Few democratic reforms that truly foster initiative and incentive. Old ways die hard, and the leaders of some nations very much prefer the status quo. They like having a few wealthy families at the top and the rest of the populous in economic subjugation.

5. Failed economic policies like communism or some extreme forms of socialism can stifle progress and hope. An economic system that does not give people some sense that things will improve in the future will ultimately lead to disillusionment, hopelessness, and despair.

6. People who have been oppressed for so long that they no longer have any hope. They can hardly conceive of a brighter future for themselves and their families.

7. Teachings fostered by certain groups, including some churches, discourage rather than promote safe and healthy birth control methods. As a result, overpopulation is literally out of control in nations like India, Pakistan, and some parts of Latin America.

I created this list to help me better understand some of the causes of poverty. But it is not to be an "excuse" list. The command of our Lord to feed the hungry, clothe the naked, and heal the sick has not changed. The timeless teachings of the Bible are not amendable. We are to heed the call of our Lord in every generation and every situation. My seminary professors used to say that in addition to running an ambulance service at the bottom of the cliff, we must also figure out how to build a protective fence at the top of the cliff. So, we must look at the causes and the effects of poverty in our world.

When I look at the magnitude of this problem, I realize that no one person or organization can solve it. I am grateful for such organizations as Lutheran World Relief, The World Health Organization, UNICEF, Habitat for Humanity, UNESCO, Catholic Charities, Bread for the World, Loaves and Fishes, Youth Works, the Red Cross, the Lutheran Volunteer Corp., Lutheran Social Services, The Salvation Army, The Peace Corps, and the Heifer Project.

They all strive to alleviate hunger, homelessness, and deprivation. Organizations like World Vision and Operation Bootstrap have greatly benefited many people. Our national church (The ELCA) also has a solid and active world hunger program and an International Disaster Relief Fund.

But some of this could be thought of as short-term help. Whole nations, like our own, have to engage in this effort. The World Bank and the International Monetary Fund (IMF) must work harder to assist poverty-ridden nations. For example, a nation like Tanzania could benefit significantly from an infusion of capital that would promote industry and manufacturing. The people are willing to work, but jobs, and industry and capital investment are in very short supply. I know we, as Americans, cannot solve all the world's problems, but we cannot ignore them. Suppose we believe that God has blessed our nation in extraordinary ways, such as enlightened leadership, stable, democratic government, natural resources, and prolonged times of peace and prosperity. In that case, indeed, we must share our blessings with others.

Let me offer you the following scenario to put this all into perspective. If we could shrink the world's entire population into a village to just a hundred people, this is what it would be like. 51% of the world's entire wealth would be in the hands of only six people. Seventy of the hundred would not be able to read. Fifty-one would be suffering from malnutrition if not outright starvation. Seventy-eight would be living in substandard houses. And only one of the hundred would have a college education.

In the Great Judgement Scene, Jesus tells us that as we have done it unto the least of these needy people, we have done it unto Him. So, indeed, we must do this as individual Christians and corporately as a Church.

This work is not an unpleasant task but an excellent opportunity to show our love for God and the hurting people of this world.

# A GOOD WORD FOR WELFARE

Society is much like a family unit in which some members depend on others. I want to say a good word for the welfare programs of our land. No, I am not a starry-eyed idealist who thinks public assistance is above question or error. The government programs designed to help poor and needy people are imperfect, and some individuals take unfair advantage of them. On the other hand, welfare programs are no more susceptible to abuse or mismanagement than any other facet of our society, public or private. Every society has a favorite scapegoat. In the United States, it is our welfare system. Everyone supposedly knows of someone who is cheating the system. I am often amazed at how quickly otherwise well-informed people categorically accept all kinds of half-truths and falsehoods about public assistance. We need to examine who benefits from assistance and dispel a myth or two along the way. Most welfare recipients are not employable. The majority of those receiving assistance are children under working age. In 1979, nearly 70% of all Aid to Families with Dependent Children recipients were children. Others receiving aid are mothers with childcare responsibilities, the aged, and persons with a disability. Only a tiny percentage of individuals could be employed if jobs were available.

**Widely held welfare myths**
- The "welfare Cadillac" has become the symbol of the luxury people enjoy receiving governmental assistance. However, a study in California revealed that three fourths of all welfare recipients did not even own a car; of those who did, most owned cars valued at less than $5000.

- The stereotype many Americans have of welfare recipients is that they are Black, Hispanic, or Native American. However, according to the Department of Health and Human Services, the largest percentage goes to Caucasians.
- Public assistance, we often assume, is the largest drain on our tax dollars. Yet, contrary to popular belief, the most significant chunk of each tax dollar goes toward military expenditures. Moreover, only a little more than half is set aside for welfare programs. The remainder goes to Social Security and other entitlement programs.

The most prevalent myth asserts that welfare programs are riddled with cheaters. On average, however, state agencies suspect about 4% of all welfare recipients of fraud. Contrast that percentage with Internal Revenue Service estimates that as many as one in five Americans knowingly cheat on their income tax returns. Some estimates suggest that theft, shoddy quality, and outright graft reduce overall corporate profits by as much as 15% in some areas of our country,

## Unfairly singled out

Two wrongs do not make a right. But public assistance fraud has been singled out unfairly among the many wrongs facing our society today. Why are we so critical of programs designed to do what our Lord calls us to: feed the hungry, clothe the naked, and care for widows and orphans?

Society is much like a family unit in which some members depend on others for help. A typical family might include young children, elderly or sick people, and those experiencing financial setbacks. A caring family does not turn its back on those in need. Why should our society do so?

Martin Luther King Jr. once observed that a nation's health can be measured by the way it cares for its elderly, its children, and its infirm. Our priorities are confused when we spend billions of dollars on a needless arms race while many in our land live in want. In a day of great human need and unprecedented military spending, the words of Jesus are more timely than ever, "blessed are you for, I was hungry and you gave me food. I was naked and you clothed me." (Matthew 25)

# Separating Needs from Greeds

I remember when President Carter asked the American people to reduce their energy consumption. Reaction to his claim that the energy situation is serious has been mixed. Some believe the energy shortage is a hoax; others are convinced it is real.

Whatever we may think of the president's proposals, he may have suggested a course of action that will strengthen our nation spiritually. In many ways, his call to learn to live with less is one of the values Jesus sets forth for the kingdom of God.

As the challenge goes out to consume less and conserve more, we are reminded of the words of our Lord to consider the birds of the air and the flowers of the field and how our heavenly Father cares for each of them. Then Jesus asks, "Are you not of far greater value than they?"

Isn't the call to discipleship a call to trust in God rather than in things? Isn't it challenging to separate our needs from our greeds? Isn't there a massive difference between what we *want* in life and what we *need?*

Can we continue to justify and support an economy that thrives on waste and built-in obsolescence? Do we need automobile engines with eight gas-hungry cylinders, or could we be just as happy with six, or even four cylinders? Do we honestly need coffee brewers with timers that burn energy all night so we can rise to a hot cup of coffee in the morning without waiting for it? Are we not fast approaching the limits of self-indulgence?

Is big always better than small? Is fast always better than slow? Is getting better than giving? What did our Lord mean when he said that we find by losing, receive by giving, and live by dying? Are these not the very foundation stones of God's kingdom?

In reducing our affluent lifestyle and learning to live with less, there is an excellent chance for us to comprehend the values of God's kingdom of love, peace, patience, kindness, mercy, and justice, which can give such strength and purpose to our lives. "For what will it profit a man if he gains the whole world and loses his soul?"

Let us then welcome the call to learn to live with less, not just for the sake of our nation but for our own sake as well.

The admonition of Jesus has a timeless quality: "Do not lay up for yourselves treasures on earth, where moth and rust consume...but lay up for yourselves treasures in heaven... For where your treasure is, there will your heart be also."

And let us live simply so that others may simply live.

# Section Eight

## AND A FEW MORE...

# FOX NEWS AND FAKE NEWS...

In the mid 1990's millionaire Rupert Murdoch came to America from Australia (via the UK) and quickly established the FOX News channel with sexual predator Roger Ailes at the helm. What most people don't realize is that FOX News is NOT in any way a legitimate news organization. Nor has it ever been. If you read their charter documents, it states very clearly that they are strictly an entertainment enterprise very much unlike ABC, CBS, or NBC. And because they are NOT a real news organization, they can say just about anything they want to, true or false, and not have to worry about any kind of prosecution. They try hard to look like a legitimate news bureau with the same "on air" trappings as the big three mentioned above but that is where the similarities end. ABC, CBS, and NBC (and even outlets like NPR and PBS) are bound by a set of standards that were established long ago by the Federal Communications Commission. Broadcasters who fill the air with lies and gross distortions of the truth can easily be fined or lose their licenses altogether. FOX News, however, being only in the entertainment business, can play very fast and loose with the truth and generally they do. For example, after the 2020 election results showing Biden to be the clear winner, FOX News stated over 2,000 times in the months that followed that the election was filled with fraud and deception. It was stated or strongly implied many times that the election was stolen and that Donald Trump was the real winner. Never once did you hear such statements on any legitimate news outlet because they are in fact bound to tell the truth and state only that which is factual. I hope you can see the difference. But it was FOX News and the social media that had huge numbers of gullible Americans believing the Big Lie and FOX News did little or nothing to tell the truth. And they or their guests are still promoting this same damnable lie!

There is also another side to FOX News that could hardly be called flattering. A few years ago, well respected Meghan Kelly came forth with bombshell accusations about having been propositioned multiple times by FOX News management for sexual favors starting at the top with Roger Ailes. Over time Ailes created (among his male staff) an office culture of exploitation, abuse, intimidation, and outright sexual perversion. In short, FOX News had become a virtual den of iniquity. (The motion picture "Bombshell" will also give you an idea as to just how sick and toxic was this office atmosphere.) And if you think I over-state the case, consider these facts:

1. Bill O'Reilly, a bright, shining star at FOX, was forced into re-tirement after it was learned that FOX had spent huge sums of money fending off all kinds of allegations that he too was a sex-ual predator of the first order. His abrupt departure validated the claims that a number of women at FOX brought against him.

2. Bill Shine, the president of FOX, was let go because he too was pressuring women staffers for sexual favors.

3. Eric Bolling, another FOX staffer, was also let go for the very same reason.

4. Woody Fraser, also of FOX News, was let go for sexual indis-cretions.

5. Jennifer Eckhart accused Ed Henry of raping her. He is no longer in the employment of FOX News.

6. Wendy Walsh was a FOX News contributor a few years ago. In a Time Magazine, interview, here is what she had to say: "When I came to work, I was put into a 'sausage dress'. The hair got blonder, the cleavage got deeper, and the heels got higher. FOX was creating a kind of Snapchat image: any woman, even one like me with advanced degrees, would be turned into what looked like an office sex toy. Part of what happened at FOX started as soon as you walked into the makeup room." (Time Mag., 12/18/2017) Glass topped desks were the order of the day to reveal more of the female anatomy. It is also worth noting

that over the last several years, FOX News has spent more than $60 million dollars to settle claims with women who were sexually harassed by more than a few FOX News male staffers. The entire upper management of FOX News fostered a perversely predatory posture toward women.

Why would anyone want to watch such a cast of sick, vile, predatory men? And lest we forget, who was it that not long ago came very close to calling FOX News the "State News Channel of America?" None other than Donald Trump himself who has been credibly accused by no less than 26 women for his unwanted sexual advances and exploits. (and can we ever forget his Access Hollywood bus recording with Billy Bush?)

Please keep in mind that FOX News has two major goals: to make money and to entertain you. Apparently their idea of entertainment takes place "on screen" and "off screen" as well, promoting an office atmosphere that is exploitive, carnal, and downright despicable. A pox on their house!

# CHILDISH BEHAVIORS

All of us have heard the phrase "arrested adolescence". It refers to someone whose path to maturity and responsible adulthood got cut short. In a phrase, they just never grew up. If ever there was an Exhibit A for this kind of person, it would be Donald Trump. Forget the politics for a moment and just look at the basic actions of this man in the last year or two.

There is an election and, fearing that he will lose, he begins spreading the damnable lie that "the only way we can lose this election is if it is rigged." These are the words of a very insecure person who is completely unable and unwilling to accept the results of a legitimate, highly scrutinized, and thoroughly validated election. And because his ego is so very fragile, he must continue to promote this lie up to, during, and following the election. All the while, he is chopping away at the tree of democracy in America, and he could not care less. He cares only about his own public image and feeding his incredibly narcissistic ego. (it is also interesting to note how fixated he is on the size of his audiences; it's almost like an obsession for him to boast of "the biggest crowd ever seen", etc.)

For the ten or eleven weeks between the election and the inauguration of Joe Biden, Trump is either moping around the White House watching FOX News (some of the days on his official presidential calendar were totally devoid of any important tasks) or he was plotting and scheming by any means available to overturn the election results and hold on to power no matter how bogus or outlandish were his claims of victory. And, as we all now know, we came very, very close on January 6th to losing our democracy. Had Mike Pence buckled under the very intense pressure placed on him by Trump, we would have had a Constitutional crisis the likes of which this nation has never seen before.

Further, when all of our past presidents were leaving office, they quickly created a Transition Team to help the incoming president and his staff learn "the ropes" of the White House. This process usually involves six to eight weeks. Trump used every delaying tactic in the book to make the Biden transition as difficult as possible. Just another sign of how juvenile and pathetic this man really is.

And finally, true to his childish behavior, he could not even bring himself to attend the inauguration of Joe Biden. His sick, utterly selfish, and fragile ego just would not allow it. This is exactly how a 5 year old acts when he does not get his way. And this is not how a sitting president of the United States of America should ever act. But then what else did we expect from Trump? Infantile behavior of the first order. And statesmanship of the worst kind.

# Some Rethinking on the Subject of Hell...

A few years ago, I was preaching at one of those many retirement communities in Arizona. After the service had ended, a man approached me and simply said (with a lot of feeling), "thanks for not preaching hellfire and damnation today". I was actually taken aback a bit by his comment partly because I have never preached that kind of sermon in all my years of parish ministry.

Because I was greeting a whole line of worshippers afterward, there was no time to further discuss his comment. And when I looked for him later on, he was gone. But you can bet a bundle that there was a real story behind that single, rather intriguing comment. And it also set me to thinking more deeply about this whole subject of hell. Just how central is this theme to the Bible's story of sin, judgement, forgiveness, redemption, and salvation?

I think it is safe to say that in recent years, the Church has been rethinking some of its teachings regarding both heaven and hell. For centuries, and especially during the Middle Ages, the Church often used the heaven/hell dichotomy as a way of literally scaring people half to death with the threat of eternal damnation, the fires of hell, and a hopeless eternity full of pain, anguish, sorrow, and not a little gnashing of teeth. The threat of hell was used like a club to beat people into submissive obedience always picturing a wrathful God who seemed to delight in judging people and then sending them to a painful and everlasting death. There was little or no proclamation of a merciful God who was much more interested in saving than slaying. Seldom was God pictured as a loving and caring Father whose will for his children was always for their health and wellbeing. And it was the Reformers like Knox, Calvin, Hus, Wycliffe, Zwingli, Savonarola, and especially

Martin Luther who called this whole misguided doctrine into question and who later on denounced it as being pretty much a perversion of the New Testament gospel message. So, let's take a closer look at the doctrine of hell and see what we can find…

People are sometimes surprised to learn that there are only 14 specific references to hell in the entire Bible. The word is never once used by any of the great prophets of the Old Testament, nor does St. Paul, the greatest evangelist of the early church, ever use the word. Half of these references are found in Matthew's gospel, likely the most legalistic of the four gospel writers. The other seven references break out in this manner: three in Mark's gospel, two in Luke, one in James, and one in II Peter. It is also worth noting that John, perhaps the most beloved of the four gospels, makes no reference at all to hell. And we now believe that the reference to hell in the Apostle's Creed could also be translated as "he descended to the dead". (You will now find this notation in the ELW, our Lutheran book of worship and hymnody.)

Now, why this potential change? There are three words in the Bible that are related to this idea of death and hell. The first word is SHEOL. This term is used exclusively in the Old Testament in reference to the underworld, the place of the dead, but it seems to carry no notion of punishment, anguish, pain, or sorrow.

The second term is HADES which literally means "not to be seen anymore". It should be noted that this term is also found in much of Greek mythology where it denotes the abode of the dead. This word could also be considered the Greek equivalent of Sheol. Again, primarily denoting the place of the dead but with little or no mention of punishment or judgement.

The third term is GEHENNA which comes to us (as best we can tell) from the literal Valley of Hinnom located outside the walls of ancient Jerusalem. Historians think it was some kind of city-wide garbage dump which burned or smoldered constantly. This term has been used to designate a place of torment for the wicked. It is also associated with fire, stench, smoke, and perhaps some degree of dread and foreboding.

(There is one other word, Tartarus, used just once in the entire Bible that seems to denote the afterlife, but it is a very obscure reference at best.)

It is also worth noting that over the centuries, Christian thought and theology has likely been heavily influenced by Dante's, *The Divine Comedy*, part one being all about the Inferno of hell. Other writings include Milton's Paradise Lost, Bunyan's The Pilgrim's Progress (1678), and Deguileville's the Pilgrimage of the Soul (1358). In addition, there have been many works of art over the centuries that depicted the Great Judgement scene with multitudes of people falling into a fiery pit, or being dragged down into the bowels of the earth by hideous looking demons, or legions of condemned people covered with boils and sores living in anguish, torment, fear, and total despair.

To illustrate further how the Church has vacillated somewhat on this doctrine, consider the Catholic Church's teaching on Limbo, a place where unbaptized children went in death who were too good for hell but not yet good enough for heaven. This centuries old teaching was totally negated by the RCC about a dozen years ago (thankfully) given that there simply was no scriptural foundation for such a farfetched doctrine.

However, the RCC still teaches that Purgatory is the place of "final purification", again denoting that somehow God's grace is not sufficient and therefore we need some degree of suffering to "clean us up" before entering the heavenly realms. For many Protestants, this teaching seems to denigrate God's ability to save us by his grace alone, his mercy alone, and his boundless compassion. Nothing cheapens the power and the wonder of the Crucifixion more than my need to say, "thanks, Lord, for your saving work; but now I need to add my own two cents worth"— as if Jesus really did not get the job done adequately on the cross of Calvary twenty centuries ago. This kind of thinking must really be a slap on the face of God.

So, do I believe there is a hell? Well, the Bible does reference the idea of hell so I would be reluctant to dismiss it altogether. It might be worth noting that over almost five decades of Christian ministry, I don't recall ever preaching a sermon focusing specifically on the threat of hell. For me, the gospel message is so positive, so life-giving, and so life-changing that I never felt the need to dwell on hell. Or as one of my profs used to say, "you don't get beans to grow by pounding them into the ground". You water, cultivate, nourish, and encourage them and one day you will see how powerful the grace and goodness of God can be in the lives of ordinary people who discover what it means to be loved by God without conditions of any kind.  Some years ago, the presiding bishop of our church was asked if she believed in hell. She answered, "I believe there is a hell, but I also believe it is sparsely populated."  I like that answer.

# THE BIRTH OF BECCA

March 18, 1981  7:30 a.m. Wednesday.  Hennepin County Medical Center

Having been up all night, I am both exhausted and exhilarated! A few hours ago, I witnessed a miracle if ever there was one. For me, this miracle eclipsed the changing of water into wine or the feeding of the 5,000. It was the miracle of birth. I have witnessed it before as this was my third opportunity to participate in the birthing process. But it was no less impressive. In fact, I stand in greater awe of this miracle now than I did the first time I experienced it.

The night holds many memories. Hours of contractions, my wife working very hard at controlled breathing, fetal monitoring, a very helpful nurse and a competent doctor, and many silent prayers for the welfare of both mother and baby.  Being a bit more at ease with this third birth, I ask the doctor about some of the things I am seeing. What causes the labor to begin? The doctor replies that "there are several theories, but a conclusive answer still eludes medical science". Later, a few moments after the actual birth, I inquire as to how the baby knows that it is time to begin breathing on its own after floating in amniotic fluid for the last nine months? The doctor replies, with a certain sense of humility in his voice, "we really don't have a definitive answer for that one either. There is still a lot of mystery in this whole birthing process".

Mystery and miracle. In an age of relentless research into the secrets of our world and our bodies, it becomes a privilege to witness a genuine mystery and miracle. Could it be that God's spirit breathes life into the nostrils of this and every other newborn as described so beautifully in the Genesis creation account?

As I drove down the freeway toward home that morning, I witnessed another miracle. A glorious sunrise appears over the eastern horizon. I think of the hymn "O Day Full of Grace" for it has already become that. A few hours earlier in the stillness of the night, God spoke a resounding word of affirmation to his creation through the gentle cry of an infant child. (much like that first Christmas in Bethlehem) Now another affirmative word is spoken in the form of a new day----a day of grace, opportunity, and celebration. Despite the fatigue I feel, my heart is just about to burst with joy and thanksgiving. God has been good, and his steadfast love does indeed endure from generation to generation.

# DEAR TEENAGERS

As I think most of you know, I am usually a very positive person and I don't like to dwell on the negative things of life. But sometimes things have to be said that are straight to the point and clear as crystal. So, I simply want to share with you today ten (10) of the most important "DON'TS" you may ever hear. Live by them and you will likely live a long and reasonably healthy and happy life. So here we go....

1. Don't speed when driving and be especially cautious on ice and snow or in a downpour of rain. When your tires are not making solid contact with the road, bad things can easily happen.
2. Never ride in any car without your seatbelt securely fastened. If someone tells you that you don't need it, tell them they could be dead wrong. Seatbelts have saved tens of thousands of lives. Also, anyone in the car who is not belted becomes a human projectile in an accident, causing harm to others in the car.
3. Never, ever, drink and drive. It's just too dangerous. And never text while driving. Driving today demands your full attention, 100% of the time. And never ride with a drunk driver!
4. Don't ever experiment with any kind of illegal drugs or mood-altering substances. Just one "hit" can leave you hooked (enslaved) for life. (Or find you on the way to the morgue.) Your body is a gift from God. Please do not abuse it in any way.
5. Don't believe the lie that premarital sex is a good thing. That lie came to us straight from hell. And begin to pray now for that one special person you hope to marry someday. God does have a plan for your life.

6. Don't mess around with gambling. It can also become very addictive.
7. Don't use any tobacco products, no matter how attractive they may seem to be. They are just plain unhealthy and harmful to the human body.
8. Don't mess around with pornography. It too can become very addictive.
9. Don't become a "screenager". Whether the TV or the computer or the smart phone, use these devices wisely and with moderation. Be selective and choose only educational or wholesome or inspirational programming. And know that much of what you find today on the internet could be totally bogus and is not to be believed. There is so much "junk" out there that you just have to be cautious and discerning.
10. Finally, don't follow the crowd. They usually have no idea where they are going. Learn to stand on your own two feet and listen closely to the voice of your conscience. It may well be God speaking to you. Stand for something or you will fall for anything. Remember, godly living has its own built-in rewards. Or as St. Paul reminds his young friend, Timothy, "Let no one despise your youth, but set the believers an example in your speech and conduct, in love, in faith, and in purity". (I Tim. 4:12) If you do this, I promise you that God will find a way to bless and direct your life.

From a fellow traveler on the road of life, Pastor Paul

# DEVELOPING THE HUMAN CONSCIENCE

Christian education is important for many reasons but I think I am safe in saying that none are more important than the development of the human conscience. Even a very cursory look at our world today will testify to the truth of this claim. Homicides, domestic violence, robbery, drug and human trafficking, tax evasion, adultery, mass shootings, etc. are all painful reminders of what can happen to the human heart and mind when it goes astray from God's guidance and instruction. I recently read that most of our big box stores now routinely add 10% or more to the cost of each item just to cover losses due to shoplifting. In four Florida counties surrounding Tampa, police were called to local Walmarts over 1,000 times in a recent, single year. How badly we need to again embrace the wisdom of the Proverbs which remind us to "train up a child in the way they should go and when they are old, they will not depart from it." And since Christian education seems to be lacking today in a large number of homes across our land, the church must take this responsibility more seriously than ever.

So just exactly what is the human conscience? One little boy summed it up this way: "it's that spot inside of you that burns when you do something that you know is wrong". I well recall Disney's Pinocchio whose conscience was Jiminy Cricket. But Pinocchio most often ignored Mr. Cricket and it got him into a whole lot of trouble. This might be the best definition I have ever found: the conscience is that in-born, God-given faculty that allows us to critique our own behavior. This is a powerful reminder that we are not puppets, droids, or robots. We mortals have a soul and a conscience. And we also have a freewill to do a great many things in life, good or bad. And this is exactly why the conscience must be trained and sensitized to guide a person onto the paths of godly and righteous living. I do not believe that the conscience is the actual voice of God speaking to us, but I do believe God can use the conscience to instruct us, convict us, and guide us as we are confronted with a vast array of choices every day of our lives.

And the Bible is no stranger to this topic either. The Bible talks about a weak conscience, a defiled conscience, a seared or dead conscience, and a conscience that testifies to the truth. When Adam and Eve ate of the forbidden fruit, they ran and hid themselves from God. Why? Because their conscience told them they had disobeyed. When Peter denied Jesus three times, he ran away and wept bitter tears. Why? Because he knew he had done wrong. And this is a good thing. Jesus surely forgave Peter, but such forgiveness would have had no meaning had Peter not first acknowledged his betrayal of Jesus. Here is the point: the human conscience is very important to our spiritual life, and it needs to be sensitized and developed as fully as possible. Again, this is the work of the church when teachers explain the wisdom behind the Ten Commandments, or when they tell the story of Joseph's brothers who repented of the hatred and jealousy, they had shown Joseph as a young boy, or when King David repented of his sin and penned those painful yet life-giving words of the 51$^{st}$ Psalm.

And if you think I am overstating the case, let me ask this question. What do we call people whose conscience is dead or was never developed in the first place? We call them sociopaths or, in the extreme, psychopaths. These are people who exploit, manipulate, or even do bodily harm to others without any sense of shame, guilt, remorse, regret, or repentance. In short, they are very sick and sometimes dangerous people because, as someone has said, the needle on their moral compass has been broken off. They have no concept of right or wrong and are therefore a real danger to themselves and to others.

Once again, let me state that the importance of Christian education in the church cannot be overly emphasized. Someone has noted that the church is always just one generation away from extinction if we "drop the ball". The Lutheran church was born on a university campus, so our long tradition of teaching goes back to the Middle Ages. Luther once wrote, "we must spare no diligence, time, or cost in educating and teaching our children, to the end that they may serve God and the world." I often think of that single verse which gives us so much insight into the developmental years of our Lord. We are told that he grew in wisdom and in stature, and in favor with God and man. Is this not the wish we have for all our children as well as for all of humanity? We are called to sensitize our conscience to the voice and to the will of God, as well as to grow daily in the grace and the knowledge of our Lord Jesus Christ.

# How To Handle Criticism Gracefully

I have always thought there should be a short course at the seminary teaching pastors how to handle the criticism that inevitably comes their way when doing parish ministry. We are, after all, flawed, broken, self-centered human beings and there are bound to be some disharmonies even in the most healthy and functional congregations. Over the years I discovered several techniques that often mitigated some of the hurts, tensions, and divisions that can occur in the course of any ministry of the church.

The first rule of thumb is to always differentiate between the criticism itself and the one offering the criticisms. No one likes to be criticized but it was helpful to try to ascertain just how valid (or invalid) was the criticism and how intense were the feelings that brought it about in the first place. But most of all, I found that sometimes these events, irksome as they may be, were also opportunities for some real ministry. Every time I got a complaint or a critique, directly or even indirectly, I responded as soon as my schedule allowed. The worst thing a pastor can do is to ignore these negative overtures. Whether it was a letter, an email, a voicemail, a text, or even just a note on my office door, I tried hard to get back to this person asap. Also, if I thought the issue was serious enough, I would invite a person to my office, or offer to visit their home, or, better yet, meet for coffee at a restaurant which always felt more like neutral ground for both of us. I wanted to hear them out. I wanted to greet them face to face. I wanted to (gently) correct any misinformation they may have gotten and perhaps even inquire as to the source of such information. I wanted them to know that I valued them as a person and certainly as a member of our congregational family. Often times these meetings were amazingly healing. Everyone wants to be taken seriously. Such meetings could be hugely beneficial for both the parishioner and for me personally. There were also some times (though not many) when people were angry enough that they chose, for whatever reason, to leave the church. I did as much "damage control" as I possibly could but their minds were already made up. In these cases, I went out of my way to thank them for whatever years of service they may have given the church, sent them forth with my full blessing, hoped they would soon find another congregation that would suit their needs and welcome them warmly, and finally, should they ever change their minds, the doors to our church would always be wide open to them. I can think of several households that left our church for some months or even some years that eventually came back to rejoin us. Of course, they were welcomed with open arms.

As a footnote, I well recall an incident from my first church years ago in Pontiac, Michigan. I apparently had offended a parishioner in some way that was never fully revealed to me. I simply received a short note in the mail saying that he and his family were leaving the church and that I should not even try to persuade them otherwise. I honored their wishes. I also felt badly about the situation but could do nothing to correct it. About a year and a half later I met this man's wife in a restaurant. When she approached me, she said, "I owe you an apology." "What for?" I asked. This woman then went on to tell me that at the time of their leaving the church her husband had lost a father to suicide, had a sister who was gravely ill with cancer, while he himself was having health issues in addition to almost losing his job with one of the big three automakers in Detroit. She went on to tell how all of this was such an embarrassment to her husband that he just could not come to church anymore where, in her words, "everyone else seemed to be having a near-perfect life."

I learned a huge lesson that day. Never judge your critics too harshly, if at all. You never know how heavy are the burdens they may be carrying. It also made me think about how the church presents itself to the world. As I believe I mentioned before, the church is not a museum for saints. It's a hospital for sinners. Over time, I once again befriended this family though they never returned to our church. Still, this incident taught me a lot and for that, I am very grateful. Without wanting to sound patronizing, one of my mottos for ministry was this: kill them with kindness. It's surely an overstatement but there is a real element of truth and goodness in those four words.

# COVID COMPLIANCE...YES OR NO?

A young man on the evening news shouted into the microphone, "since when does the government have the right to tell me I have to wear a mask?" Well, let's think about it. The government tells me how fast I can drive on the highway. The government tells me I cannot smoke in public buildings. The government tells me I have to pay income taxes, property taxes, and other taxes as well. The government tells me I have to buckle up when driving or else pay a fine. The government tells me I have to send my children to school or home school them. I have to have a valid Passport to travel in and out of the country. I have to go through security before I can board the airplane. I have to pay a toll to travel on certain roads and bridges. Americans have often prided themselves on a rugged individualism fostered in part by one too many John Wayne or Dirty Harry movies. But now is not the time for such thinking. Now is the time for ALL Americans to start thinking communally. Mask, social distance, wash hands, tracing, self quarantine, for my good but also for the good of my neighbor. We have no other choice right now if we are to contain this virus. It is also a very Biblical concept. "Love does no harm to a neighbor." (Romans 13:10)

# Some Words of Wisdom...

1. The good Lord didn't create anything without a purpose, but mosquitos came close.
2. When you get to your wit's end, you will find God there.
3. Opportunity may knock once but temptation bangs on your door all the time.
4. God does not propose to judge a man until his life has concluded.
5. "Be fishers of men", Jesus said. You catch them and God will clean them.
6. Coincidence is often when God chooses to remain anonymous.
7. Don't wait for six strong men to take you to church.
8. Forbidden fruits create many bad jams.
9. God doesn't call the qualified; he qualifies the called.
10. God grades on the cross, not the curve.
11. God promises a safe landing but not a calm flight.
12. He who angers you also controls you.
13. If God is your co-pilot, you are in the wrong seat.
14. The task ahead of us is never as great as the Power behind us, as believers.
15. Humility is not thinking less of yourself but thinking of yourself less.
16. People don't care how much you know until they know how much you care.
17. There are two kinds of speakers in the world; those that have something to say and those who have to say something. And the difference is like that of a lightning bolt and a lightning bug!
18. Said the robin to the sparrow, I should really like to know, why these anxious human beings rush about and worry so. Said the

sparrow to the robin, sir, I think that it must be, that they have no Heavenly Father such as cares for you and me.

The poem was written by M. Cheney.

# It's A Popular Theology,
## and it's Deeply Flawed

For those of you who spend time with television evangelists, you have perhaps noticed a rather frequent theme in much of their preaching. It's called Prosperity Theology, and it seems to sweep over the land like a prairie fire. And why not? It offers so much and appeals to so many. Some of the most popular of this bunch include Benny Hinn, Creflo Dollar, Paul Crouch, Joel Osteen, Kenneth and Gloria Copland, Jimmy Swaggart, Joyce Meyer, Mike Murdock, and, to some extent, now retired Robert Schuller. The message is quite simple (and very appealing): If you pray hard enough, or if you send in enough money, or if you follow these four (or more) principles, or if you adjust your thinking, or if you buy my latest book or CD, etc., God will richly bless you. And you can rest assured those blessings will come in a material form (i.e. a bigger paycheck, a better job, a bigger house, a thicker portfolio, a new car, or some unexpected inheritance from a long, lost relative.)

Well, let's "test the spirits" here to see how valid or how bogus Prosperity Theology really is. Here are four of my major concerns:

One, Prosperity Theology seems to picture a very passive God who is out there somewhere but who only becomes active when we do X, Y, and Z. And if you don't do X, Y, and Z, then you have no right to expect God to do anything in your life. This is not the active God of the scriptures that I read about who is deeply involved in the affairs of his world.

Two, sin, according to Prosperity Theology, is simply a wrong way of thinking about life. And if I change my thoughts and my habits, then God will give me an abundance of health, wealth, and happiness. But this is a very shallow understanding of sin, to say the least. Sin is humankind in open and hostile rebellion against God. And we are such flawed and broken beings that we cannot "fix" ourselves. In fact, we are sick unto death, and it is only the saving work of Jesus Christ that can restore us to health, and not some "four steps" to fame and fortune. And if you doubt the seriousness of our true human condition, we need only pick up the morning newspaper for proof.

Three, while the Old Testament contains some passages that are conditional (if we do such-and-such, then God will bless us), the New Testament has a very different understanding of the word "blessing". For example, of the nine Beatitudes, not one promises any kind of material wealth as a blessing. Of the seven petitions of the Lord's Prayer, only one asks for something material (give us this day our daily bread). The other six are concerned with spiritual matters. In fact, one could conclude that the very lack of material wealth could be seen as a blessing. The blessings of which our Lord often spoke (recall his own very simple lifestyle) were definitely non-material, such as love, peace, joy, hope, forgiveness, kindness, mercy, faithfulness, gentleness, and self-control (see fruits of the Spirit, Galatians 5:22). These are the building blocks of the Christian life that we should be most interested in acquiring. And have we not been told that it is more blessed to give than to receive?

And finally, Prosperity Theology raises the whole question of material wealth in our lives. These so-called TV evangelists often live in multi-million-dollar homes, fly around in privately owned jets, spend huge sums of money just to maintain their TV ministries, and off screen often live lives that seldom reflect the values of our Lord. The Bible does not condemn wealth, per se. But it offers many stern warnings about the hypnotic power of wealth to corrupt our lives. It is the love of money that is the root of all evil. Of the 34 parables in the New Testament, in almost half of them, Jesus is teaching about the proper or improper use of our wealth. The parable of the Rich Man and Lazarus, the Rich Young Ruler, the wealthy farmer who took his leisure only to have his soul required of him that very night, the widow and her two mites.... these timeless stories should give us all pause. Money can be a wonderful servant but also a terrible master. And money can so easily become the one true god of our lives lulling us into spiritual complacency and a lethal idolatry. Someone has noted that we should always ask these two questions: what am I doing with the wealth that God has entrusted to me and what is my wealth doing to me? I have always liked the acronyms for MINE and GOD'S. More Is Never Enough and Giving Our Daily Share.

In his book, *The Cost of Discipleship*, Bonhoeffer states Christ calls us to come and to die: die to sin, die to selfish pursuits, and to die to the corrupted values of this present world order. This thought alone should make us all very wary of any get-rich-quick theology.

# Why Donald Trump Must Be Held Accountable for Breaking the Law

Many people today are unaware that democracies around the world are very much under attack. Authoritarianism, despotism, totalitarianism, and dictatorships are on the rise, and this is a very scary development. Democracies are a fragile commodity and can be lost almost overnight unless there are those who will preserve and protect them by upholding the rule of law and by denouncing and prosecuting those who would undermine or circumvent such laws. On January 6, 2021, we came within inches of losing the world's oldest democracy. We were one vice-president away from an overturned election that was otherwise as transparent, as valid, as scrutinized, as recounted, and as audited as any election in our nation's history. The 2020 election was not stolen and anyone who tells you otherwise is flat out lying.

Our founding fathers (Jefferson, Adams, Madison, Franklin, Washington) understood human nature well enough to expect the day when one of our presidents would become so drunk with his power and his own sense of self-importance that he would seek to establish himself as an unquestioned dictator or despot in America. This is precisely why we have a tripartite form of government: legislative, judicial, and executive. Power is always to be shared. And this is exactly why our democracy has now lasted for two and a half centuries. Our laws and our founding documents, if obeyed, are specifically designed to maintain the health and wellbeing of our national government. Democracy can be very messy because of this power sharing, but it is a thousand times better than a dangerous dictatorship like we are now witnessing in Russia and other parts of the world as well.

And Donald Trump admired and even befriended some of the world's worst dictators. He wanted (and still wants) the power they have, and he has even said so on more than one occasion. He envied them and he despised anyone in our federal government who tried to legally limit his power. Recall also how poorly Trump treated many of our most trusted allies while cozying up to some of the world's most brutal and despicable despots. Vladimir Putin was one of Trump's best buddies and Putin played Trump like a violin. Trump's massive ego needed stroking every day and Putin used the power and the prestige of our presidency to promote himself on the world stage while Trump was too dense to fully realize what was going on. North Korea dictator Kim Jung Un did the same thing. He wrote "love letters" to Trump and once again Trump freely gave him the world stage and the full endorsement of the United States presidency. Trump also admired Recep Erdogan of Turkey, who has now taken his democratic nation into a rapidly developing dictatorship. Trump loved Viktor Orban from Hungary. Other dictators who have been flexing their muscles in recent years include Rodrigo Duterte of the Philippines, Daniel Ortega of Nicaragua, Nicolas Maduro of Venezuela, Abdul Fattah al-Sisi of Egypt, Crown Prince Mohammed bin Salman of Saudi Arabia, and Bashar Assad of Syria who has now witnessed the killing of over 500,000 of his countrymen in a horribly bloody civil war. Other despotic nations now include Iran, Thailand, Cuba, Burma/Myanmar, and of course Xi Jinping's China, likely one of the worst of the bunch. All murderous men and all apparently admired by Trump.

Some say that if Trump escapes prosecution for the dozens of laws that he and his family have broken (now including 4 indictments from three states and the District of Columbia and 91 criminal violations of the law), it will be a serious blow to people all around the world who still believe in the democratic way of life and who still trust, admire, and wish to emulate "the American way". If Trump evades prosecution, it will send a powerful signal to the world that our democratic way of life has been a failure, and that any power-hungry sicko can get elected and can so easily destroy the work that it has taken over 250 years to build. It is no exaggeration to say that if Trump is re-elected, we can kiss our democracy goodbye forever, and this would be a catastrophic disaster by any standard. Because no one is above the law, not even Donald Trump.

If you haven't noticed, Trump's language has become ever more violent and deranged. He said that General Mark Milley, one of our most highly respected and decorated military officers, should be "executed!" He said he would quickly "weaponize" the Dept. of Justice to go after anyone who has ever challenged his decisions while he was president. He recently used the Nazi dog whistle "vermin" (a word Hitler used often to describe the Jews) in one of his most vindictive speeches. In another recent speech, Trump said, "If I am president and I see some-body...beating me badly... I would go and indict him. He would be out of business and out of the election." A blatant misuse of presidential power. If elected, he says he will pardon all of his supporters who have been criminally charged in a court of law and convicted by a jury. This alone would make a mockery of our entire judicial system. Impeached twice. Indicted 4 times. Charged with 91 criminal offenses. Says that a president does not have to abide by the constraints of the U S Constitution. Wake up, America, please wake up!

# About the Author

**Pastor Paul L. Harrington**
My family moved six times as a boy because the Burroughs Corporation frequently promoted and transferred my father. Family and faith became the hallmarks of my youth through all of these moves, ranging from Miami to Minneapolis. Following my graduation from Bentley High School in Livonia, MI, I attended a Bible college for one year in Minneapolis, MN. The next four years were spent at Concordia College in Moorhead, MN, earning a B A with a major in English. Another five years were spent at Luther Seminary in St. Paul, MN, where I earned a Master of Divinity degree and a Master of Theology degree. The focus of my master's thesis was on chemical addictions and how they might be best treated in today's society.

During my seminary years, I met my wife, Margaret, a student at the University of Minnesota majoring in Elementary Education. Following a brief courtship, we were married in her home church in Dunnell, MN, in December of 1968. Following ordination, I spent nine years serving a parish in Pontiac, Michigan, a suburb of Detroit. It was not a large congregation, but there I learned many important lessons about how best to do parish ministry. Then, in 1980, I received a call to become a mission church developer for the former American Lutheran

Church. The proposed site was Apple Valley, MN, one of several communities in northern Dakota County poised for significant expansion and rapid growth. Dakota County swelled to well over two hundred thousand residents in a few years, meaning congregational growth was undoubtedly expected. Love, leadership, and location soon made a congregation of over nine thousand members possible.

True to my formative years of faith and family, Margaret and I were blessed with three children who grew up, married, and blessed us again with twelve beautiful grandchildren, the "Dozen Cousins". My retirement years have thus far been filled with travel, family, friendships, writing, reading, walking, worship, grandchild care when needed, and more than a few afternoon naps.